BLACK BRITISH LIVES MATTER

EDITED BY
LENNY HENRY & MARCUS RYDER

faber

First published in the UK and USA in 2021
by Faber & Faber Limited, Bloomsbury House,
74–77 Great Russell Street, London WC1B 3DA

Typeset by Samantha Matthews
Printed and bound by CPI Group (UK) Ltd, Croydon, CR0 4YY

A CIP record for this book
is available from the British Library

ISBN 978–0–571–36849–5

MIX
Paper from
responsible sources
FSC® C020471
www.fsc.org

10 9 8 7 6 5 4 3 2 1

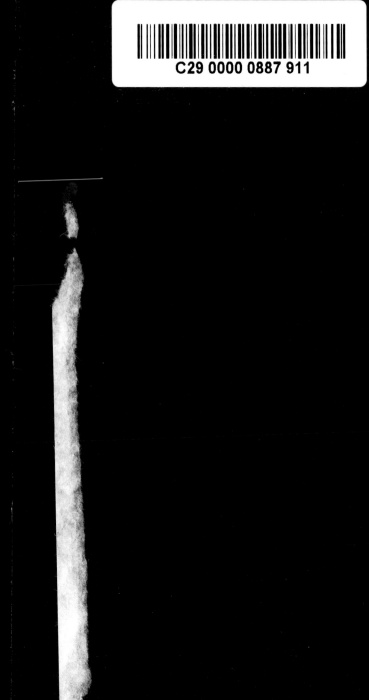

BLACK BRITISH LIVES MATTER

To the Windrush Generation,
including my mother Marlene Ryder,
who paved the way.
We will be forever in your debt.

M.R.

I want to dedicate this to my mum, Winifred Henry,
who arrived here ten years after the *Windrush*
and was really cross that there wasn't a Pathé News
crew on the docks to greet and interview her.
This is for you, Mum. Love you. Len.

L.H.

CONTENTS

INTRODUCTION

LENNY HENRY AND MARCUS RYDER

Black lives matter.

It is easy to say, but what does it mean?

From starting as a simple hashtag in 2013, the phrase is now a political movement. But, at its most basic, its power stems from its simplicity.

Black lives must be valued and viewed as equal to those of any other race; it is a clarion call for equality.

Often, when we discuss the meaning of the phrase, we point to how our lives don't matter and are not valued. As a rallying cry for equality, we highlight the examples of inequality, we draw attention to the overt and systemic racism we face as a people.

The fact of the matter is, the racism we face is shocking.

When it comes to Black mothers, we can point to the statistic that Black British women are four times more likely to die in pregnancy than White women.

When it comes to education, Black British Caribbean children are twice as likely to be permanently excluded from school as White pupils.

The UK Black unemployment rate is double that of our White counterparts.

Black British people are over four times more likely to be detained under the Mental Health Act.

Black families are five times more likely to be officially homeless than White families.

We earn less. If you compare like for like, Black Londoners earn a fifth less than White Londoners and, if you take the country as a whole, Black and other ethnic minorities earn £3.2 billion less every year compared to their White counterparts.

We are nine times more likely to be stopped and searched by the police, which also means we are over three times more likely to be arrested. And when we are arrested, we are more likely to be denied bail if our case goes to court. If found guilty, we face 50 per cent longer prison sentences.

Finally, despite making up less than 5 per cent of the population, nearly one third of all deaths in police custody are Black. And, for the vast majority of us who do not die in police custody, we still disproportionately inhabit areas of the country with a shorter life expectancy – 9.2 years less for men and 7.1 years less for women.

These facts, and many others, bear repeating, because too many people want to deny the depth of racism we face.

We saw that denial following the Oprah Winfrey interview with Meghan Markle and Prince Harry in March 2021, when the Society of Editors – a powerful media organisation representing the interests of the majority of Britain's national newspapers – issued a statement denying the existence of bigotry in the media despite all the evidence to the contrary.

We saw that denial in the British government-backed report by the Commission on Race and Ethnic Disparities published also in March 2021, effectively gaslighting the Black community by telling us that institutional racism didn't exist.

We see that denial every time we look up at a statue of a former slaveholder and are told that we should celebrate the 'great' history they represent and forget the history of what they did to our ancestors.

In the struggle to ensure our lives matter, we must never forget the racism we have endured, especially in the face of people actively trying to deny it.

But all too often, pointing out racism is where the discussion ends.

For us (Lenny and Marcus), ending the discussion there is not good enough. We do not want our lives to be portrayed as a negative – shaped by the very bigotry and prejudice that try to constrain it.

Recently many people have pointed out the need to be 'anti-racist' as opposed to simply being 'non-racist'. Tackling discrimination must be active rather than passive. But even that is not enough.

For example, being anti-sexist is better than being simply non-sexist, but it is far better to be feminist. In looking at women's lives, it is not enough to simply view them through the prejudice they face.

Similarly, if Black lives really *do* matter, we must go beyond simply defining our lives as a reaction to racism.

That's why we've curated this book. It's an attempt to reframe the debate around Black Lives Matter – fully acknowledging racism and its pernicious effects – but also articulating clearly why and how our lives are important.

Black British people have unique perspectives and experiences that enrich British society and the world. Our lives are far more interesting and important than the forces that try to limit it.

So, we commissioned seventeen prominent Black British figures, all leaders in their fields, to explore our unique contribution and importance in various aspects of British life, drawing from their own personal experiences – often taking racism as the starting point, but always moving the debate beyond the discrimination that attempts to limit us.

For example, in the UK only 2.6 per cent of British tech company board members are from ethnic minority backgrounds, despite making up roughly 14 per cent of the population as a whole. While corresponding numbers for Black people are not available, related figures are dire – only 0.7 per cent of university professors and 15 of the 445 people who graduated with postgraduate research degrees in computer science in 2018/19 were Black.

In the face of this kind of reality, we thought it was vital to speak to Dr Anne-Marie Imafidon, named the Most Influential Woman in UK Tech for 2020. She speaks to the prejudice far too many people face in the sector while explaining why we are more than just the sum of the struggles we face.

Many of the issues we have picked are areas directly affected by institutional racism.

In architecture we have a thought-provoking essay by the world-famous architect Sir David Adjaye, responsible for the Stephen Lawrence Centre in London and the National Museum of African American History and Culture in Washington DC. According to the industry bible *Architects' Journal*, Black architects remain 'hugely under-represented'; according to a survey in 2020, 33 per cent of people of colour working in the sector said racism was 'widespread'. But what does our architecture say about our lives beyond the racism we face, and how do our unique experiences literally shape the buildings we design? David provides the answers.

Even before the Black Lives Matter movement came to global prominence in the summer of 2020, the role played by history has been central in the so-called culture wars and the place of people of colour in British society. Hence our interview with one of Britain's leading historians, David Olusoga. He gives us an understanding of Britain's history through Black eyes, not just from an anti-racist perspective.

Many of the themes brought out by David Olusoga are also echoed by Dr Kehinde Andrews, who established the UK's first undergraduate Black Studies degree. We would personally recommend reading these two chapters together as they build on each other, but with the proviso that we think you will get something different out of them, depending on the order in which you read them.

Recognising the importance of different power dynamics in British society when it comes to how different under-represented groups are treated, we had to talk about why Black British politicians matter. Dawn Butler MP contributes an intimate piece detailing the parallels between an event involving her brother and the Metropolitan Police, and George Floyd – and what this means for her own mission and role as a legislator.

It was not until 2020 that *Why I'm No Longer Talking to White People About Race*, by Reni Eddo-Lodge, took the overall number one spot in the UK's official book charts. It was only the year before that Bernardine Evaristo won the prestigious Booker Prize with *Girl, Woman, Other*. This illustrates the struggles that British authors of colour face in the publishing industry, so we commissioned the highly acclaimed novelist Kit de Waal to go further. Kit explains exactly why Black writers matter to shaping narratives read by British people.

When we discovered that Nels Abbey, author of *Think Like a White Man: A Satirical Guide to Conquering the World . . . While Black*, used to work in the City, he was an obvious choice to

write why Black British business matters. He did not disap-
point. By the time we read his essay, we started to see patterns
and recurring themes of why Black people having power and
agency over our lives can be transformational to British society.
We similarly hope that you too will start to see links and simi-
larities between what at first appear to be quite disparate topics.

There are obvious links between why Black British lawyers
matter and why Black British police officers matter, written,
respectively, by Alexandra Wilson, the author of *In Black and
White: A Young Barrister's Story of Race and Class in a Broken Justice System*, and Leroy Logan, the Black former superintendent
in the Metropolitan Police whose life story was featured in the
BBC *Small Axe* dramas directed by Steve McQueen.

There are huge connections between some of the issues raised
in the essays on Black British arts brought out through a conversation between Lenny Henry and the artistic director of the
Young Vic, Kwame Kwei-Armah; why Black British comedy
matters, written by Lenny Henry; and why Black British journalism matters, written by Charlie Brinkhurst-Cuff. All three
contributions address how they tackle the individual burden of
representation, while telling unique stories and recognising that
the Black British community is not one homogeneous whole.

Other essays that naturally fit together include why Black
British athletes matter, written by former athlete, coach and
campaigner Michelle Moore, and why Black British charity
matters by Derek A. Bardowell, a former senior manager at the
National Lottery Community Fund. After seeing how people
like Marcus Rashford are working with charities to address critical issues in our communities and government policy, we are
convinced that both issues will be increasingly important over
the coming years.

Lastly, we were surprised at how some essays we thought might be similar actually diverged, yet still illuminated our overall themes. For instance, we were eager that the book did not just look at different professions and so were delighted when Baroness Doreen Lawrence, the mother of murdered teenager Stephen Lawrence, agreed to contribute an essay on why Black British mothers matter. To complement this essay, we commissioned the author Colin Grant to write about Black British fathers. Both pieces draw out the importance of Black parents but are very different in their approach.

The same is also true for why Black British mental health matters and why Black British health matters, written by two award-winning journalists. Marverine Cole takes us on a deep personal journey into her own battles with mental health, while Nadine White reflects on her reporting of and experience of the Covid-19 pandemic, as well as various historical themes around Black health.

While the contributors more than rose to the challenge of explaining why Black British lives matter, we still had concerns.

We worried about using the phrase 'Black British lives matter', and as we began to receive the essays from the various contributors, we even worried about the frequent references to George Floyd's death, knowing how publishing cycles work and whether this might seem like an 'old issue' by the time the book hit the shelves.

But we came to the conclusion that even by thinking that this was a concern, we were playing into the hands of people arguing that the protests of 2020 were a 'moment' as opposed to a 'movement'.

Our apprehension about using the phrase 'Black British lives matter' was centred around nervousness that we were hijacking a specific political term coined in America addressing police brutality. However, after speaking to various people, including David Olusoga and Kwame Kwei-Armah, we realised that the strongest advocates of Black Lives Matter believe that the phrase's usage goes beyond mere survival and simply avoiding physical death in majority White societies.

If that is the case, then recognising Black British experiences adds to the Black Lives Matter movement; it does not detract from it.

Our intention is for this book to serve as a primer not only for every one of its readers to go and discover more about the amazing people featured within, but also for thinking carefully about the questions they raise through many other aspects of our lives and industries.

Black British lives will always matter and must be celebrated.

Enjoy . . .

BLACK BRITISH WRITERS MATTER

Doing the work with power and agency

KIT DE WAAL

The importance of being able to tell our own stories, in our own voice, goes to the very heart of who we are as a people and our place in British culture. In collecting essays for the anthology it was clear from the start we needed to explore the importance of Black British writers.

Kit de Waal is an award-winning author who has championed the importance of representation in storytelling, using some of the advance she received for her debut novel, My Name Is Leon, *to set up the Kit de Waal Creative Writing Scholarship to help improve working-class representation in the arts.*

I started this essay so many times. I kept thinking, 'Who is this for?' When we write about why Black British writers matter, is it really a defence of our place in the literary landscape? Is this what Toni Morrison meant when she said:

> The function, the very serious function of racism is distraction. It keeps you from doing your work. It keeps you explaining, over and over again, your reason for being. Somebody says you have no language, and you spend twenty years proving that you do. Somebody says your head isn't shaped properly so you have scientists working on the fact that it is. Somebody says you have no art, so you dredge that up. Somebody says

you have no kingdoms, so you dredge that up. None of this is
necessary. There will always be one more thing.[1]

So, should I write this 'thing' at all? Morrison's quote provided me with an entry point. What exactly is the work that we
Black British writers must not be distracted from?

I started thinking about the American South and the many
prohibitions on Black slaves learning to read or write, the
anti-literacy laws that were passed in response to the rise of abo-
litionists in the North. Slave owners didn't want literate slaves.
Reading 'tends to excite dissatisfaction in their minds', they said.
And anyway, slaves might discover the truth about the sanitised
Biblical narrative used to keep them in their place, abolitionist
literature might get into their hands and their heads, they might
hear about successful revolutions like the ones in Haiti and
Jamaica and make plans, write those plans down and distrib-
ute them. Organise. They might, worst of all, start speaking for
themselves, might record their stories and tear down the flimsy
corruption on which slavery is based and prove to be not brute
but human. They didn't want that.

Slaves fared no better on the British-owned plantations of the
Caribbean and, in the absence of writing, they fell back on the
cultural apparatus of oral storytelling; the tongue was their pen,
paper and notebook. Spoken word, proverbs, ballads, myths
and folk tales passed from person to person, generation to generation, to preserve something of their history and memories,
rites, rituals and traditions, some of which survive in one form
or another today. Such storytelling – and interestingly, deliberate silence – was in itself a form of resistance, many narratives
articulating and celebrating the Black struggle in the language
and patois of the islands.

But we did learn to read and write (not that we hadn't been doing it in our homelands for thousands of years). So, by the mid-1700s, Black British writers like Ignatius Sancho, Olaudah Equiano, Mary Prince, Ottobah Cugoano and others used their new-found agency to do the very thing that the slave owners were terrified of. They told their stories and made the case for our freedom and equality. With millions still enslaved, that was work of the utmost importance.

Four hundred years later Black British writers are still doing the work started by those first Black Britons: putting themselves and their talents at the forefront of political activism and change; publishing bestsellers, polemics that pick apart colonialism, the denigration of our history and the continued oppression of our people and our voice. Today's journalists, historians and activists such as Reni Eddo-Lodge, Afua Hirsch, David Olusoga and Akala dedicate their time, energy and considerable intellect to writing about our place in the world, celebrating our achievements, helping us understand the architecture of the society we live in, its foundations built so often on the bones of our fathers and mothers. They give us access to the facts and figures, the reasons and arguments, making the case. They write for us, so we can feel supported, uplifted, seen and known. And they often do so at personal cost, vilified and abused by an increasingly right-wing press, at the mercy of invisible attackers on social media, bullied, abused and patronised. Writing continues to be a risky business.

Another part of that 'work' is writing not for edification but writing as entertainment, making things up, writing fiction. But herein lies a problem. What we may *want* to write about and what we are *allowed* to write about are different things. In a world where we are seen as Black first and writers second, where even the term 'Black writer' appears to dictate the content of our writing, where the space we are allotted in the publishing landscape has been getting smaller every year and where one Black writer can knock another off that spot, it is becoming more and more difficult to write whatever we want. The industry expects something of us – especially in this time of Black Lives Matter where it feels under intense scrutiny – it wants a Black story from a Black writer with a Black cast of Black 'types' it recognises and a message that will ultimately be approved by the white gatekeepers' eye and sensibilities.

A friend of mine wrote a poem that featured the typical Caribbean front room. She mentioned the ubiquitous plastic flowers. 'Were they exotic flowers?' asked the tutor. 'No,' said the poet. 'I think they should be,' was the advice. That's us, exotic flowers.

It's not that we don't want to write 'Black' stories. After all, it's who we are, our identity and experience will shape every story, bleed into every poem, inform every essay whether it's about Black 'issues' or not. But we also want the freedoms extended to white writers who are given the space and expectation to write about anything they like (including us), and be applauded for it, awarded for it. Black British people write about gardens (with or without exotic flowers); see Wesley Kerr and Advolly Richmond. Black people write about food; see Jimi Famurewa and Melissa Thompson. About fashion; see Edward Enninful et al. Johny Pitts writes about travel, as does Nana Luckham. Maggie Aderin-Pocock writes about space, physics and mechanical engineering. And once we get into fiction, we let loose our imagination and really spread our wings.

Romance, science fiction, crime, thrillers, stories for children, stories about sex and relationships, families (Black, white, other), literary fiction of the highest calibre by the shelf-load, graphic novels and poems and the intersection of all of the above, we do it all. We have range. These are not 'Black' stories – or not only Black stories. They are universal stories – a phrase so often synonymous with the white story. This is writing that spans the breadth and depth of the human experience.

Black British women's stories, so often left out of history, tell of the interior and exterior struggle for autonomy, from the domestic to the most critical frontiers of social and political change. And these women are finally being recognised, from Booker Prize-winning Bernardine Evaristo to the many talented debuts and short-story writers across the spectrum. Dialogue Books, under the leadership of Sharmaine Lovegrove, regularly finds and nurtures new Black British talent; and the indefatigable Margaret Busby edited *New Daughters of Africa* in 2019, 200 stories of writing by women of African descent covering over a century of Black British writing. Behind the scenes, there are also enablers and publishers such as Jacaranda Books, publishing twenty novels by twenty Black writers in 2020, and Stormzy's #Merky Books imprint.

Writing books that reflect the experiences, characteristics and aspirations of Black children has never mattered more. Malorie Blackman's *Noughts and Crosses*, published twenty years ago, depicts an alternative reality with power in the hands of the Black people, with white people at the poorer end of society. Action and adventure books like these allow children to see the pointlessness and danger of racism, while Alex Wheatle places children's stories in the urban environment many of them recognise, giving validity to their lived experience, putting them firmly on the page – not the absent father, not the convict, not the sidekick, not the also-ran. Those of us who grew up without ever seeing ourselves in the books we had to read will know the value and importance of authentic representation, how it empowers and validates our existence. It pushes back against the narrative of white normalcy and gives us the reins; gives us control and the opportunity to tell the nuance, the truth and the complexity of our lives, past, present and future, not 'the single story' Chimamanda Ngozi Adichie describes. When we share our stories with one another, verbally or on the page, we create a safe space where we can be vulnerable, grounded and receptive, no explanations necessary.

Black British writing is not only for us and about us. Out of the corner of our eye, there is another audience that needs to understand and appreciate our lives at least as much as we do. These stories are also for the white child who has never read a book with a Black boy as lead character, a Black astronaut, a Black girl with a fabulous afro, never seen a book that celebrates the contribution made by Black Britons to Roman Britain, to two world wars, to science, to law, to art, to medicine. Books that celebrate the range of Black sexuality, Black people with superpowers and agency, not the ever-present images of Black youth on television and news channels – members of gangs, dangerous, aggressive with slack morals and low IQs. In our books we are proud and present, who we truly are. What kind of world do we live in if these stories are left out?

Another part of the work, another reason we read and we write, is to get under the skin of the other person, whatever the colour – not just what they do, but why they do it, the reasons they give others and, importantly, the reasons they give themselves. Because when we read about fear and shame, aching and longing, our hearts meet somewhere just beyond the page and we recognise the humanity and sameness of that other person. The woman who loses her child, the man in chains, the girl

without her father, the hungry boy; whatever it is, there's a part
of us that says 'I know how that feels' or 'I believe that.' Through
storytelling, the space between us shrinks down to a place where
we can meet one another. As James Baldwin said, 'You think
your pain and your heartbreak are unprecedented in the history
of the world, but then you read.'

The seeds of the many-headed Black Lives Matter movement
came to fruition in Britain in the Windrush scandal, the forced
detention and deportation of Black Britons made possible by a
discriminatory immigration system and Hostile Environment
policy. In 1956, Samuel Selvon wrote *The Lonely Londoners*,
detailing the lives of some of the first post-war Caribbean
immigrants in London, and the late Andrea Levy's *Small Island*
explored the same subject in 2004. Today, as always, writers are
trying to capture the spirit of the day and the mood of the times,
and the ongoing effect of the Windrush scandal does not escape
our attention. Colin Grant's deeply moving *Homecoming: Voices
of the Windrush Generation* is a compilation of over one hundred
Windrush stories, allowing us to witness the journey of men like
my father, from the optimism and energy of his first arrival in
England to anger, regret and ultimately disappointment at his
place in a country that no longer needed him.

That such writing matters goes without saying. If we do not
tell these stories and place these accounts in the context of colonialism, we do a disservice to ourselves and our children, to
those who still suffer the disadvantages of second-class citizen-
ship, to the white communities we live in, our friends, allies and
to history itself. This is no distraction; it is the work itself.

Things are better than they were in the 1700s. We are further
along, singing different songs, telling different stories with more
power and agency. Not there yet; there's still work to do.

I'm scratching the surface here. I'm thinking of the writers I haven't mentioned, Caryl Phillips, Zadie Smith, Ben Okri, Dorothy Koomson, Grace Nichols, James Berry, Benjamin Zephaniah, Diana Evans, Sara Collins, Raymond Antrobus, Courttia Newland, Aminatta Forna, Jay Bernard, John Agard, and the hundreds of Black British writers I know and admire, often overlooked and under-recognised, poets, biographers, playwrights, journalists, editors, spoken word performers, bloggers, novelists, historians, academics, short-story writers and you there with the little something-something in the drawer.

We all matter.

BLACK BRITISH HEALTH MATTERS

Racism is the biggest threat to our health

NADINE WHITE

This book was started during the middle of a pandemic that dispro-portionately affected Black people in Britain. One study revealed that Black Covid-19 patients were almost a third more likely to die within thirty days of hospital admission, compared to similar White patients, and 80 per cent more likely to need intensive care.

Nadine White is an award-winning journalist and has been rec-ognised for her work covering how Covid-19 has impacted the Black British community. But she recognises that the health inequalities affecting Black British people are wider than just Covid-19, with roots that go much further back into history.

A visit to the doctor, for people who look like me, is far too often a negotiation with what harms me the most, when it should be a sanctuary from the biggest threat to our health and well-being.

I am talking, of course, about racism.

I have lost count of the number of micro-aggressions, and macro-aggressions, I have experienced at the hands of Brit-ish doctors and healthcare practitioners. It's also common for friends and family to tell me about negative health experiences. And as a journalist I have written far too many stories covering Black people being treated badly by the medical profession.

Too often it seems that, as Black people, we have to literally justify why our health matters, why Black health matters. Which is why, when I was approached to write a chapter for this book, I jumped at the opportunity, because for me the political is also personal and the matter has deep resonance with me.

I believe Black British people's health actually reveals far wider issues of how we are treated in society – from our relationship with the government to our relationship with our own culture.

And through understanding and prioritising our health, we can fundamentally change every aspect of our lives. If we can ensure Black British health matters, we will ensure Black British lives matter.

Black health and the government

Black people's experience of maintaining good health and accessing care where needed is all too often blighted by racism and systemic inequalities. This denotes a requirement to fight for our very lives even while incapacitated by ill health and at our most vulnerable.

In November 2020, an explosive report by the parliamentary Joint Committee on Human Rights was published. Entitled *Black People, Racism and Human Rights*, the forty-five-page document highlighted the racial inequalities that blight the lives of Black British people across health, criminal justice, immigration and democracy.

Like so many reports before it, it seems to be collecting dust on Westminster's shelves as action points have yet to be fully implemented.

As a journalist I was genuinely shocked at its conclusion: Black people's human rights are being ignored in the UK. It was utterly damning stuff and yet there was next to no media coverage around it – which prompted me to harness my righteous anger to write a piece entitled 'When will you admit that Black lives don't matter?' for HuffPost UK's opinion desk.

Among other things, the report showed that over 60 per cent of Black people in this country do not believe their health is equally protected by the National Health Service (NHS) compared to white people. Within this cohort, women (78 per cent) are substantially more likely than men (47 per cent) not to believe that their well-being is protected – a significantly higher number that underpins the startling outcomes as evidenced across the following examples.

Respondents involved in the committee's work called for more Black-focused initiatives from ministers and the NHS, including mental health support to better protect their health outcomes. No such undertaking has been rolled out by the government – which speaks volumes.

Unfortunately, disparities in health outcomes are part and parcel of inhabiting Black people's bodies across the UK and beyond.

Black men are three times more likely to develop prostate cancer than their white counterparts, according to NHS data. Yet they are consistently under-represented in research studies around prostate cancer despite being disproportionately affected by the illness.

Black women are more likely to have more aggressive forms of certain cancers than our white counterparts, according to Cancer Research UK.

For example, Black women over the age of sixty-five are at a greater risk of cervical cancer, are generally prone to more deadly forms of breast cancer – and death from endometrial cancer is highest in Black women.

Discrimination and subpar treatment are also part and parcel of the Black experience when accessing healthcare – or trying to, anyway.

Black, Asian and minority ethnic communities face other barriers to healthcare access. For example, there is some evidence of unequal access to pre-hospital care.

A 2015 study by the Race Equality Foundation cited 'stereotypical views among providers'[1] were one reason for this disparity, as well as 'problems of cultural awareness in professionals; language and communication difficulties; and a limited understanding of how the healthcare system operates for some minority groups'.

To borrow a medical term, many of these issues are chronic and have been ongoing for years. But obviously Black Britons' health – along with everyone else's globally – was hit with a new acute problem. Covid-19.

The Covid-19 pandemic is far from the 'great leveller' that government ministers initially suggested it was, affecting rich and poor alike. Very early on, it became apparent that the outbreak's impact on Black communities would be disproportionately severe – and as anticipated, so it has transpired.

On 9 April 2020, the Intensive Care National Audit and Research Centre found that a third of coronavirus patients were Black or Asian, despite those groups making up only 13 per cent of the UK population.[2] Despite this, the government failed to take action until June 2020 when it asked Public Health England (PHE) to look into the relative risk of Covid-19 to ethnic minority groups.

However, after the PHE review was published, it then transpired that the government had removed a key section from the review which confirmed what many of us had long suspected:

the disparity was due – in part – to racism and social and economic inequalities.

The probe concluded:

> The unequal impact of COVID-19 on BAME communities may be explained by a number of factors ranging from social and economic inequalities, racism, discrimination and stigma, occupational risk, inequalities in the prevalence of conditions that increase the severity of disease including obesity, diabetes, CVD and asthma. Unpacking the relative contributions made by different factors is challenging as they do not all act independently.[3]

It would appear that unpacking the issue altogether has been near-impossible; the government has failed to consistently tackle the disparity in Covid-19 health outcomes while Black communities have been left to languish amid sickness, growing mortality rates and anxiety regarding future prospects.

Throughout the pandemic I've reported on how it has affected Black communities around the country. This earned me an award and a place at Downing Street's press conference, where I held Health Secretary Matt Hancock to account with questions about the government's handling of the outbreak.

However, this has never just been about work for me; I've had first-hand experience of the devastating impact of the virus. Since the beginning of 2020, I've lost Black friends and family members to Covid-19, most recently my older sister. When this pandemic started, I didn't for one second envisage the devastation it would wreak upon my life, Black lives and society at large.

At the time of writing this, Black people are currently more than four times more likely to die from Covid-19 than white people, while vaccine uptake is significantly lower in Black communities due to mistrust in the government and concerns around health ramifications.

UK Prime Minister Boris Johnson said that campaigners were 'right to say Black Lives Matter' but questions have rightly been raised about how far his own cabinet believes that, given the clear lack of regard for Black health during a pandemic.

Black health and our culture

I love being Black. I know that sounds so obvious as to be almost banal. I love my Jamaican heritage and I love the wider Pan-African culture of which I am part. But exploring our health also forces me to examine that relationship with my culture.

It has long been an established fact that Black people are more likely to develop diabetes and hypertension, which are both serious health conditions. Evidence suggests that lifestyle choices have a lot to do with this outcome, but poverty plays a part too.

Black households are most likely to be in persistent poverty; food bank usage is soaring among them, as they are usually priced out of being able to afford the most nutritionally rich food. Healthy food in the UK is three times more expensive than unhealthy food, a 2018 report by the Food Foundation highlights.[4]

However, there are important cultural considerations to bear in mind also. Popular culinary dishes, which are traditionally consumed across many Black households around the world, have a tendency to contain high amounts of starch, which has links all the way back to slavery.

While in captivity, enslaved Black people were given starchy scraps – such as corn meal, lard, molasses and flour – discarded by their white owners who kept the best, most nutritious foods for themselves.

Slaves were given what was left of the animal remains and offal once the owners devoured the best of the meat. These foods were no healthier to eat on a consistent basis then than they are now – it wasn't uncommon for our enslaved ancestors to develop health deficiencies as a result of this poor diet, on top of being stressed and overworked.

Centuries later, we regularly consume similar foods and celebrate it as culture while still being overworked and stressed. Do you see where I'm going with this?

And I want you to know that I am not writing anything here that I haven't discussed with my family members plenty of times.

As Black people living in the West, surely a big part of maintaining good health has to be self-love and the formation of new traditions which serve us in a wholesome way – though granted this is a radical act, in and of itself, in a world that can often be so cruel to us.

What does this new culture look like? There's no rigid 'one size fits all' approach to good health – it is ultimately about figuring out what works and what is most healthy for the individual. After all, everyone's different.

Perhaps for some it's a case of less curry goat, white rice, macaroni cheese and salt when preparing our food.

For others it could mean more salad, steamed fish and water while cutting back on the old Wray and his Nephew liquor or simply tweaking family recipes so they're healthier.

As I said earlier, I'm right there with you all. These are all musings I've turned over in my own head as I assess my life and well-being. The appropriate saying is 'dance a yard before you dance abroad', in other words ensure your own house is in order before preaching to others.

Eschewing lifelong, deeply ingrained habits is oftentimes a lifelong journey which I'm on myself. I love fried chicken, festivals (traditional Jamaican sweet fried dumplings) and homemade coleslaw as much as the next person.

Yes, that's right: I've been in a place where I'm frying plantain at two in the morning or cooking up a starchy storm at *what o'clock* to self-medicate after a traumatic day at the office or after a Twitter troll called me the N-word for the umpteenth time.

Frankly, where Black people are constantly othered within the country we call home and are faced with the trauma of grappling with racism every day, the temptation to lean into what feels familiar, comforting and safe – such as 'soul food' or your favourite cultural recipe – is strong. It may be dripping in oil and full of sugar but, man, doesn't it taste good and doesn't it provide sweet, albeit temporary, relief? I am aware that I just made comfort eating sound very complex but that's because it often is – as are the consequences.

Recognising that Black health matters forces us to explore difficult parts of our culture. We have found ways to find joy in the most traumatising experiences – nothing could be more traumatising than chattel slavery – and that's admirable. But does that mean it needs to be continued? Should we venerate parts of our culture that are literally killing us?

Black health and sleep

'Sleep is that golden chain that ties health and our bodies together,' Thomas Dekker once said. During a 2016 survey by insurance company Aviva, more than a third of Brits (37 per cent) said that they do not get enough sleep.[5] The study assessed the rest habits from within thirteen English-speaking nations.

Women were more affected by this than men, with 52 per cent of females feeling they are too tired to exercise, compared to 35 per cent of males.

The main reason cited was stress. Black people are more likely to be stressed than our white counterparts. The Race Disparity Audit in 2017 revealed that Black adults reported the lowest ratings for life satisfaction – the feeling that things they do in life are worthwhile – and happiness.

It is a well-documented fact that stress can cause sleep disruption.

An earlier study by the University of Pennsylvania and the University of Delaware assessing the 'ethnic differences in sleep duration' (2015) found that Black people were twice as likely as their white counterparts to have a short sleep.[6]

Restlessness and insomnia were also common among this cohort, leading to an increased likelihood of dying from heart diseases.

Strong links have been established between sleep problems, physical health and psychological issues. Racism and discrimination are depriving us of sleep.

Yet being sleep-deprived is often made to appear cool; it's as though burning the candle at both ends is viewed as an indicator of productivity and a strong work ethic. This attitude permeates our norms and values as Black people. Sleeping 'too much' can be viewed with suspicion or downright disgust.

Far from just needing the rest, lying-in often invites the question of whether you are unwell or just lazy. Even during a day off or time of quiet, to nap outside of allocated bedtime hours is shameful for many Black people across the diaspora.

I'm reminiscing as I write this, thinking about how often my grandparents' and – to an extent – my parents' generation were conditioned to think this way. At times I'd see my late grandfather Joseph dozing off on the sofa – each time his head would droop downwards, he'd instinctively wake up fighting the urge to sleep.

'Grandad, why don't you put your feet up? You're tired,' I'd ask.

To which he'd laugh and reply, calling me by my nickname: 'Country gyal, I'm not tired. I'm just resting my eyes.'

To this day, my Nana will very seldom admit that she's actually submitted to rest. I often watch her snooze in front of me while playing Candy Crush on her iPad and she'll swear blind that she's wide awake.

They raised my mum and aunties not to 'lounge about' or 'lay lay' – certain hours shouldn't catch you in bed and woe betide you if this should happen. Tired or not, it was unbecoming.

My siblings, cousins and I were duly raised in a similar way, though the rules relaxed slightly in our case as our parents had slightly mellowed out over the years.

In one sense, one can admire the discipline and sense of routine this forged, I suppose. However, more alarmingly – like our starchy culinary customs – fear and rejection of sleep within Black communities is rooted in colonialism and serves as yet another example of dangerous norms which we've reappropriated and baked into our culture.

Similarly, in his autobiographical slave narrative *My Bondage and My Freedom* (1855), abolitionist Frederick Douglass wrote: 'More slaves are whipped for oversleeping than for any other fault.'

Racists have propagated the idea that Black people are inherently idle and have weaponised sleep in order to keep us subjugated.

Writing about Black people in 1851, American doctor Samuel Cartwright said: 'Left to pursue their natural inclinations, Black people devote a greater portion of their time to sleep.'

For me, sleep illustrates how there is simply no aspect of our lives that racist ideology and disinformation hasn't invaded. Sleep is literally a basic human need and yet even in sleep we are fighting discrimination.

Black health and mental health

Lauryn Hill once sang 'How you gonna win when you ain't right within?' in her chart-topping hit 'Doo Wop (That Thing)'. In other words, inner well-being, good mental health, is just as important as physical health. I submit that L-Boogie is absolutely correct.

People from Black communities face a higher risk of serious mental illness – largely due to the disproportionate impacts of socioeconomic factors, such as poverty and marginalisation.

In particular, Black men from African and Caribbean backgrounds are over-represented in mental health services. They typically come into contact with these organisations through the police and the criminal justice system, and are more likely to receive the harsher end of services including control, constraint and seclusion.

The toll of living with discrimination and racism is high – yet the Race Equality Foundation reveals that Black communities are less likely to be referred to talking therapies and more likely to be medicated for mental ill health; less likely to access mental health support in primary care (for example, through their General Practitioner); and more likely to end up in crisis care.[7]

In 2016/17, known rates of Mental Health Act 1983 detention

in the Black or Black British group were over four times higher than those of white people, and rates of community treatment order use were eight times higher.

While the national discussion around mental health has rightly thrived in recent years, it's been encouraging to see more and more high-profile Black men open up about their own thoughts and experiences around mental health.

Stormzy, for example, has been vocal about his battle with depression. 'I always saw myself as this strong person who just deals with life, I get on with it – and if something gets me low, I pick myself back up. [Depression] was a world that was so alien to me. I just used to think, you get up and march on. So for me, I felt that I needed to address that, what I was going through.'

How many of us Black people have fed ourselves similar destructive self-talk that we must be 'strong' and soldier on, come what may? I know I have.

We're no nearer to closing the disparity gap, though. Meaningful conversation, for all its importance, must translate into tangible action taken by those with the power to engineer this change. So, one must ask the question: to what extent has Black health been prioritised in the upper echelons of society? And how far do we, as Black individuals, prioritise our own psychological well-being?

Black health and Black mothers

The death rate for Black women in childbirth is four times higher than for white women. The NHS acknowledges this disparity but has no target to end it.

In response to sustained Black-led campaigning around this startling maternal mortality rate, the NHS recently launched a

Long-Term Plan to take 'a concerted and systematic approach to reducing health inequalities and addressing unwarranted variation in care'.

This is being carried out as part of the Maternity Transformation Programme, which aims to implement an 'enhanced and targeted continuity of carer model for Black, Asian and minority ethnic (BAME) women'.

The idea is that by 2024, 75 per cent of 'women from a BAME background' will receive continuity of care from their midwife throughout pregnancy, which it is hoped will go some way towards tackling the disparity.

However, aside from the fact that 2024 is three years away as I write and lives are at stake in the meantime, the lumping together of all women from ethnic minority groups in addressing this matter is most unhelpful; particularly when Black women are more likely to die during childbirth than Asian women (who are twice as likely to die as white women) and mixed-race women (who are three times as likely to die as white women).[8] So, how 'targeted' is the NHS approach, really?

Anecdotally, we know that many Black women have experienced micro-aggressions and racism during their pregnancies, yet this is typically glossed over by institutions such as the government and the NHS. All we keep hearing is that the reasons for the disparity are not known.

Meanwhile, the UK's leading Black women's lifestyle platform, Black Ballad, conducted the Black Motherhood survey last year which yielded more than 2,500 respondents.

It was the first study of its kind and uncovered harrowing stories of substandard care, discrimination and micro-aggressions that marred the experiences of many pregnant women.

From the wrong dosage of medications being administered

to jibes being made from healthcare practitioners about their ability to speak English, Black women have revealed deeply disturbing experiences of being abused and placed at risk during pregnancy.

Not only did the experiences leave expectant mothers hurt and humiliated, but many also reported feeling scared as health concerns went undetected and they were rendered voiceless while facing an increased risk of death during a time when they were most vulnerable.

So, there's a wealth of anecdotal evidence which supports the notion that racism is the core reason why so many Black mothers are dying.

Dr Christine Ekechi, co-chair of the Royal College of Obstetricians and Gynaecologists' (RCOG) Race Equality Taskforce, said: 'Poorer health outcomes and experiences are not only seen within maternity care, but have an impact across a woman's life. Black women with breast cancer have a higher mortality rate than white women; we see similar disparities in cervical cancer outcomes, endometriosis diagnosis, and in mental health outcomes, to name just a few.

'Racial bias, both implicit or unconscious and unintentional, can hinder medical consultations, negatively influence treatment options and can ultimately result in Black, Asian and minority ethnic women avoiding interactions with health services,' she added.

Endometriosis is now seen in greater numbers in Black women and at more advanced stages, with implications of chronic pain and infertility; RCOG studies find Black women also have poorer outcomes from fertility treatment.

Black women are at greatest risk of a premature delivery and subsequent death of their newborn, according to a study by the Maternal and Child Health Research Centre.

Black women have a higher risk of miscarriage, an Elsevier study shows[9] – and, for full-term pregnancies, stillbirth is also twice as likely to occur in Black women compared with white women.

Reproductive conditions such as fibroids – non-cancerous growths that develop in or around the womb – are three times more likely to occur in Black women than white women. While awareness around endometriosis is rightly growing – a conversation spearheaded by prominent white women – very little is generally known about fibroids because the issue is clearly not deemed prevalent enough for in-depth research to be funded.

Black health and Eurocentric values

Racism is deeply entrenched in medicine. The Eurocentric nature of the profession has historically been at the expense of Black people's lives – particularly Black women.

For example, Dr James Marion Sims – who is widely regarded as the 'father of modern gynaecology' – performed experimental surgeries on enslaved Black women without anaesthesia between 1845 and 1849 as he perfected his method of fistula operations. Because they were enslaved, and seen as the property of white men, they were not afforded the right to consent to these procedures on their bodies.[10]

During slavery, it was common for white doctors to be present on plantations and 'treat' slaves, both for genuine and experimental purposes. It is worth mentioning that many of them were financially invested in the slave trade. Therefore, any genuine medical procedures they conducted were usually so they could keep their slaves – deemed as assets – in working condition to get their money's worth, as opposed to out of the goodness of their hearts.

Colonialists held the belief that the African anatomy was different to that of Europeans; that is to say, inferior and animalistic. As far as they were concerned, Black people didn't feel pain in the same way, could bear torturous treatment and easily live another day. Or not. Either way, who cared?

The writings of these doctors became foundational texts for racial stereotypes that placed white people as superior. For example, William Wright, an Edinburgh-educated plantation doctor and slaver, wrote in his memoir (1828) that African slaves were 'rescued from . . . a state of barbarism' and referred to Africans as a 'dark race'. And the scholar Rohan Deb Roy tells us:

> Prominent Victorian scientist Sir Francis Galton argued that 'the average intellectual standard of the negro race is some two grades below our own (the Anglo Saxon)'. Even Charles Darwin implied that 'savage races' such as 'the negro . . .' were closer to gorillas than were white Caucasians.[11]

Through science, these captors forged the concept of different races – as opposed to one human race – which legitimised slavery and dehumanised Black people.

Nowadays, this archaic, toxic legacy may still be polluting healthcare and sullying Black people's experiences of it.

For example, Black women are too often not believed when they complain about being in pain; this notion of them having a higher threshold for pain, and these discriminatory credences, mean that timely opportunities to detect serious health conditions in Black women are missed and they end up paying the ultimate price.

Indeed, a Boston University study in the US revealed that Black patients are about half as likely to be prescribed pain medication as white patients.[12]

Following an emergency operation, aged twenty, I had to beg for pain relief during my recovery. My requests were repeatedly ignored by white and Asian nurses and consultants who did not believe it was as bad as it was . . . until I was literally on my hands and knees in agony. I was made to feel like a liar; cast aside and unimportant.

A year before, I had a physical examination and was poked and prodded by a sneering white nurse. I was taken aback by the borderline aggressive way in which she had handled me – as though I'd somehow offended her without saying a word – and the abrupt manner in which she addressed me. I noticed she didn't once make eye contact either.

When she escorted me back to the waiting room, she completely transformed, calling the next person's name in a friendly, shrill and almost girl-like tone. I looked around and a white woman came bouncing towards her.

Just the other day, I attended a medical appointment and the doctor, who I have never met before and knows nothing about me, implied that I have a high pain threshold. Too many of us have similar accounts.

Black health and the ongoing pandemic

Racism is a pandemic within this ongoing pandemic – and has been affecting Black health outcomes for centuries.

It is an established fact that stress and poor mental health can impact physical health. However, the correlation between racial discrimination, stress and physical illness is lesser known.

A recent US study shows that the stress caused by experiencing constant racism can shorten the lives of Black people, by triggering genes that cause chronic inflammation and deadly illnesses.[13] That, to me, makes a whole heap of sense. The research, published in the journal *Psychoneuroendocrinology*, found genes that promote inflammation are expressed more often in Black people than in their white counterparts.

For me, it also raises important questions about whether intergenerational trauma can either increase the likelihood of the onset of certain health conditions or exacerbate them.

Academic Michael J. Halloran has argued that this type of trauma, caused by 300 years of slavery – alongside poor economic circumstances and social prejudice – has led to the poor state of physical, psychological and social health among African Americans. Could the same be true for Black Brits who are also descendants of slaves?

In his 1952 semi-autobiographical novel *Go Tell it on the Mountain*, Black author and activist James Baldwin asked the question: 'Could a curse come down so many ages? Did it live in time, or in the moment?'

With all of the inequalities we face – specifically health in this context – how many Black people have asked the similar question: 'Am I salt/prone to bad luck or is something else at play?' Fascinating.

As the world saw a resurgence of the Black Lives Matter movement in the summer of 2020, Prime Minister Boris Johnson announced that the government would set up a commission to look at racial inequality.

Writing in the *Telegraph* to announce the Commission, the Prime Minister said: 'It is no use just saying that we have made huge progress in tackling racism. There is much more that we need to do; and we will. It is time for a cross-governmental commission to look at all aspects of inequality – in employment, in health outcomes, in academic and all other walks of life.'[14]

Following the backlash against the Commission's widely contested report, published in March 2021, marginalised groups continue to bear the brunt of healthcare disparities.

Additionally, Black people continue to be grossly underrepresented in vital, potentially life-saving research studies while funding is allocated to every clinical cause but ones tailored to our well-being.

The fight for our lives is not some imagined iteration of Black people's predisposition to victimhood as some bigots would have everyone believe; a plethora of anecdotal and statistical evidence clearly illustrates this bleak reality.

However, the absence of solutions-based research and remedial initiatives means that the problem continues to be widely overlooked across society – from the decision-makers at this country's helm even to parts of our own communities.

The lack of awareness around this means that every day encompasses a missed opportunity to save lives. But, in spite of this, Black health has always mattered and will always matter.

There is something about growing older and, with each passing year, embracing life's lessons as it unfolds. As I continue to see my people needlessly suffering and sometimes dying in utterly preventable circumstances, often exacerbated by systemic inequalities, I'm reminded more and more of the need to take stock and prioritise self-care while being louder still in calling out the injustices that bring about our collective plight. As far as I'm concerned, the two are not mutually exclusive. At twenty-eight years old, I've never felt more strongly about advocating for Black health than I do now. You know what they say – health is wealth.

BLACK BRITISH HISTORIANS MATTER

A conversation between

LENNY HENRY AND DAVID OLUSOGA

It would be impossible to create a collection of essays titled Black British Lives Matter *and not look at the role of Black historians.*

History has become a major battleground in how we think of Black people's place in British society. The role history plays has come to the forefront in discussions around Black Lives Matter as protesters topple statues of former slave owners and the National Trust examines how it incorporates the history of slavery in presenting the country's past, to name just two examples.

However, in a chapter covering Black British historians we were eager not just to repeat some of the historical facts about Black people's presence in Britain, which dates back to at least the Roman Empire, or highlight the 'complex past', to put it politely, of some of our national heroes. Instead, we wanted to take a wider perspective and get dispatches from the 'frontline' of the current so-called culture wars and talk to a Black historian about how he sees his role in these politically charged times.

We also thought it was important to recognise that the struggle for systemic evaluation of Black British lives dates back much further than the recent Black Lives Matter slogan, and to put recent events into a historical context.

We asked Britain's most famous Black historian whether he would give us his perspective on why Black British historians matter

– no bribes were made, apart from the promise of a large cappuccino and a stack of patisserie as high as the top of his twisty dreadlocks.

David Olusoga's list of achievements is far too long to print here. He has written seminal works on the First World War including The World's War *(2014), which won First World War Book of the Year. He presented and produced the BAFTA award-winning* Britain's Forgotten Slave Owners *for the BBC. And I should also mention my own personal favourite, which is currently on my bedside table,* Black and British: A Forgotten History *(2016), which was awarded both the Longman–History Today Trustees' Award and the PEN Hessell-Tiltman Prize.*

Luckily for us, he agreed to talk over Zoom, and we covered everything from how we should view eating toffee in Edinburgh to why we should not focus (too much) on toppling statues. But we started the conversation with Lenny asking how a Black kid growing up in the North-East of England became obsessed with Britain's past.

Lenny Henry: Thank you so much, David, for agreeing to talk to us about the importance of Black British historians. You are one of the most pre-eminent Black historians in the UK and definitely the best-known – for me and millions of Britons you are literally the superhero of history. So a simple question to start. How did you become interested in history? I mean, Bruce Wayne became Batman because a bat flew in through a window. Spider-Man was bitten by a radioactive spider. Was there a similar experience? Were you bitten by a radioactive history book?

David Olusoga: (*Laughing*) Not quite.

Growing up in the 1970s and '80s, in the North-East of England, my family lived in a council house in Gateshead.

Everybody was obsessed with history; well, to be precise, all the boys at school were obsessed with the Second World War because it was what was on television all the time. We used to play all the time with our plastic Airfix soldiers. The magazines and comics we read were all about it. So, I got into the Second World War because all my friends were into it and it was a major part of British culture growing up.

Then one day my mother, who is white and British, told me that in Lagos, the city of my birth, the place where my father lives, there is a memorial to Nigerians, just like me, who fought and died in the war.

And I had absolutely no idea about this and struggled to believe that this was the case.

To give an example of how much I struggled with this new bit of information, I had loads of plastic Airfix soldiers, and I remember very clearly going back and scrutinising these soldiers, *very* carefully. I had a box of British Eighth Army soldiers. The Eighth Army was the army that fought under Montgomery in North Africa. And on the cover of the box was a picture – a painting of those soldiers fighting in the desert – and I remember spending hours looking at that box and seeing all those white soldiers. And so, I naturally presumed that the Eighth Army was made up of white men.

In reality, the British Army was actually one of the most multicultural forces ever brought into existence; it was full of Indian soldiers, soldiers from all over the Empire. But there was nothing about this aspect of the Second World War in the toys, or the films I watched on television; nothing in the magazines and comics I read that suggested for a second that it was anything other than all white people involved in this most brutal of conflicts.

So, my mother telling me about Nigeria was aptly discordant.

When she said people of your father's ethnicity, Yoruba Nigerians, fought in that war, fighting alongside Indians and people from the West Indies, and other parts of the British Empire, it didn't make sense.

So that was a catalytic moment for me. It was my white mother, saying *both sides of you, not just the British white working-class side, but both sides of your heritage, were involved in this history.*

Lenny: I'm always blown away when I see pictures or footage of people that look like me in the Second World War, in army uniform, signing up in the Caribbean. Interestingly, at school, history was just facts and dates and, similarly, I probably had the same distorted view of the past. So, what's your job as a historian? Is it to correct these perceptions?

David: Well, I think the job of an historian of Black British history is very, very different to the job of other types of historian because the job of an historian of Black British history is one of recovery.

For people who are studying historicised parts of British history, their job is often to try to find new angles into stories that are familiar or histories that are well recorded.

But Black history is about recovery. It's about finding people in the past, finding connections that have been deliberately obscured and trying to draw these links. Simply knowing that those connections are there and knowing that these biographies exist, in some ways, isn't enough, because we are so trained to think of history in these compartments that we can still be blind to it. So, I'm constantly rediscovering the extent to which the 'programming' worked on me.

I know how the trick is done. I've been behind the scenes and

I've seen the smoke and mirrors, and yet sometimes the trick has been done so effectively that every so often it still works on me.

I'm still thinking things through and realising connections that are obvious once you think them through, but they had never occurred to me before. One example is the Black connections to my Scottish ancestors on my mother's side of the family.

As a kid we had no money, so for our holidays we would go up to Edinburgh on day trips. We would go to the castles and we loved it, and one of the reasons we loved it so much was because we got loads of sweets. We associated Scotland with sweets – tablet, toffee and shortbread, it's all sugary. So, a lot of the time we were on a sugar high, climbing and clambering around castles.

My favourite sweets were called Highland toffees. They had a green tartan wrapper. And it was only when I was at university studying slavery, and discovering the disproportionate number of slave owners in Jamaica who were Scottish, that I worked out that my Scottish sweet tooth was connected to slavery.

The reason that there's Highland toffee is not because they're growing sugarcane somewhere in the Highlands. It's because Scotland was disproportionately involved in sugar slavery. So, my associations of everything that made going to Edinburgh great as a six-year-old are actually connected to slavery.

Similarly, there are connections when I think about another love of mine, music. At university one of my favourite bands, and they should be everyone's favourite band, was Bob Marley and the Wailers. And if you think about it, the names of the original three members of that group are all Scottish. Robert Nesta Marley – Marley is a Scottish name because Bob Marley was half Scottish. Peter McIntosh (Peter Tosh) – well, that is obvious. And Bunny Livingston, who has just sadly departed.

Marley, McIntosh and Livingston – three Black guys on an island in which a third of the slave owners were Scottish means a third of the people have ancestors who were owned by Scottish slave owners. And the connections never occurred when I was younger, sitting at university listening to Bob Marley and the Wailers and eating my Highland toffee. I was utterly blind to it.

Lenny: I imagine it's like having a massive penny drop on your head from a great height when you see those connections.

David: When you're a Black historian, it's a very different arena of history to be in because most of history is about fighting against accidental obscurity, the natural way in which the past is forgotten, and historians reclaim aspects of the past and make them into history. However, I think what you're dealing with when you come to stories of Black history and empire is a process of *deliberate* amnesia, *deliberate* forgetting, *intentional* obscuring.

Lenny: I guess these are things that affect us all, we're looking at the world through a different lens. But how important is it that a Black historian addresses Black history versus 'normal' history?

David: Well, I would absolutely fight for a Black historian to be able to study any aspect of history that has no obvious connection to the story of their African heritage. But the problem is that for the past 500 years the entanglements between Europe and Africa and Africans in the New World, mean that it's impossible not to acknowledge an African connection in most aspects of history.

From the Age of Exploration onwards, it's pretty hard not

to bump into Africa and Africans, because Africa is part of the world. And in some ways, that's the heart of the problem with the way we envisage Black history. Africa has been taken out of the world.

These connections were deliberately severed, so it's about taking this continent and plugging it back into all of these connections. And the more you do it, the more you realise that you can't understand any European country, and particularly a country with an imperial past like Britain; you will fail to understand the United States and multiple other countries, without understanding their connections to Africa.

The other big penny-drop moment for me is the story of Britain's North-East, and the industrial revolution, which, growing up in Gateshead opposite Newcastle, was a big part of my education.

It's the only period in British history when the North was richer than the South and we're not going to forget that in a hurry because it ain't coming back anytime soon. It's at the heart of our culture, our working-class Northern identity, forged in the industrial revolution. And I remember being told that the mills of Lancashire were being fired by the coal of the North-East, the Tyne Valley, from under our feet, that was cut from the earth by our ancestors, and by machines invented in Newcastle, Jarrow and other places, by these great industrial heroes, and we learned about those heroes and great inventions, the water frame, the spinning jenny.

And all of the time we were taught this, we were never once told where the cotton for these mills came from. And once you know that the story of the industrial revolution cannot be honestly told without the story of American slavery, and the almost two million African Americans who struggled and eventually died to produce that cotton, then you realise the whole under-standing of our past is dishonest.

You couldn't tell the story of the industrial revolution with-out talking about coal. So how the hell can you write about it without talking about where the cotton comes from? And so, what you're fighting against as a Black historian is obscurity, it's forgetting. But it's also a deliberate need in this country to take out these parts of history that are uncomfortable.

History to me is like a stone that we need to pick up and look at the underside and see the bugs crawling around there, because that's where you find the interesting bits of history. You are literally there with a big magnifying glass.

Lenny: You are right, some parts are uncomfortable. I grew up in Dudley, in the Midlands, and chains are part of the Black Country flag. I remember an event once, when I opened the Black Country archive, and a man came up to me and said, 'Hold this flag'; I looked down, and I saw these chains. And thought to myself: 'We're talking about how the Black Country participated in the industrial revolution and oh s***, we made chains here: what was the predominant use for chains during that period? It must have been for the purposes of slavery' – that whole thought process for me was shocking. A massive penny drop from on high.

Now I want to talk to you about the George Floyd tragedy. As a person of colour, and a historian, how did you view it? Can you separate those two things?

David: When it first hit the news, I tried to hide. It was during lockdown. Everything was difficult. I couldn't watch it. And I still haven't watched it. I just watched parts of it on the news.

And I initially presumed that the normal script would play out.

The charges would be dropped or there'd be a court case and there would be no convictions. And that all that would happen was that another Black person had been killed in front of cameras and those involved would not face the consequences, which, in some ways, is a real expression of power.

But then the normal script wasn't followed. And I watched this phenomenon of protests growing. What was really interesting was watching how the normal response from the authorities, the traditional strategies of obfuscation and defensiveness that usually work in Britain, didn't work.

What Black people were told in the weeks after the murder of George Floyd is that you can't compare British racism to American racism. That's what we heard on *Newsnight* [BBC nightly current affairs programme] as one commentator after another said that Black British people were wrong to look to African American examples for inspiration. We were told the UK police aren't armed and therefore it is not the same. They said this, despite the fact that guns had nothing to do with George Floyd's death. And when Black British people talked about the long list of Black people who have died in police custody, again, it was all dismissed. And this normally works.

But for some reason, and I still don't fully know what the reason was, it didn't. It just didn't *take* this time.

The fact is, it's historically illiterate to put forward these arguments. For decades, Black people have looked to the African American example for inspiration. I'm from Newcastle, a city that Frederick Douglass [African American abolitionist] came to in the 1840s. And, you know, his manumission, his freedom from slavery, was purchased by two Quaker women in a square in Newcastle.

Martin Luther King was given an honorary degree from Newcastle University.

Malcolm X came to Britain, Stokely Carmichael came to Britain. Black people have always looked to the African American struggle, as an example, and for inspiration. So, it was historically illiterate, but the most important thing was that it was ineffective this time.

I can only put it down to two things. One is that the difference between what happened with George Floyd and all of the other depressingly long list of murders at the hands of American police was the pandemic. I think the pandemic did a couple of things. It took old people off the streets, giving the streets to the young, who used it for protests. And the pandemic also turned down the volume on everything else.

My depressing conclusion is it took something like lockdown, in which so many other things that would have been in the news weren't, to turn down the volume enough for our society to actually hear the protestations of Black people. You had to turn off so many other sources of distraction to hear us. And this weird historical juncture meant that there was enough background silence for Black people, finally, to be heard.

Lenny: I know you've talked about it before but as a Black historian I have to ask you about the issue of statues and the Black Lives Matter protests.

David: I am worried how the issue of statues – even though I supported the toppling of the statue of Edward Colston [a major slave trader], here in Bristol – how that has been weaponised by people who wanted a very useful distraction. And I wrote a slightly pleading piece in the *Guardian*, saying that the statues are a distraction. It is racism, that's the thing we've got to topple.

So, I don't want to get too distracted about the statue incidents, but talk about the other thing I find fascinating about this moment we're living in – the demonstrations are being led by a generation who think about race differently. And what strikes me when I talk to people in their twenties, people who are students, people who protested, they have aspirations and ambitions that literally never occurred to me to even entertain. So, when you talk to those kids, their aim and what they regard as their generational mission is to destroy racism and to weed it out of their society. It never occurred to me.

Lenny: That's a big job.

David: It never occurred to me that it was even possible. And maybe I'm right and they're wrong, or the other way around. The fact is I put limitations on what I thought was possible; I always presumed racism would always be here, that it was a given. But the truth is, it was not always here, it was invented. So, in some ways, my own position is historically dubious. The fact that I never even dreamed of having the aspirations that these young activists think are their normality and their generational mission shows me something is radically different.

And it is not just the younger Black generation. Talking to young white kids now about their fervour for anti-racism is just astonishing. I think we have a moment when there's a generational shift. To me, this generation appears to be a group of people who believe that they have a mission, focused on equality in all its forms: sexual, racial, gender, sexual orientation. And they are frighteningly committed to it. It's remarkable. I wrote loads about Black Lives Matter and this generation – they topple statues, they organise literally hundreds of marches, hundreds of thousands of people on the streets. It's impressive.

Lenny: We've talked a lot about Black Lives Matter during this conversation and you've linked it almost exclusively during our chat to George Floyd. So here comes the confession. In putting this book together, Marcus, my co-editor, and I have actually argued about the title and whether it is right to use the phrase 'Black British lives matter'. How do you feel about using the phrase?

David: To me, the job of Black British historians at this moment is to fight against the deep and deliberate toxification of ideas and phrases that are not beneficial to us.

Black Lives Matter has been dismissed as political. It's been made into a pejorative, it's been attacked with counter phrases like 'all lives matter', because that's what's happened to every Black political movement that you can think of over the last hundred years and further back. In 1919, when Black soldiers from the US army returned to America after fighting in the First World War, they fought in some cases in the French army because the American army wouldn't allow them to fight. And they came back filled with ideas by W.E.B. Du Bois [African American historian and Pan-Africanist], and a belief that they had earned the right – as had their ancestors who fought in the US Civil War – to have their civil rights taken seriously. And their movements were absolutely discredited, they were said to have been Marxists because they had been on the Western Front; even though this was a long way from the Eastern Front where the Russians actually were, they were dismissed as Marxists. They were said to have been ruined by the liberalism of France, and the fact they'd been 'allowed' to have relationships with French women, and therefore couldn't fit back into American society.

And that movement, that political moment of those soldiers who came back with very modest reasonable demands, they were absolutely discredited, because that's what happens. Instead of a moment of reckoning with American racism and rewarding people for their service in the war, what you got was the red summer of 1920, the mass lynching of African Americans, both soldiers and civilians, a spate of race riots and violence in America, because that's how people have coped with Black politicisation.

They've taken our organisations and have made them toxic. They've made white people frightened of them. They've made us scared to say the names of our organisations, or to acknowledge our leaders. They've made everything, even the most basic demands for equality, seem extreme.

The fact that Black Lives Matter is being discredited as a Marxist organisation is exactly what happened in 1919. And the tragedy is, think where America would be now, how America could be leading the world on these issues, if it had only listened to those Black soldiers in 1919 and not dismissed them as Marxists. This history is a history of missed opportunities. This history is a moment of forks in the road and being pushed down the wrong avenue.

Well, we know how it's done. We've seen the trick done thousands of multiple times before, and part of it is by discrediting our organisations, by making us scared of embracing the organisations that are there, that we built to fight for our rights. So, I embrace Black Lives Matter. And I think the stories need to point out the process being used to attack it. We've seen this before. Our job as Black historians is to say this has been done in the past and look at what it costs all of us.

Lenny: So, I guess we'll stick with the title of the book. You've given the example of how you view Black Lives Matter through a historical lens, but how does your life experience impact on how you view and analyse history?

David: I think as a Black person. I find myself seeing tropes that my colleagues often don't see, and having to point out what to me causes discomfort – ways of seeing the world that are unexamined and come from a place of racism or a colonised mentality. And as an historian, I'm often pointing out different issues. I see myself as a politicised Black person who is an historian. But the complication is that while I'm fascinated by Black history, also the thing I'm most passionate about in all of history is the First World War.

And this goes to the heart of why Black British historians matter. The reason we matter is that we are creating and recoupling parts of our history.

OK, hold on – this is one point of this conversation that I want to get right, so let me phrase this better.

Black British historians matter, because we are the people who uncover the lost lives and the lost histories that were deliberately concealed; we are showing the chapters of British history that are relevant to all of us.

Most people who read my books are white. Most people who watch my television programmes are white. And that's fine because this is a shared history. Black British history for too long was seen as something only for Black people. It was marginal, it was dismissed, it was something to have in Black

History Month, 'let them have it'; you know, let's make a quick programme or cheap book. The idea that this is actually at the heart of British history, and that it's a shared history that belongs to all of us – that's the thing that's been denied. That's the thing that was dismissed, and it was dismissed out of ignorance. It was a presumption that we didn't really matter, that we hadn't been anywhere important or done anything significant. But we were there at every critical event in British history in the last 500 years because the Empire was the biggest story of British history for the past half a millennium. And Black and brown people were at the centre of it. But because it was uncomfortable, those connections were broken and many of them were broken deliberately.

My job is like rewiring a house. The way I see it is: British history is like a rambling mansion. There are some rooms that are occupied and some that are forgotten. So it's about opening the doors to those rooms that are cold and forgotten. They've been boarded up. And showing people the stories and the phenomena inside those rooms that affect all of us, that's my job.

It's about getting us out of that tiny portion of the great massive mansion in which we all live and with which we are so familiar – in that we know every detail of every inch of wallpaper, because we've looked at it too much – and looking at the rooms that we never set foot in.

And finally, while it might seem like one of the most simple and banal of phrases, it doesn't make it any less true or important: Black British history is British history.

Lenny: David, thank you for letting us into some of those boarded-up, forgotten rooms.

Thank you for showing us that as Black people we have a unique perspective and that can help all of us, of all races, understand our past better.

And thank you for helping Marcus and me settle a bet on the title of the book. I'm not going to say who was arguing what, but one of us is now owed a very expensive bottle of Appleton rum.

BLACK BRITISH ARCHITECTURE MATTERS

Emerging a Black British architecture

SIR DAVID ADJAYE

It is hard to think of an award for architecture that Sir David Adjaye has not won during the course of his illustrious career. He was the lead architect responsible for both the National Museum of African American History and Culture, in Washington DC, and the National Cathedral of Ghana. He was awarded the Royal Institute of British Architects' Royal Gold Medal 2021, becoming the first Black architect to win the prize.

David was one of the first people we approached to write an essay for this book. His positive response gave us the confidence we needed to approach many of the other writers, highlighting the importance of documenting precisely why Black British lives matter in so many different and varied parts of British culture.

What is a Black-British architecture? What are the material expressions of a people with such a complex history? What do we mean here when we say 'a people'? To have a Black-British architecture is more complex than a single signifier, more complex than a single image. You have to overcome the idea of looking for an aesthetic that cannot exist without the complex entanglements between movement, continuity and becomings – the material essences of a diasporic motion unleashed in an urban sphere. From this develops a visual culture which Jamaican-born political and social theorist Stuart Hall once called for when he spoke of the formations of identity, ethnicities, new possibilities and the re-articulation of Britain's cultural sphere. This visual culture is an architectural force, and a re-articulation of space where Hall says

> Cultural Identity . . . is a matter of 'becoming' as well as 'being'. It belongs to the future as much as to the past. It is not something that already exists, transcending place, time, history and culture. Cultural Identities come from somewhere, have histories. But like everything which is historical, they undergo constant transformation.[1]

The question of membering and re-membering plays a prolific role in what it means to be a part of the diaspora, to be both Black and British, to be at the hyphenation of those words, in which, like Hall said, it's not a matter of history alone but of the constant transformation it must undergo. It's the mission of memory to situate us both in and outside of time; the mission of a cultural hybridity, recognising the entanglements that create the special space of Black-Britishness; and the mission of emancipation where Blackness is understood as a political space. From 1948 onwards, a new language was forming to make visible the previously invisible histories and from this language came a methodology for architecture.

Memory (Bernie Grant Arts Centre)

I remember watching television in my youth and seeing Bernie Grant appear in the same agbada, traditional West African garments, as my uncle. The only difference was that one garment

was in the British Parliament and one was back home. Bernie
Grant was the first person of African descent to win election to
the House of Commons. He was history in the making, a left-
wing figure speaking out on issues of race, education and policing. Everything about Bernie was noble and unapologetic. He
made it a priority to reach Black communities throughout Britain and often brought the concerns he witnessed to the floor of
the House of Commons where he spoke out against discriminatory policing methods and unfair immigration control, despite
receiving critique from the public and Labour Party members.
Bernie was an ecologist in his own right. He didn't fragment
the world, but he saw how things connected. He understood
how education, institutionalised racism, health, housing, greater
resources for inner city areas, refugee rights and artistic expression operated together as an ecosystem. His approach to life was
multiple and the embodiment of his legacy became the Bernie
Grant Arts Centre, a cultural training ground and centre for
excellence serving the many facets of the wider community.

The Bernie Grant Arts Centre, located in Tottenham, North
London, was a project commissioned by the Bernie Grant
Trust. At the heart of the centre's programming is the intention to develop strategies to tackle institutional racism and
create community cohesion within the Tottenham area, which
Bernie Grant himself saw as a nexus for a significant number of
actors, musicians and writers. Through this, the idea for a performance centre and a centre for excellence within the community became a major aim of the project, along with the inclusion
of an educational space. It was clear that in creating a space for
Black-British identities to be, the project was creating a space
for Black-British identity to become. Therefore the centre had
to be multiple in its design to accommodate the flexibility of a

Black public challenging the superstructures of power previously seen in cultural and media representations before them. There are two main elements to the project: the auditorium, and the surrounding buildings – which represented significant aspects of the Trust's work – supporting the auditorium. The situating of the auditorium within the three buildings and the lowering of the roof to improve sight lines of the space's entirety created cohesion and both an informal and formal public space. Spaces where gathering, both organised and spontaneous, occurs, spaces where the real learning happens.

Historically speaking, in Black architectural traditions globally, the veranda or the porch would act as the blurring between the public and private realms. As a threshold or an in-between – it was a space that held the tension between an interior and exterior, giving it a transitory character. These were the spaces in which the education between communities and people of various ages would take place, where homeowners and passers-by would stop, and gather to tell stories at the in-between. Stories that transformed, stories that warned, stories that inspired and mythologised the experience of life into a comprehensible map of guidance. Gathering, and designing for gathering, therefore becomes an incredibly important characteristic for Black-British architecture, where the coming together to tell these stories, to receive education, to have wisdom passed down from generation to generation was and is the seed of culture being passed from one elder body to an upcoming youth, from one timeline to the other. To portray this within the centre was a literal deconstruction from within, where the permanent qualities of architecture as it met the transient becomings of Black-British people created the performance space of multidisciplinarity.

The auditorium itself included three main spaces: a foyer and bar, the performance hall and a large rehearsal space, all linked by an efficient circulation system. The front building was occupied by teaching spaces and small offices where the exterior suggests a transitory relationship between the old and new construction, embodying that generational intertwining of elders and ancestors imparting wisdom to youth. The Enterprise building, a long, thin building, contained the second rehearsal space, an enterprise unit for young businesses and shared support facilities. The design of the Bernie Grant Arts Centre, therefore, portrays the type of multiplicity and collectivity necessary for the Black-British community. It's a design that embodies what Black cultural theorist and poet Fred Moten once described as 'figuring it out'. Moten invoked Walter Rodney's 1969 book *The Groundings With My Brothers* to think about what it really means to 'figure it out', to 'work it out', to see if we can 'get together and figure this thing out'. It's a transformational thought, a spatial thought, because when the realm of architecture becomes subject to the realm of not just figuring through thought but figuring as a material exercise in space, you have a realisation of what Moten so eloquently describes – which is that 'what we've been trying to figure out how to get to, is how we are when we get together to try to figure it out'.[2]

We need to gather. Gathering is the radical act, the *figuring out* of our future from fragments of the past. The architecture becomes a space for those collective memories and a multiplicity meant to facilitate their complexity. In the same way that Bernie fashioned and figured himself out as a representation in the House of Commons for his community, when we say 'Black-British architecture' we think of the spaces in which we figure ourselves out, outside of the difficult realities that were laid before us.

Cultural hybridity (the Idea Store)

What differentiates the Black-British experience from an Afro-Caribbean experience or African American experience is that the language of race cannot be separated from class. In fact, the structures of class were largely in place when the migrations of cultures to Britain occurred, which only highlighted the fact that we have to think about both race and class together. As Stuart Hall says, 'race is the lens through which people come to perceive that a crisis is developing. It is the framework through which the crisis is experienced. It is the means by which the crisis is to be resolved.'[3] From this space, everything that was 'other', everything that was outside the eyes of Britain – Asian, South Asian, African and Caribbean bodies – formed as a political space of Blackness in alliance against the dominant narrative that viewed them as a problem. The act and power of coming together in community as a political force is the very idea that created the architecture for the Idea Store. Cultural hybridity as a method is about the interconnectivity between life and the creating of something new and more complex that says there isn't one way of doing or being in the world.

The Idea Store – commissioned by the London Borough of Tower Hamlets for two libraries located in Whitechapel and Chrisp Street – became a public architecture that didn't dominate over its inhabitants. Instead – through its infusion and situatedness in the surrounding community – it became a representation of its surroundings. In a moment where the idea of the library was thought to be dead due to the rise of technology and free information, Tower Hamlets Council decided to replace the traditional library format with seven 'Idea Stores' in order to improve access to a wider range of information and educational facilities.

The Idea Store Whitechapel presents an example of what it means to challenge the dominant both within its architecture and within its programming. It is located on the north side of Whitechapel Road where a wide pavement is occupied by a busy street market in a multicultural and multi-ethnic area of London. Rather than moving against the market, it moves with the market, as an expression of the community where, like the market stalls which have striped drapes, the building exterior contains a framed superstructure draped in green- and blue-striped sheets – an experience of the building which allows a community to see themselves within space. The library breaks from the typology of a Victorian municipality that discourages participation and, instead, is designed with two types of connecting. Firstly, it contains an escalator that opens directly onto the street, and secondly, the library facility itself is combined with adult-education facilities, a crèche, a gallery for exhibitions and a café. If the Bernie Grant Arts Centre touched upon notions of gathering through many functions, then the Idea Store, through hybridity, creates a new area of negotiation and representation. The architecture of the Idea Store ruptures the dominance of what a civic building had previously been and instead situates itself in the reality of the streets, constructing and reconstructing itself in discourse with a growing community.

Blackness in Britain's past created a language for speaking about identity as empowering and multifaceted. It emancipated identity from skin and showed us that the democratic solution we are looking for could be understood within this language. Now, taking this to the realm of architecture means that if 'Black-Britishness' is multifaceted, our structures must contain a multiplicity, and this multiplicity can be achieved through a type of generosity. Things change. People and communities grow. And within each moment of change is a type of growth in conversation with the external environment that begins to posit architecture's response.

Blackness as a political space (Rivington Place)

The mid-1980s to 1998 was an incredible period for the cultural and political interventions of British 'Black Arts'. There was an explosion of Black visual arts in the form of photography, painting and film in particular, with the rise of prolific figures and collectives such as Isaac Julien, Sankofa, John Akomfrah and the Black Audio Film Collective. This was the generation to extend the debate of expressive culture, this was the generation of the children of Empire coming of age – they didn't 'come from' the land of their parents, they were born in Empire and yet their longing for home was just as prescient, just as precious. The affirmation of this generation was that a new politic was forming which needed new forms of expression to represent these intertwining identities. As historian and academic Paul Gilroy explained, 'Black expressive cultures affirm while they protest'[4] and the protest of visual culture presented by Black diaspora film-making at the time created new imagery to counter the dominant imagery. A functional identity was not only re-imagined, but re-imaged. The genre of diaspora film-making as an experimental arts practice was often characterised through a non-linear narrative form playing with an asynchronous montage and always including multiple perspectives. These elements also became a prompt for the urban space because from this comes the creation and re-creation of new narratives for multiple lived experiences.

Rivington Place Arts Centre is a space to champion this

multiplicity. This was the legacy of Stuart Hall, who pioneered a new language and need for new visual media representations for the Black-British community. As one of the most influential intellectuals of his time, there may not be enough words to describe the work of Stuart, but like Bernie Grant, he saw the ecology of life and its problems operating as an ecosystem. Within the academic spaces, Stuart redefined issues of culture, race and ethnicity and showed us the reality of what was really happening in London at the time. With occasional appearances on the BBC, he critiqued the media for the way it created stereotypes and representations and he was a huge influence for the Black arts movement where his understanding of the power of the arts forged new cultural institutions into existence.

Rivington Place was the first arts building in London to be backed with public funding since the Hayward Gallery, a testament to the importance of the arts and centres for the arts within Black-British communities. Rivington Place is the permanent home for two arts organisations: Iniva (Institute of International Visual Arts), which houses the Stuart Hall Library; and Autograph ABP, which formed a strategic alliance to make a permanent centre to champion artists of different backgrounds and support them at various stages of their career. Rivington Place set the standard for all other arts institutions in London to follow. Iniva, for example, was first launched at a conference at Tate Britain entitled 'Towards a New Internationalism', which explored the necessity for diversity and difference in the role of curatorial practice and the arts. The very ethos of the organisation stood for something radical – a recognition that the dominant discourse couldn't account for a universal experience of life and art without recognising the strategic workings which had filtered out the Black and diasporic experience.

Rivington Place is located in Shoreditch, East London, where the historic fabric includes a number of industrial warehouses that have been repurposed by cultural organisations and small businesses. The building acts not only as a key addition to the London arts scene but it also provides a space for practitioners specifically from culturally diverse backgrounds and marginalised groups to present ideas and practices in the contemporary visual arts. The building's external lattice pattern, thinking back to the asynchronous montage feature previously discussed in Black-British film-making practices, was informed by Sowei masks of Sierra Leone. This influenced the way light entered the space, pointing towards a dialogue between African, instead of European, perspectives as foundational for the structure. The building includes a double-height project space, gallery, lecture theatre, café, library, digital media lab and offices for both organisations to continue running and supporting the communities of ethnic minorities.

Rivington Place is a space envisioned for figuring it out and imaging the future through art. As an example of a Black-British architecture, it demonstrates a new type of institution of the arts saturated by and within a 'new vocabulary and syntax of rebellion'.[5] The history of the mid-1980s to 1998 demonstrated the emergence of new art forms to accommodate journeys of transformation, weaving commonalities and differences into something revolutionary. As an institution based within the diasporic identity of Britain, Rivington Place portrays an architecture that can both hold a space from which to speak and become a place to speak from.

The process of designing a Black-British architecture is a two-part mission of encapsulating within design the recognition of a violent history and transient migrations, but also the needs of communities to figure themselves out, outside of the dissonant realities once set before them. Black-British architecture demonstrates that the materials of memory, intertwining of cultures, and the shared politic created out of alliance are the means by which what was previously othered now sits at the forefront. As Kobena Mercer, Yale professor of History of Art and African American Studies, once said, 'Becoming liberates our perception of time from the beginnings, middles and endings of narrative codes that privilege the moment of closure.'[6] The architecture doesn't just liberate the Black-British experience in real space, and in real time; it also demonstrates that what was once perceived as a moment of closure is now and continues to be our new beginning.

BLACK BRITISH POLICE MATTER

An act of defiance

LEROY LOGAN

Leroy Logan was described in the Guardian *as 'the man who risked everything to fight racism in the police force – from within'. He was the first chair of the National Black Police Association. His life was adapted into a film by the director Steve McQueen for the BBC drama series* Small Axe, *marking key moments in contemporary Black British history. Leroy is the author of* Closing Ranks: My Life as a Cop.

When we decided we needed an essay on the importance of why Black British police matter, Leroy was not just our first choice, he was our only choice. We are incredibly grateful that he agreed to contribute to the anthology.

Introduction

Norwell Roberts, officially the first Black – African Caribbean – British police officer, joined the Metropolitan Police Service (the Met) over fifty years ago in 1967. I was privileged to attend his leaving reception, where he was piped in by Scottish bagpipes. Despite the fact that he had endured a hostile working environment, Norwell was wearing a massive smile, literally ear to ear. During that joyous occasion, I asked him why he was beaming in this uncharacteristic way and he summed it up as a strong signal of defiance – especially to the people who had tried to grind him down – that they hadn't succeeded. Norwell's comments lived with me until I retired sixteen years later in 2013, when I unashamedly copied his entrance with bagpipes and a wide defiant grin.

Unfortunately, there is nothing to suggest that Black British police officers today feel any more valued than I did or even during Norwell's era. This is a real disappointment and I don't make this comment lightly; in fact, it's with a heavy heart that I do so.

All themes highlighted in the Met can easily be transferred to the same challenges other constabularies face in the UK.

Scene setting

I equate the death of George Floyd with one of those iconic US moments in recent memory. You may find this surprising, but I see it in similar terms to the 9/11 terrorist attacks and the inauguration of the first Black president, because I am sure most of us can remember where we were as our gaze was transfixed by these historic events. The examples I have shared conjure up bittersweet memories and we can definitely agree the last nine minutes and twenty-nine seconds of George Floyd's life was a bitter moment in American history but, at the same time, it had widespread implications for wider society in each of the fifty states, and allied countries. The UK is no exception.

Tears ran down my face as I watched the video footage circulated within a few short hours of George Floyd begging for his life, while the officer carried out a cold-blooded lynching and his colleagues made no attempts to prevent or stop it from happening, despite the gut-wrenching repeated cries he made – 'I can't breathe' – echoed by concerned bystanders. Those officers swore an oath to protect and serve, which is not far removed from the oath I swore as a police recruit in 1983, the starting point of my thirty-year career in the Metropolitan Police Service.

What made it worse for me was how the officer used his knee to end George Floyd's life, because kneeling is generally accepted as an act of reverence, devotion and duty – from church communion and marriage proposals to being knighted by the Queen. As a commonly accepted, important and positive gesture for many nationalities, I am not surprised the officer's illegal use of his knee in taking the life of a fellow human caused global revulsion. The devastating irony did not escape me when I immediately reflected on the peaceful protest of Colin Kaepernick, the San Francisco 49er NFL player who, in spring 2016, began taking a knee during the pre-match playing of the US national anthem, in response to the ongoing scourge of racially motivated police killings in the United States over decades. It is not surprising this act of solidarity has spread across the sporting world as a protest against acts of racism, including the English Premier League, since that fateful day on 25 May 2020 in Minneapolis.

One of the main issues emerging from the George Floyd killing is the widespread implications for police reform, particularly in the context of the global reach of Black Lives Matter (BLM) since its formation in 2013 as a movement for freedom, liberation and justice. In 2020 BLM was seen as the largest movement of people in US history, which had a ripple effect across the globe primarily through the mobilisation of young people of all backgrounds, ethnicities and cultures peacefully protesting. From 25 May until mid-November 2020 there have been protests in 4,446 cities and towns worldwide, including across the length and breadth of the UK.

Without any hesitation I attended one of the first London

protests in early June 2020, as an act of solidarity for George Floyd and my personal act of regret on behalf of Black officers who wanted to be there, who shared their feelings with me and could not attend due to the restrictions of police regulations. It was also an act of defiance that 'A Change Is Gonna Come' – as Sam Cooke famously sang almost sixty years ago and recently re-celebrated in the film *One Night in Miami*.

It was the first protest in which I had taken part since retiring in 2013, giving me a unique sense of freedom, because I was totally unconstrained by my previous role as a police officer. This strange sense of exhilaration remained with me as I saw the multicultural body of young people gathering in Hyde Park who were energised by a series of inspirational speakers, culminating with actor John Boyega whose speech went viral, adding more kudos to the BLM cause. I took the opportunity of joining them in taking a knee as an act of commemoration of the tragic events in Minneapolis and in solidarity to the call for racial equality, before setting off for Parliament Square and winding through the streets of central London energetically chanting 'I Can't Breathe' and 'No Justice, No Peace, No Racist Police'.

Throughout this time I observed that my ex-colleagues had generally given us – the protesters – a very wide berth, as an explicit attempt to avoid the tactical mistakes seen in the US that occasionally resulted in violence. I saw these more passive tactics as somewhat unorthodox for the Met. I had policed many protests in this setting and, generally, the response was tightly run with police being more hands-on to maintain the speed and direction of the march. I welcomed this new light-touch approach to reduce conflict, even with the more boisterous young people on the march. It was reassuring to see Black officers policing the march, showing their shared and common experience with the multicultural gathering. It was a perfect example of why the police service needs to reflect the population it serves – a visualisation of Black Police Lives Matter.

I also took the opportunity to observe some of the multi-ethnic officers assigned to our event more closely; I sensed they had a greater empathy with the marchers and this was confirmed when I struck up brief conversations with a few of them at certain points along the route. It became clear to me that George Floyd had been a significant discussion point in Met circles, but a real concern for me was how it was impacting Black officers in the workplace culture of the police.

While on the march I tried to put myself in the position of those young Black officers by reflecting on a few iconic events involving the Black community, where police were heavily criticised for their corruption, incompetence or racism – or a combination of these factors.

Bristol seminars

I recalled one particular experience when the occupational culture was most toxic for me as a young officer, which I now liken to having a metaphoric knee on my neck. It occurred during the summer of 1990, when the head of the Met's HR department, Assistant Commissioner Wyn Jones, recognised that Black officers were far more likely to leave in the first two years than their white counterparts and significant changes had to be made. The best way of finding out the experience of Black officers was to speak to them, so he organised two-day seminars outside London in Bristol.

As one of the officers who attended, I finally felt that my concerns, and those of my seminar colleagues, would be heard, making us feel our lives mattered and the hostile environment we had to endure would be changed for the better. We opened up our veins and bled out the pain we suffered on a regular basis in the culture of the workplace. One officer told how whenever he radioed his colleagues, they would make monkey noises back at him. Every N-word we'd ever been subjected to while at work – be it in the staff canteen or on the football pitch – came out. For everyone who spoke, the experience was cathartic and soul-searching.

As far as I was concerned, I wasn't going to go through this process and then go back to business as usual. I didn't see Bristol as just a series of seminars; for me, it was a call to action. This drive for change energised me to apply for a position on the working group tasked with writing up a report on the seminars. In 1991 our report was published, but in fine Met tradition it got shelved, around the same time Wyn Jones was subject to an inquiry for criminal misconduct. Despite this setback, the report was the embryonic stage of the Black Police Association (BPA), resulting in its launch in 1994 based on our overarching aim of 'improving the working environment of Black personnel with the intention of improving service delivery to the Black community'. Recognising the police service has a problem dealing with race equality issues both internally and externally, our intention was to get the Met to realise there is an inextricable link in the way it treats its diverse personnel, so that it is better equipped to serve the needs of a diverse public.

Macpherson Inquiry

No Black officer can forget the extra burden they felt on the lead-up to, during and after the Macpherson Inquiry looking into the racist killing of Stephen Lawrence and the botched investigation. It came in many forms, but I outline four of these below.

Firstly, Black officers became the focus of white officers' misplaced frustrations over the label of institutional racism applied to the Metropolitan Police Service by the inquiry report.

Secondly, some senior leaders took a different stance and were willing to give Black officers special status as experts in race equality issues, only because of the colour of their skin. In some instances, it was a potent form of exploitation, because in many cases it was against the Black officers' wishes.

Thirdly, if Black officers like me were willing to shine a light on the institutionally racist policies and practices, there were attempts from sections of the top team to undermine our honesty, integrity and other parts of our good character.

Finally, a combination of the above caused an unbearable and demoralising burden on Black officers, which could eventually precipitate a premature end to their career.

The inquiry recommendations had a significant focus on achieving a more reflective organisation through close monitoring of recruitment, retention and progression of Black officers, followed by a commensurate culture change, to ensure the Met would not only attract the best Black talent but also nurture the individuals through a robust Positive Action – not positive discrimination – programme. These initiatives were underpinned by independent oversight given by the Stephen Lawrence Steering Group (SLSG), chaired by the then Home Secretary, Jack Straw, in the presence of Doreen and Neville Lawrence, together with Heads of Ministries, Chief Constables and me, as first Chair of the National BPA. This was a continuation of political intent to explicitly show the Labour government's ownership of the Macpherson Inquiry in the first place, followed by ownership of progress around the recommendations. This oversight remained in place from the report's publication in 1999 through the following decade, chaired by subsequent Labour Home Secretaries, making it clear to Black officers like me that we were valued and we mattered.

During this ten-year period, the Met showed the greatest growth in the number of Black recruits, with more than a five-fold increase, based on the principle 'what gets measured gets done'. This resulted in greater representation up the ranks, including the appointment in 2004 of the first Black Chief Constable, Mike Fuller, who served in that role for six years. Since 2010, no other African Caribbean officer has followed in Mike's footsteps. It's not a surprise to know this initial progress levelled off once the SLSG was dissolved in 2010 and not replaced with any form of tangible oversight. It is totally clear to me that the wider race and equality issue was no longer a priority in the era of austerity that came in with the Tory government. Then the Brexit referendum result in 2016 saw a right-wing shift in the wider public; the police is a reflection of this – we witnessed a greater emphasis on heavy-handed racial-profile policing and a more hostile occupational culture for Black officers to endure and navigate through.

The death of Sir William Macpherson in February 2021 has caused us to reflect on how, for decades, Black people's lived experience was through the prism of institutional racism. This has invariably manifested itself through the disproportionate use of stop and search, which is in turn correlated with the excessive use of force. Before the inquiry report, senior leadership and politicians spoke about the 'bad apples in the barrel' scenario, which implied there were no systemic failures responsible for police misconduct. However, the report's definition of institutional racism faced the police with the uncomfortable

truth that it needed to reform, according to the inquiry's recommendations. The need for reform was not exclusive to policing
but throughout society, and the report provided a watershed
moment which all public institutions had to confront.

Twenty-two years later, the BLM protesters are carrying the
Macpherson torch and renewing the demand to confront systemic racism that is alive and kicking, especially in the police
force, which is in desperate need of transformation into a mod-
ernised, more reflective organisation, better equipped to deal
with the challenges of the twenty-first century.

The Damilola Taylor case

As I advanced through my career, I grew increasingly frustrated
by the fact that Black officers' cultural intelligence and com-
petence was underused in terms of their culture, experiences,
education, languages, etc. This was mainly because of the Met's
tunnel vision obsession that only in-house training was appropriate to policing London, even when the population was growing
more and more diverse. Consequently, I submitted a paper outlining how these untapped skills and abilities could be accessed
through a secure database, resulting in bespoke deployment of
Black officers in operational settings such as kidnappings, hos-
tage negotiations, murders and so on; what I eventually classed
as Affinity Policing (AP) deployments.

Unfortunately, the report was not seen as a priority by Deputy
Assistant Commissioner Bill Griffiths – head of the CID training
school at Hendon – during rollout of the Macpherson Inquiry
recommendations in 1999. Not easily deterred, I saw this as an
opportunity to show the advantages of this previously untested
model of policing in a high-profile investigation. Through a

complex sequence of events, I took the opportunity of apply-
ing the AP model to the Homicide Investigation Team of the
Damilola Taylor case in 2000–1, by introducing a team of Black
officers known as the Cultural Resource Unit (CRU). Damilola
Taylor was a ten-year-old Nigerian boy who was killed on a London estate in 2000; his death, in many ways, opened a public
discussion around how society treated young Black men, not least
the police. Nothing could have prepared me for the dramatic
impact the CRU would have within hours of their deployment. It
was with great anticipation that I attended their initial debriefing
sessions; they never failed to amaze me each time they shared their
achievements. I observed how they drew together as a cohesive
and dynamic team.

An example of the CRU's immediate impact was the experience of two officers, Debbie and Jimi. During their first wave of
house-to-house enquiries, they went to homes where repeated
visits by white officers had not even elicited a response from
the occupants. When they went, they had the presence of mind
to shout through the letterbox, 'Auntie (or 'Uncle'), it's me,'
in Yoruba, a Nigerian language predominantly spoken in the
southern regions of the country, especially in Lagos, the largest
city. From within the veil of silence would come the cautious
voice of an occupant saying, 'Ah – you're Nigerian?' to which
they would respond, 'Yes, Uncle' or 'Yes, Auntie' (in Nigeria
and many other African countries, addressing an older person as
'Uncle' or 'Auntie' is seen as a mark of respect). This would be
promptly followed by the unbolting of a secured door and the
occupant gesticulating anxiously for them to enter the prem-
ises quickly. Within a couple of hours, Debbie and Jimi would
emerge with critical intelligence for the investigation. The AP
model was already proving its worth, showing the benefits of

Black officers who broke down the wall of silence to secure witnesses, identify forensics and secure convictions.

It was essential that I was fully objective about the CRU's performance, so I left it to the investigation operation's supervisors to assess the team's outcome. Their summary report was very complimentary on behalf of the Senior Investigation Officer. It noted, among other things, that within the first few days of their deployment, the CRU had gathered potentially important intelligence and passed it on to the enquiry team thanks to people's willingness to speak to them. The only negative feedback they'd had was members of the community saying, 'Why has it taken so long for you to arrive? You should have been here the day it happened!'

Thanks to the quality of intelligence gathered in such a short time, the CRU was asked to carry out more important actions and allocated vehicles to do so. This gave the unit a level of unforeseen respect, and facilitated its seamless integration into the Homicide Investigation Team. The CRU officers grew enormously in confidence and in their investigative abilities. I saw an appetite for complex investigations that had been lying dormant in them surface fully, as newly found skills and abilities blossomed. This case was also a catalyst of change in breaking down the internal barriers Black officers faced when joining the CID and other specialist operations units, because I was able to qualitatively assess their impact in an operational and tactical setting.

To get such immediate results, despite the inherent risks, vindicated my total confidence in the CRU officers. I was pleasantly surprised that the initial scepticism Homicide Investigation Team colleagues exhibited was eventually replaced by a more positive – if somewhat grudging – tone of support. They never explicitly vocalised their support in my presence or in the meeting minutes; instead, they implicitly conceded defeat in their general disposition towards the CRU and me. Over the sub-sequent weeks and months, I wasn't surprised to see many of them owning these breakthroughs in the investigation. Success has many guardians; failure is an orphan.

Morris Inquiry

The Macpherson Inquiry had improved the Met's service delivery to the public, with a particular emphasis on the Black community in order to level the playing field in comparison to white members of the public. It led to changes such as the Race Relations Amendment Act 2020, which outlawed race discrimination in areas not covered by the 1976 legislation and required public authorities, such as the police, to promote racial equality. Other outcomes of the inquiry included: community and race relations training for frontline officers, chief inspectors and lower ranks; Senior Investigation Officer critical incident training, to reduce race bias in major investigations and critical incidents; placing Hate Crime on the statute books and developing Family Liaison Officers focusing on these forms of crimes; and the creation of Independent Advisory Groups – critical friends – centrally at Scotland Yard and, locally, on borough-based Basic Command Units.

Disappointingly, we did not see any tangible change in the Met's culture regarding recruitment, retention and progression, despite the Macpherson Inquiry recommendations. A critical indicator of the cultural hostility was the disproportionate number of Black senior leaders subject to misconduct investigations (three times higher than their white counterparts); sadly, it is still the case in 2021. I have been subject to a formal misconduct investigation and trial by media for an allegation about which my white counterparts did not even get verbal warnings. Unfortunately, I was not the only one; therefore, when I was Chair of the BPA Executive, we successfully lobbied for an independent inquiry, headed by Sir Bill Morris, a well-recognised champion for equal rights in the Trade Union movement. The Morris Inquiry was our way of influencing change from the bottom up, thus putting a strong value statement in our continued fight against institutional racism.

While setting up the inquiry, we had to be very specific in terms of reference, to expose the evidence of disproportionality. The points that we wanted to emphasise were that it was the BPA commissioning it, that it should have independent oversight and take into account the long-standing employment tribunals. It had to take in the critical matters concerning Operation Helios – a witch hunt against the BPA – in comparison to other investigations, and question whether the central Independent Advisory Group was truly independent of the Met, as it was supposed to be.

We also wanted the inquiry to look at how the Met's Department of Professional Standards carried out its role of monitoring police conduct. What checks and balances did it have when looking at cases? How did it decide whether it was in the police interest or the public interest for a case to be heard? Was it really objective or even fit for purpose? Then there was the question of how the Director for Public Affairs (DPA; the Met's media wing) often reinforced certain false narratives. For instance, when I was being subjected to trial by media, there was a lot of concern about the DPA leaking information to the press. What were they doing to counter false narratives?

Ultimately, we wanted to ensure that there was a root-and-branch review of the policies and practices of the Met, a confirmation that proper community impact assessments were being done for these cases (and if not, why not?), and a reassurance that whatever strategy the Met employed, it should have the least amount of disruption to community trust and confidence.

It was unprecedented that Black police personnel had called for and got an inquiry of this nature. People might wonder why it was such a big deal for us. For me, it was about understanding that we were willing to speak up; to ensure that people knew that we weren't self-serving but were speaking out about all the issues of inequality and injustice that needed to be addressed, for the Met to progress as a modern police service; one that the community trusted and had confidence in. For us, these were critical matters that needed to be dealt with.

The inquiry officially launched on 21 January 2004, and over six months, the panel gathered evidence, received over 1,400 documents and heard evidence from 109 people. On 14 December 2004, *The Case for Change*, the 288-page report on the Morris Inquiry, was published. Never in our wildest dreams did we think we would have an inquiry of this nature. Even though it had Bill Morris's name on it, the BPA movement was the main driver pushing the agenda. We had made history. We felt vindicated that, despite all the challenges, we were able to formulate a report that evidenced the hostile police culture. We were speaking truth to power; we were getting more clarity on areas of the organisation that most people would never know about. Sometimes we'd think, 'Is there any more that we don't know about how the organisation operates?' but at least we had a greater idea of the scale of the problem.

The views of serving officers

I have made it a priority to make regular contact with Black officers in the Met, especially through my membership of the Met BPA and continuing on from my retirement in 2013. Additionally,

I liaised with them through my advocacy and activism work in the community, primarily through the BPA charitable trust I helped set up in 1998 – rebranded as VOYAGE (Voice of the Youth and Genuine Empowerment) in 2016. Even though I felt totally confident in my understanding of what Black officers go through, I didn't want to leave any stone unturned, so I decided I must hear from a few strategically placed officers to ensure my understanding was current, reliable and informed. In particular, I wanted to know how they felt valued internally and externally in this current Black Lives Matter era. For this exercise I called them my Officers Reference Group.

After the George Floyd killing and the reinvigoration of the BLM movement, acts of solidarity for greater equity – like taking a knee – were important to individuals and organisations across the public sphere. Policing was not exempt and we saw isolated cases of officers of all ethnic backgrounds doing likewise across the country, without any central directive, whether it was the College of Policing or the National Police Chiefs' Council.

However, these isolated examples of solidarity came to an abrupt end when Chief Constables took the lead of Metropolitan Police Commissioner Cressida Dick, the most high-profile cop in the land, who made it a lawful order on 7 June 2020 that such actions would be prohibited, suggesting Met officers who did take the knee may have felt pressurised by crowds. I was at the 6 June march and I didn't sense that officers were pressurised to take the knee. This was like putting a knee on the neck of Black officers who felt prohibited by such orders, especially when this diktat was made in isolation, without consultation from police staff associations like the BPA or reaffirming the Met's anti-racist commitment in its Diversity, Equality and Inclusion (DEI) policy. It was a contradiction in terms because, at the same time, Cressida Dick was suggesting the force was sympathetic with the BLM move-ment. She talked it but didn't walk it, unlike other constabularies such as Essex, where the Chief Constable ensured their DEI strat-egy reflected their anti-racist commitment with the backing of the Police Crime Commissioner and the staff associations.

The Met's Management Board stance put pressure on some of their Black officers on a borough level, when they were in con-tact with the Black community and had to defend this lack of action. This pressure was exacerbated by acts of tokenism which were being put forward as a point of expertise with the public and/or with their colleagues because of the colour of their skin, not because of their skills and experience in these critical mat-ters. What one officer described as being 'part of a pet project'.

At the peak of the BLM protests across the country, I felt compelled to publicly criticise Cressida Dick when she made it known the Stephen Lawrence investigation would be shelved, because the timing could not have been worse; the decision did not have to be made in public at such a crucial time for the Black community. I called it a crazy decision – on Twitter – that added insult to injury for the Lawrence family, the wider Black community and the Met BPA that has explicitly supported the Lawrence family from their unsuccessful private prosecution against the murder suspects in 1996 until the present day.

Other findings from my Officers Reference Group were equal-ly enlightening. It emerged that the Met was stuck doing old tricks and unwilling to learn new ones, in terms of how it values Black officers and the type of policing it provides to the Black community. This reinforced perceptions that the Met has not significantly progressed on issues of race equality, both internal-ly and externally, since the Macpherson Inquiry, especially since the independent oversight provided by the Stephen Lawrence

Steering Group was removed around 2010 and with the lack of political will from central government. In fact, the current Home Secretary, Priti Patel, is into the sort of dog-whistle politics that emboldens senior officers like Commissioner Cressida Dick to state that the Met is no longer institutionally racist, when it is above her pay grade to suggest anything of this nature. The Commissioner needs to wait until the Home Affairs Select Committee – chaired by Yvette Cooper – reports back with its inquiry entitled *The Macpherson Report: Twenty-one Years On*, which is already well overdue.

Even though some force areas have made strong positive communications, accompanied by the infrastructure and capacity to learn, the Met appears to stick to the same old tactics with the expectation of getting different results. This gives many people like me the distinct impression it not only suffers from institutional racism but also institutional amnesia, creating an analogue attitude that creates a flawed foundation for a public service to build on in a digital age.

Despite this gloomy backdrop, there are glimmers of hope that show pockets of progress in force areas across the country, including the Met – although it is patchy and not a corporate approach. For example, the Met has introduced 'Listening Circles' to look at the issues emerging from the massive impact of George Floyd and BLM. But these circles are not underpinned by a tangible organisational response; while the Met declared these 2020 events a critical incident, here we are, well into 2021, without any transformational leadership. This has an impact on an individual basis when some Black officers candidly state how they feel isolated and conflicted by the fallout from May 2020, compounded by senior leadership's ambivalence to their need for support and feeling valued.

One of the most profound comments that my Officers

Reference Group made about the senior leadership is: 'If they don't think racism exists, their sense of denial has made them blind.' I couldn't sum it up better if I tried.

To add insult to injury, the wider police culture has adopted the 'Blue Lives Matter' mantra, which is code for extreme right-wing views dominating the lower ranks represented by the Federation – the statutory staff association – that has been consistently pushing back and is out of step with progressive change. From my own experience, I observed directly their adversarial stance to the formation of the Met BPA in 1994 and the emerging issues from the Macpherson Inquiry report, in particular the definition of institutional racism. Surprise surprise, twenty years later they are part of the problem in fuelling the toxicity of the occupational culture and their sense of being emboldened by the political leanings of the current Home Secretary.

The present narrative is a growing concern for me, knowing how it can become more extreme, as we have observed in the US. There we have seen how the populist hard-line narrative has developed into an ideology of white extremism that has polluted enforcement agencies and the military, including the Capitol Police Department that withstood the 6 January 2021 insurrection even though over twenty officers within that unit are alleged to have been co-conspirators and have been suspended pending further investigation and trial. I'm a strong believer in the comment 'when the US sneezes the UK catches a cold', hence my concern.

Concluding remarks

Joining the Metropolitan Police Service in 1983 was a massive culture shock for me, because I was a career scientist responding to the calling of policing and entering a hostile police environment – reinforced by a macho-driven militaristic ethos that didn't celebrate difference, that demanded everyone assimilated into the ranks by stripping themselves of their identity and being a slave to the culture, commonly known as the 'Thin Blue Line'. I knew I had to make a significant standpoint before joining, clearly making it known when appropriate that I'm a Black man who happens to be a cop and not a cop who happens to be Black. This meant I had no inclination to assimilate, but I chose to travel a road that is much less travelled since it requires a strong sense of identity, self-confidence and strength of character based on cultural values and principles. On top of that, I had a clear purpose to change the organisational culture, eventually becoming one of the founder members of the Black Police Association and its community-facing charitable trust, VOYAGE.

Unfortunately, far too many Black officers find the hostile police culture extremely toxic with insufficient support from supervisors and senior leaders, resulting in them leaving in disproportionate numbers. This has been confirmed by an ongoing review by the Police Foundation, the UK's policing think tank; its findings are devastatingly worrying and clearly show that Black officers are not a priority, because, if they were, the wider police family – including Police Crime Commissioners – would do something about it. The sense of isolation and negative experience faced by Black officers nationally are reflected in the Police Foundation's data:

- There has been only very small growth in the numbers of Black police officers. As a proportion of the total police force it has grown by just 0.3 per cent, from 1 per cent to 1.3 per cent, over the past thirteen years.
- Since the 1981 Scarman report – one of the first reports to look at the policing of the Black community – national

growth has only been 0.9 per cent, during which time twenty-eight out of the forty-three force areas across the country have shown no progress.

- National projections suggest it would take ninety years for the percentage of officers in the organisation to reflect public demographics and it would take the Met seventy-two years to do likewise, which is approximately twice as long as the projections made by the Home Office when the Macpherson recommendations were issued in 1999.

- The few Black police officers who do exist are twice as likely to suffer dismissal as their white colleagues.

These terrible retention figures are mirrored by disappointing recruitment and promotion performance, where the success rate at each of these assessment levels for Black officers is approximately half of their white counterparts, suggesting an inherent racial bias in the selection process.

If these findings do not kick-start significant and sustainable change, nothing will. I hope the plight of Black officers will improve dramatically as soon as possible, through an acknowledgement of the hostile environment they face on a daily basis and the sustainable actions required to remove the systemic failures that keep them down.

If we care about how our Black communities are policed, we must care about Black police officers. Black British police lives matter.

BLACK BRITISH LAWYERS MATTER

Bridging the trust deficit

ALEXANDRA WILSON

In 2020 barrister Alexandra Wilson, a Black woman, made international headlines when she was mistaken for a defendant three times in one day at court by a security officer, a solicitor and a clerk. Her experience highlighted the conditions facing too many Black people working in the legal profession and the lack of diversity.

Alexandra is the author of In Black and White: A Young Barrister's Story of Race and Class in a Broken Justice System. *We feel incredibly fortunate that she agreed to contribute an essay detailing not only her personal experiences at the bar, but also the wider consequences of racism and discrimination in the legal system.*

Introduction

As a barrister specialising in criminal and family law, I am on the frontline when it comes to witnessing the justice system's trust deficit with the Black community. The consequences of the lack of trust in our legal system, most notably the criminal justice system, has devastating consequences for many of the Black people who are dragged through the courts every day. When I walk into a criminal courtroom, I am often met with the same faces: a white judge, a white opponent and, sadly, too often, a Black defendant.

In 2020 many of us were forced to confront the issue of the

over-criminalisation of Black people in the UK's criminal justice system. While the focus started on the US in the aftermath of the killing of George Floyd, the Black community in the UK rightly pointed out that we have to open our eyes to how our country also fails Black people. Unsurprisingly, our criminal justice system was brought into the spotlight and forced to confront the over-representation of Black people as suspects, defendants and prisoners, yet the contrasting under-representation of Black people as lawyers and judges.

The differences between those who are powerless in our criminal justice system and those who wield the power are alarming. As a barrister, I know that I am in a privileged position in that I provide a voice to the powerless in an attempt to ensure that the powerful exercise that power in the fairest way possible. In a system where people like me are over-represented as defendants but under-represented on the other side, I try to bridge the trust deficit.

The trust deficit in the Black community

The phrase 'trust deficit' was used by David Lammy in the Lammy Review. He described the trust deficit in many Black, Asian and minority ethnic (BAME) communities as revolving around the fact that '[m]any BAME defendants trust neither the advice of solicitors paid for by the government, nor that the CJS [criminal justice system] will deliver on the promise of less punitive treatment in exchange for prompt admissions on guilt'.

The Lammy Review was an independent review into the treatment of, and outcomes for, BAME individuals in the criminal justice system. It was established to 'make recommendations for improvement with the ultimate aim of reducing the proportion of BAME offenders in the criminal justice system'. Many of the findings from the Lammy Review inform this essay.

However, whilst David Lammy's report focused on the experiences of those across Black, Asian and other ethnic minority groups, this essay focuses on the experiences of those of Black heritage only. This is not to disregard the importance of looking at how the criminal justice system treats people from other ethnic minority groups but rather to focus on the issues that disproportionately affect Black people. It is important to note that sometimes a breakdown is not available and hence I rely on statistics for people from BAME backgrounds. These statistics will have to be treated with caution as they represent the experiences or treatment of Black, Asian and other ethnic minority groups, not just Black people.

My overarching message is this: it is crucial that Black people have trust in the criminal justice system. Anecdotally, many of my Black clients don't; they don't think that they will be treated fairly by judges and believe that their fate has already been decided. Many have experienced discrimination from 'authorities' since childhood, whether this is being unfairly excluded from mainstream education or being harassed by police officers who have stopped and searched them on numerous occasions.

It's hardly surprising that many Black people do not have faith in the criminal justice system and we must act now to bridge this trust deficit.

The police

Only 1 per cent of police officers are Black.[1]

A police officer's role is to protect members of the public by enforcing the law. The United Nations sets out a basic principle, the rule of law, which applies in the UK. That is: 'all persons, institutions and entities, public and private, including the State itself, are accountable to laws that are publicly promulgated, *equally enforced* and independently adjudicated, and which are consistent with international human rights norms and standards' (emphasis added).

It is fundamental that the law is equally enforced. In the UK, many people have rightly questioned whether the law is equally enforced on Black people compared to white people.

Black people in the UK are stopped and searched at a higher rate than any other ethnic group. The three Black ethnic groups (Black Caribbean, Black African and Black other) had the highest rates of stop and search out of all eighteen individual ethnic groups identified. The police choose who they decide to stop and search and it cannot be concluded that the law is equally enforced when Black people are nine times more likely to be stopped and searched than their white counterparts.[2]

It doesn't end with stop and search. Perhaps unsurprisingly, given the over-policing of Black people, they are also arrested at a higher rate than any other ethnic group. Black people are more than three times as likely to be arrested as white people.[3] The three Black ethnic groups (Black Caribbean, Black African and Black other) and Mixed White/Black Caribbean had the highest arrest rates of all eighteen individual ethnic groups.

This over-policing of Black people is not inadvertent; it is a product of racist ideologies about the criminality of Black people. The Macpherson Inquiry report on the Metropolitan Police's handling of Stephen Lawrence's death details some of the racist attitudes historically prevalent in the police. Inspector Leroy Logan recalled being in the back of a car with a white female police officer who, upon seeing a Black person driving a nice car, exclaimed, 'I wonder who he robbed to get that?'[4]

Historically, the 'rotten apple' narrative has been used to justify these attitudes, turning a blind eye to the issue of systematic and institutional racism. In the Macpherson report, Dr Robin Oakley claimed in his first submission to the Inquiry that racism is a 'problem specifically of individual officers, of "rotten apples" within the service'.[5] This was challenged by Sir Paul Condon, who states: 'Racism in the police is much more than bad apples . . . [it] can occur through a lack of care and understanding . . . it can occur almost unknowingly, as a matter of neglect, in an institution.'[6]

The Macpherson report provided a helpful definition of institutional racism: 'the way the institution or the organisation may systematically or repeatedly treat, or tend to treat, people differentially because of their race'.[7]

It was recognised that many white police officers, living outside of the city they work in, only interact with Black people at work, in often negative situations. This limited interaction reinforces their existing negative stereotypes of Black people. Dr Robin Oakley, in the report, added: 'Police work, unlike most other professional activities, has the capacity to bring officers into contact with a skewed cross-section of society, with the well-recognised potential for producing negative stereotypes of particular groups.'[8]

The clearest example of these stereotypes can be seen in the Metropolitan Police's Gangs Matrix. The Gangs Matrix was created in response to the London riots in 2011. It is a database where individuals are recorded as 'gang nominals' and flagged with a green, amber or red ranking of violence. In October 2017, 78 per cent of the 3,806 people on this database were Black.[9]

There has since been a review of the Gangs Matrix, ordered by the London mayor Sadiq Khan. The review led to a thousand young Black men under twenty-five years old being removed from the database. He recognised how this matrix impacts the trust deficit in London:

> We simply cannot ignore the fact that Black Londoners have less trust in the Met and that is why my comprehensive over-haul of the Gang Violence Matrix is so important to improving the trust and confidence London's diverse communities have in our police . . . it's vitally important that the police continue to evaluate, improve and communicate how it [the Gangs Matrix] is used to address concerns from communities about the disproportionate number of Black Londoners and young men on the Matrix.[10]

Whilst the review has improved the Gangs Matrix by removing 40 per cent of the people recorded on the database, there is clearly still more work to be done as currently eight out of ten listed on the database are from an African or Caribbean background.[11]

On a personal level, I grew up with a feeling of deep mistrust for the police, yet my parents raised me to be nothing other than law-abiding. From a young age, I knew that my aunt and uncle had been physically and verbally assaulted by the police and subjected to racist slurs. As teenagers, my younger brothers would constantly be harassed by the police. The elder of my brothers was often searched on his way to work, clad in a formal suit, often rendering him late. He started to resent the police and I felt that too. My cousins and friends recited lyrics from songs which expressed hatred of the police. I felt conflicted; I couldn't see any positive that could come from a worsening relationship with the police but I understood the frustration that my family and friends felt. Then one day I too was stopped by the police whilst I was driving and I learnt what it felt like. I was petrified and I concluded that the police clearly didn't like people like me.

Whilst many of the studies in this area focus on Black men, who are more than three times as likely to be arrested compared to white men, it is important to remember that these issues affect Black women and Black children too. Black women and Black boys are significantly more likely to be arrested than white women and white boys.

I cannot pretend to be surprised that Black people continue to have little faith in the police. Significant work still needs to be done, there needs to be more recruitment of Black police officers, and the disproportionate rates of stop and search and arrests need to be tackled. In the Metropolitan Police, the Gangs Matrix needs to be overhauled. The trust deficit in the Black community's attitude to the police pours into a trust deficit for the wider criminal justice system.

The Youth Court

Whilst Black people make up only 3 per cent of the population, in 2018, 29 per cent of under-eighteens in prison were Black, and 40 per cent were Black or mixed ethnicity. Black people are hugely over-represented in the Youth Court.

In my experience in the Youth Court, children are criminalised far too young. There is also a lack of understanding among children and their families about the implications of their criminal records, particularly if they reoffend. Sometimes children are happy to just plead guilty to something (regardless of whether they did it) so that they don't have to sit around waiting in a youth court all day. Youth courts are often badly organised with multiple cases listed at the same time in each courtroom. Children and their parents are often forced to wait outside the courtroom, many feeling terrified, for hours. On one particular day, I remember attending a youth court to discover more than thirty children sitting outside waiting for their case to be heard, all of them Black or mixed race. That image will never leave my mind.

There is, of course, a continuing narrative around 'Black on Black' crime, which the media perpetuates and which particularly affects young Black people. Groups of Black boys who are friends are often mislabelled as 'gangs' in a way that their white counterparts are not. In my own cases, I have represented young Black boys who have been branded 'gang members' for their associations with other Black boys with no evidence at all of any gang affiliation.

I am not denying that there are criminal gangs and organised crime networks, of course there are. However, the narrative needs to shift to recognise that the young children who are so often being branded as 'gang members' are either not associated with any gang at all or are associated but as a vulnerable victim of child exploitation.

A real positive is that even in the few years that I have been at the Bar, I have noticed that the courts have become more focused on the Modern Slavery legislation and guidance, and more attention is being paid to those higher up in the chain of command, those responsible for what has been commonly termed 'county lines' criminality. In my experience, the courts are recognising that many of the children who are caught up in the criminal justice system are there because they have been forced into that lifestyle by people who threaten them or their families. The problem is that the approach is inconsistent between courts; some judges have a brilliant grasp of how children are often exploited, as do some practitioners, but there is still a wider lack of understanding by many across both professions.

There are numerous children who continue to be criminalised for things that could easily have been dealt with outside of court. The Lammy Review recommends that the criminal justice system works harder with services outside of its boundaries. It reports that 'the system must do more to work with local communities to hold offenders to account and demand that they take responsibility for their own lives'. I agree that the youth justice system should be based in local communities, not in courtrooms across the country. It is disappointing that David Lammy's suggestion of 'hearings' taking place in local neighbourhoods using non-traditional buildings such as libraries or community centres has not been more widely utilised. Courtrooms are intimidating and it isn't difficult to imagine that making children accustomed to courtrooms from a young age, as defendants, is likely to have negative consequences for them as they get older.

We know that Black children are hugely over-represented in the Youth Court. More intervention is needed at and before this stage to prevent a continuation of this over-representation in the adult courts.

The Magistrates' Court

Black adults, particularly Black men, are over-criminalised and over-charged. The numbers of Black people forced through magistrates' courts continues to rocket.

I was mistaken for a defendant in the magistrates' court multiple times in one day, and it's an experience that most of my Black colleagues (solicitors, barristers and even judges) are familiar with. One Black aspiring barrister reached out to let me know that he was mistakenly asked to step into the dock when attending a court on work experience.

I had two issues with being mistaken for being a defendant that day. The first was that it is frustrating and disappointing that a number of people saw a Black woman and assumed that I must be there as a defendant. This highlights both the over-representation of Black people as defendants and the under-representation of Black people in the legal profession. The second issue was that it shouldn't have mattered who I was that day; the fact that my experience of being mistaken for a defendant was so unpleasant highlights how badly we treat defendants in our criminal justice system. I was shouted at and ordered about in a way that other court users were not.

This wasn't the first time that I had seen or experienced Black people being treated differently in court. A particular magistrates' court hearing stands out in my mind where I represented a young Black man charged with dealing drugs. Whilst it doesn't particularly matter for the point of this anecdote, the Crown eventually dropped the charges against him as there was no evidence. That day, in a magistrates' court in a predominately white area, I represented him for his first hearing. My client had no previous convictions and had never been in trouble with the police before. I waited at the back of the courtroom to let the magistrates know that my case was ready.

The case before his concerned a white female defendant, who was treated courteously by the magistrates and the court staff. She entered her plea and the hearing proceeded smoothly; each person had a smile on their face. It was then my client's turn. I ushered him into the courtroom and immediately one of the magistrates shouted at him to take his hands out of his pockets. He was terrified; he had never stepped foot in a courtroom before. I led him to where he needed to sit. Within seconds the magistrates were shouting at him again, this time to stand up. The tone completely differed from the tone offered to the previous white defendant. My client had been polite and nervous and did not deserve this hostility. It is experiences like these that erode any remaining trust that the Black community has in the criminal justice system.

The trust deficit has enormous implications in the magistrates' court. As the Lammy Review recognises, many Black defendants 'see the system in terms of "them and us"'. There is a huge disconnect between the people who need legal representation and the people who are representing them, which has real consequences. Many Black defendants do not trust the legal advice they receive from mostly white, privileged lawyers, which sadly means they often disregard it. A good example of how this can exacerbate existing racial disparities in the criminal justice system is with regards to credit for pleading guilty. Black, Asian and other ethnic minorities are less likely to plead guilty for offences than their white counterparts.[12] More specifically, Black men are more than one and a half times more likely to enter a 'not guilty' plea than white men. There are explanations for this. The first is that far greater numbers of Black people, proportionally, are being forced through the criminal justice system and hence statistically there are bound to be more innocent people than compared with white people. The second reason relates directly to trust: if Black defendants don't trust the advice that they are being given, they are less likely to follow it. This includes legal advice that it would be in their interests to plead guilty and benefit from the credit given to those who plead guilty at an early stage.[13] If a person pleads guilty at the earliest stage, they will be entitled to up to one-third credit off the sentence they would have received had the case proceeded to trial and they had been convicted. If Black people are less likely to plead guilty, they are less likely to benefit from this credit.

Black people often do not feel that they are treated fairly by the police or the criminal justice system. I have sat in numerous client conferences where the client has expressed their worry that the judge will look at them, a Black person, and see a 'criminal'. They are all too aware that they will be walking into a courtroom and will likely be faced with a white judge, a white prosecutor and they will often be the only Black person in the room.

When I was mistaken for being a defendant, I appreciated what it felt like to be criminalised based only on the colour of my skin. I felt that there was very little that I could say to change people's perceptions of me. I can only imagine the extent to which this is amplified when you consider the power imbalance of a defendant and legal professionals or a judge.

The Crown Court

In my personal experience, many of my Black clients have been keen to elect Crown Court trials on the basis that a jury will decide their fate rather than a judge. The rationale is often that a jury, which may be comprised of people from backgrounds similar to their own, is less likely to discriminate than a judge or magistrates.

Juries, even all-white juries, have been shown to deliver similar results for BAME and white defendants.[14] On a twelve-person jury, it is far more likely that there will be individuals who are from BAME backgrounds themselves or regularly interact with Black, Asian and other ethnic minority people.

Whilst juries are undoubtedly a thing that we can be proud of, sentencing in the Crown Court is not left to a jury. Sentences are determined by Crown Court judges.

It is important to state at this stage, only 1 per cent of judges are Black.[15]

Statistics show that Black people are more likely to receive a custodial sentence than their white counterparts, for the same offence.

There are two likely reasons for this. The first is, as discussed above, Black people are less likely to plead guilty than their white counterparts and hence are less likely to benefit from the credit given for pleading guilty. The second is that judges are sentencing Black defendants more harshly than white defendants.

The statistics show that Black people have had a consistently higher average custodial sentence length for indictable offences than white people since 2014. The average sentence for Black people is 28 months compared to 18.3 months for white people.[16]

Drug offences are the largest category for which people from BAME backgrounds are convicted. Half of the convictions of Black people (in 2019) were for drug offences or possession of weapons (compared to under a quarter of convictions of white people).[17] A Black person is 1.4 times as likely as a white person to receive an immediate custodial sentence for supply-related drug offences.[18]

These patterns can be seen across a wide range of offences and are not new. The *Guardian* newspaper did a study in 2011 which revealed that Black people were 44 per cent more likely than white people to be given a prison sentence for driving offences, 38 per cent more likely for public order offences or possession of a weapon and 27 per cent more likely for possession of drugs.[19]

The sentencing guidelines have improved the uniformity of sentencing; however, so much is still left to judicial discretion. Sentencing is not transparent enough, which makes it more difficult to hold judges accountable and ensure that they are sentencing in a fair and unbiased way.

One of the recommendations of the Lammy Review was that all sentencing remarks in the Crown Court should be published in audio and/or written form. I think that this should go further. It shouldn't just be the Crown Court but also the magistrates' court. In the latter, magistrates or judges have the power to send people to prison for up to six months per offence (capped at twelve months in total). If they have the power to deprive people of their liberty in such a substantial way, they should also be held accountable.

Bridging the trust deficit: the law must be fair and must be seen to be fair

It goes without saying that the law should apply equally to all, irrespective of race. What might be less obvious is the importance of the law appearing to be fair.

This is particularly important in the UK, where historically the law has not applied equally to all; Black people have been subjected to racism from the police (as recognised in reports such as the Macpherson report) and unequal application of the law for years.

Black people make up just 3 per cent of the population in the UK but over 12 per cent of the prison population. Theresa May, the former prime minister, recognised that if you're Black you're treated more harshly by the criminal justice system than if you're white.

The legal profession is still disproportionately white and fails to represent society. The Bar is getting better at the junior end but fails to retain Black practitioners and they are not properly represented at the senior end of the profession, particularly as Queen's Counsel. The judiciary is similarly poor: only 1 per cent of judges are Black and there are few, if any, Black judges in the senior judiciary, certainly not in the Court of Appeal or the Supreme Court.

It is impossible to ignore the consequence of how this looks to the public and more importantly to Black defendants. Those who are dragged through the system are confronted by the prospect of knowing that their fate will likely be determined by a white person who is unlikely to have any understanding of their background. As with the criticism levelled at the police in the Macpherson report, many judges live outside of the city they work in and only interact with Black people at work. Their perception of Black people is skewed by the fact that the only Black people they meet and interact with are those who have been charged with a crime. Again, as with the police, this limited interaction reinforces existing stereotypes of Black people.

A criticism posed may be that the importance of seeing fairness is exaggerated, what really matters is whether or not there is substantive fairness. This criticism overlooks the crux of the issue – Black people do not have faith in the 'system' and this lack of trust means that sometimes they will make decisions that will result in them having unnecessarily harsh outcomes. Most people who are caught up in the criminal justice system do not sit there analysing comparative statistics of how Black people are treated compared to their white counterparts; rather, they base their views on the fairness they perceive. This is why it matters that the system looks fair as well as being fair.

In the short term, lawyers, as individuals, can help to bridge the trust deficit between Black people and the criminal justice system by showing understanding and appreciation of the issues that disproportionately affect their Black clients. Research for the Lammy Review showed that 51 per cent of people from BAME backgrounds born in England and Wales believe that 'the criminal justice system discriminates against particular groups and individuals'.[20] I have no doubt that this figure would be even higher among the Black community. As lawyers we should not shy away from this fact; it is important to acknowledge this failing and commit to changing it. It is imperative, and the responsibility of every lawyer, to consider the way that Black defendants are treated in court. Lawyers must always check and ensure that their clients are being treated fairly.

In the longer term, the public perception of bias can be addressed to some considerable extent by diversifying the legal profession and the judiciary. This has the obvious benefit of ensuring that lawyers and judges alike are not only intermingling with Black people in the dock, who have been charged with crimes. Of course, it shouldn't have to take interacting with Black lawyers to humanise Black people, but it certainly cannot be a bad thing to diversify a profession that prides itself on being the voice of the most vulnerable in society.

The increased diversity in the legal profession has important consequences for Black defendants. First, the white judges who determine their case are less likely to have negative unconscious biases. Second, the Black people coming to court might be reassured by the fact that they can see people who look like them among the 'decision-makers'. Both of these results are important in creating fairness and ensuring that the system also looks fair.

As a mixed-race barrister from a 'non-traditional' background at the Bar, I am aware of how important it is for me to be visible. My visibility helps to bridge the trust deficit, not only for my clients but for the wider public who might be reassured that there are people who look like them working tirelessly to tackle racism in the criminal justice system. I have had clients who are reassured to be represented by someone who looks like them or even speaks in a way that they feel is familiar. There are many senior Black barristers who inspired me from afar and some have mentored me personally, and I hope to do the same for the next generation of aspiring lawyers. My hope is that the profession continues to diversify and the number of Black lawyers and judges grows. When the balance in the courtroom is fairer – in that we see proportionate numbers of people on the bench and in the dock – that's when the trust deficit will narrow.

BLACK BRITISH MENTAL HEALTH MATTERS

Will we ever win the war against racism to preserve our well-being?

MARVERINE COLE

According to official government statistics, Black women are almost twice as likely as their White counterparts to have experienced a common mental disorder in the past week. In general, Black people are more than four times more likely to be detained under the Mental Health Act and eight times more likely to be subject to a community treatment order.

Marverine Cole is an award-winning journalist who has opened up about her own experiences with mental health and pushed back against the idea of the 'strong Black woman' and the harm the common stereotype does.

The moment I first saw Moira Stuart and Sir Trevor McDonald reading the news on TV when I was a little girl, I knew that was the job for me. I took my first step to becoming a television news journalist at the age of twenty-two. After working as a volunteer on the wards of Birmingham Children's Hospital, taking requests for songs that poorly youngsters wanted to hear on Radio Lollipop, the station manager gave me my own show. I could not believe my luck. Me, a DJ, a job I had craved for more than a decade. And to DJ in the city where I was born and raised was an amazing feeling. It might have only been children and staff listening and they might have not cared but I loved entertaining them and keeping spirits up.

I had a full-time job as a PA at Cadbury's but still used all my spare time during the evenings, at weekends and even during my lunch break building up my live radio and TV experience wherever I could. I carved out a spot for myself as an entertainment reporter, researching and planning weekly features on arts and culture around the city for Birmingham Cable TV. I was chuffed when I landed a role as a stand-in presenter for a three-hour African Caribbean show on Saturday nights at BBC Radio WM. With all of this experience under my belt, finally I quit my day job and went back to university to study broadcast journalism.

Things were going well in my life. I was in a steady relationship and working my dream job as a broadcast journalist – so my first brush with mental health came out of the blue. It happened during the summer of 2001 after I lost both my job and my boyfriend in the same week. Devastated, I danced and drank away the hours, partying every night at a local club called Bobby Browns. Actually the partying was only meant to last the summer, but it went on for months as I tried to drown out how I was feeling. After all, this was me, Marverine, strong and independent, sassy and in control. Us Black girls are impenetrable, aren't we? And so, I told no one. Not even the girls I was partying with. Not even my family. I continued like this until the nightly crying got too much, and then I visited my GP. I was diagnosed with depression and prescribed fluoxetine.

After that episode I got my life back on track. I continued to do well in my career in the media, landing some top-profile jobs in London. I worked as a Sky TV anchor, BBC TV reporter and a presenter on popular home shopping channel QVC. But years later, as I thought back to that summer, I wondered, why did I wait so long to ask for help? Why didn't I tell anyone? What was going on with me?

Around the time I was exploring these questions, I was back in Birmingham and in between jobs having left a TV contract in London the year before. I freelanced as a reporter and did a bit of lecturing, but the job situation was not what I wanted it to be and that was impacting my mental well-being. I was struggling to keep up with my financial commitments. Feeling low, I tried to figure it out in my own head, not going to see the doctor, or talking to anybody other than my husband. I thought, 'Maybe I'll go to Holland & Barrett and get some St John's Wort, I've just got a low mood and that will pick me up.' When I wasn't able to sleep, I tried natural remedies like Yogi tea and valerian root. I even tried some private therapy but couldn't afford to keep that up. I was in a bad way, but at the same time I was acting like everything was fine. It was not fine. If it wasn't for my husband, an absolute rock, and me being open to him about how I was feeling, I don't think I would have been able to move forward.

Documenting depression

It was out of this experience that I decided to pitch the idea for 'Black Girls Don't Cry' to BBC Radio 4. I'd made radio documentaries for the BBC before – for Radio 4 about female gamblers, and for 1Xtra about female rappers and MCs. But this was not just going to be any ordinary documentary for me. I knew this was going to require me to finally confront some of the most difficult issues in my life. Issues that I'd skirted over and pretended I was fine about. Issues I'd decided had been handled. But 'handled' was really shorthand for 'buried' in my case. And the process changed my life.

It took a while to get commissioned. Coming on about a year or thereabouts. And what I didn't bank on was the intense emotional toll producing the documentary took on me. Crawling back over your own experiences when they might be best left under the bed was not something I was able to stomach very easily. But the documentary finally aired in July 2018 and explored the story around Black women's mental health. I wanted to know why I was going through all of this experience. Why did I go through what I went through during that summer of 2001? Why did I try to solve it alone? I wanted to explore what lay behind it all. The women who shared their experiences with me for the programme to this day will always be a million times stronger than I will ever be.

Jay Mountford, a social media friend I'd met on Twitter almost a decade ago, agreed to be one of my contributors. Candid about her depression to the point of 'Wow, she is revealing all' was one thing that bound her to me. She was demonstrating extreme courage: This is me, take it or leave it. Her posts could lurch from 'I am in the depths of despair' to 'Hey life is brilliant': unsettling and captivating in equal measure. Jay was a busy wife and mother of two boys, who was appointed principal cellist with a local orchestra in Birmingham. So when I put my questions to her she immediately knew why I waited so long: she had done the same.

'There is so much expected of us because we are supposed to be this Black strong woman who powers her way through everything, and is fierce and indestructible, and can take on the world,' Jay said. 'More often than not we don't have anyone to fall on or lean against because we're supposed to be the pillar that everyone leans against.'

And not that there's anything wrong with that in itself, she made clear. It's great that people do: 'But we also cry. We're tired. We are frustrated. We are exhausted.'

Jade Laurie Hart from Moseley was my second contributor. Calling her brave might sound overzealous here, but that's what she is. She was vlogging about her experiences, writing songs and tweeting, which is where I first came across her. She jumped right out at me from her page with a rawness and an honesty about her own mental health that took my breath away. Jade is in her early thirties and suffers from borderline personality disorder. She was diagnosed with depression at sixteen but that did not stop her going to university, where she studied drama. Then, in a sequence of events – eerily similar to mine – it all became too much when she split up with her partner, lost her job and was made homeless – except that Jade ended up in a very different place.

'I was like a strong, independent Black woman and nothing would ever get me down,' Jade said. 'I would be defiant to anything negative, I was gonna do this. That was my attitude. I guess it was a mantra that I lived by and, for a long time, everything came true.'

But one day it all became unbearable.

'I had suffered with self-harm, but never to the extreme that happened on that day,' she said. 'I was half asleep, I think, when I was doing it all. And when I kind of realised, I phoned 999 and they took me in the ambulance. And that's when it was decided that I needed to go into a ward for the first time. It was the scariest experience of my life. There was a note outside the door saying this door must be locked at all times, so patients cannot go in and patients cannot get out. But I did get out.'

Jade's story made me see where my own could have ended

up, but also that the Black strong woman trope isn't helping us. I thought about the culture I come from, where there is this unspoken rule, especially among my parents' generation, that you don't talk about these things. My mum came from Jamaica as a qualified nurse as part of the Windrush generation. She worked hard to give me and my brothers the best she could. She wanted us to do well, and we did. We had a good life, and I guess I felt I needed to be strong, not to complain and to get on with things just as my mum had.

But externally, society also has a tendency to place certain expectations on us as Black women. We are seen as strong, steely, the angry, aggressive Black woman – or on the other hand, we're 'sexy', 'sassy' and yet unworthy of romance.

As Black women we're good at and used to the giving of ourselves to both stereotypes – often to the detriment of ourselves. We play the game. We don't talk about how we feel, about our mental health, or if we do it's not taken seriously. We're expected to just get on with it, and so we do. At least we try. And we do this often, thinking of others before ourselves and too often neglecting ourselves. We're now seeing how this is dangerous. We need to squash this trope. And more needs to be done to prevent Black women from getting so desperate. It cannot be, as Jay described it, that either you're well or you're sectioned.

The many routes to healing

As part of my documentary, I caught up with one of the many experts who believe Black women's resilience runs far deeper than the strong Black woman trope. Dr Erica McInnis, a clinical psychologist and academic for fifteen years, says we're exhibiting symptoms of generations of trauma from the transatlantic slave trade, which has been handed down to us.

'There are the number of ways that the legacy of enslavement and colonisation affects us,' she says. 'Women were working on the plantations, just like the men were. So there's that sort of self-determination, working and doing things for yourself, not necessarily relying on other people to give you opportunities. That's built in within Black women.'

She calls it post-traumatic slave syndrome, similar to the stress a person experiences after trauma. It's a coping behaviour Black people developed to survive, because at any time we could be suddenly separated from family members by being sold or murdered. This trauma has been passed down through generations and has been used to explain why we feel we have to maintain this tough persona.

With more and more Black women entering the mental health system, Dr McInnis talked about the atmosphere Black people have to live with today. 'We're thinking about the seventieth anniversary of Windrush, about the hardships that the generation before us faced, but perhaps not quite realising that there's a different form of hardship that we're experiencing today.

'And sometimes it's the illusion of inclusion that can be quite psychologically damaging, the idea that you can achieve. And you're all meant to be able to do anything. Then when you don't achieve, you hit yourself over the head thinking, "Oh, I have the opportunity and I still couldn't do it." But sometimes every barrier has been put there to that opportunity as well. And sometimes the covert ways in which White supremacy can operate can be so much more damaging than the overt ways.'

Unconvinced that generational trauma and cultural stigma could be the only reasons why I and many Black women I know put on a mask and hide their emotions, I turned to yet more research. The data was clear. Findings from the government's Race Disparity Report published in 2017 show it is more common for Black women (29.3 per cent) to suffer from what the National Health Service (NHS) calls common mental disorders, such as depression, anxiety and obsessive-compulsive disorder, than non-British White women (15.6 per cent) and White British women (20.9 per cent).[1] And, along with Asian and mixed or other ethnic groups, Black women were more likely to suffer from panic disorder, although it was difficult to see how each ethnic group compared because sample sizes were so small. Common mental disorders did not vary significantly by ethnic group in men, but Black people are over four times more likely to be sectioned under the Mental Health Act. In 2019/20, the act was used to detain 321 Black people per 100,000 head of the population – in comparison to 73 for White people. Ministers acknowledge that this is because the Act is disproportionately used against Black people. Black people are also eight times more likely to be subject to a community treatment order (CTO) – under which a person is discharged from hospital but placed under supervised conditions around treatment and certain restrictions around where they live.

The number of people detained under the Mental Health Act increased by 40 per cent from 2005/6 to 2015/16.[2] According to a study released in 2018 by the *British Journal of Psychiatry*, there has also been an increase in reports of self-harming, with young women between the ages of sixteen and thirty-four most at risk.

Following the release of these figures, the government promised to overhaul the mental health service to make it a system fit for the twenty-first century. Its White Paper was eventually published in January 2021, outlining changes that many, including mental health charity Mind, said cannot come quickly enough.

The charity described treatment under the current system as 'poor' and sometimes 'appalling'.

As part of the proposals, all NHS mental health trusts will have a Patient and Carers Race Equality Framework. With experienced practitioner Jacqui Dyer involved, it will seek to tackle disparities and improve outcomes for Black and ethnic minority people. It will give more say and power to patients and carers who really understand the perspectives on race that some professionals might not, reflecting that race does have an impact on access, experiences and outcomes. By all accounts 'culturally appropriate advocates' will be introduced to support patients. Patients will have more say in their care with the introduction of 'statutory advance choice documents'. The idea is that it will hopefully redress the imbalance in the system between the state and the individual by empowering patients to discuss their needs before they reach a crisis and require hospitalisation. I applaud the plans. They all sound promising, but the journalist in me holds flickers of cynicism. Why? For me, big plans and ideas from a political party that has rarely been 'for us' as Black people are ones to be viewed with caution.

There are also proposals to introduce tougher measures around decisions to issue CTOs. Clinicians will have to meet more stringent conditions to justify their use and there will be more frequent reviews, and by more professionals. Finally, when CTOs are issued, they will be limited 'to two years unless a person has relapsed or deteriorated'.

But although the changes have been welcomed by those advocating for users of the service, some are sceptical that it does not go deeply enough to tackle the systemic racism that underpins much of the experiences of Black people.[3] Hári Sewell, a social worker by background, former mental health trust director and now a consultant in mental health and equalities, described the changes as 'improving treatments' while people are 'still having to drink contaminated water'. Without proper training around racism many diagnoses of what constitutes mental health symptoms and the role racism plays in these diagnoses will continue, he feared.

He is not alone. Professor Kamaldeep Bhui, a professor of psychiatry at Oxford University, echoed his concerns in the health and social care press, arguing that more work was needed to 'really unpack, expose and remove drivers of race equality in care systems'. He said we need to look at all the pathways that have led a person to the place of being detained – the 'legacy of heritage' and 'life course adversity'.[4]

There are also concerns that some changes may simply cause discrimination to pop up elsewhere; for example, lower numbers of CTOs being issued may result in a higher proportion of detentions and longer lengths of stay for people who have been sectioned.

And while the Race Equality Framework remit to gather and monitor data and implement changes at an organisational and structural level was welcomed, there are also concerns over the lack of empirical evidence that this is effective.

Overall, experts believe that we need more than a change of the law. The government needs to support these changes with a commitment to tackle the underlying cause of the distress many Black people experience from living in a society where racism is systemic. There is a 'weathering that occurs from living with constant stereotyping and images of self and othering, often under the guise of benevolent racism',[5] said Sewell.

This all reminded me of a clip of Professor Kimberlé Crenshaw I found in the BBC archives for my documentary. She is the US-based leading law scholar and renowned feminist who coined the phrase 'intersectionality' to explain how Black women are affected by double-barrier discrimination where race and gender collide. During her academic research back in 1989, she uncovered a distinct pattern of discrimination while investigating the outcomes of a range of employment tribunals.

> I wanted to imagine a framework where people could see that there might be discrimination. I use the metaphor to identify that discrimination as 'traffic': going in one direction which might be race and racism or flowing in another direction which might be sexism or patriarchy. And the idea would be that you could be in any number of these thoroughfares and encounter racism or encounter sexism.[6]

George Floyd's killing

Black women, being right in between, are experiencing both of these things at the same time. And intersectionality can have dangerous consequences for us. They can be very deep-rooted and manifest themselves in different ways. For me, it comes in the form of my inner rage, which I often keep a lid on. Other issues can easily add to that complexity. Life-changing events, like past or current trauma, the domino effect of losing a job and being out of work, the feelings of insecurity that most of us feel when we use social media, or being physically unwell in some way. Any one or all of these can trigger mental illness at any time.

Given my experiences in 2001 and 2017, I'm protective of my mental health and try not to allow anything to get to me. Although anger over the unfairness of it all rises up every so often, I manage it well. And I had pretty much buried most of the memories of times when life felt difficult for me – then George Floyd's murder happened. Right then, many of those buried emotions rose to the surface.

I was working in the garden on a hot summer's day in May 2020 when I heard the news about it. I was shell-shocked. I could not bring myself to watch any of the video of him taking his dying breath that was being shared across social media. My phone was pinging every moment with many of my friends and professional associates sharing the video. Still I could not watch. Outrage and heartbreak ripped through me.

The worldwide Covid-19 restrictions last year meant the eyes of the world were glued to screens for more hours than ever. If you're 'old skool' like me you were watching TV news on a regular basis, or you were getting news online or from posts shared via social media. It meant that there was no escaping the horror of his death, as it unfolded before our very eyes. The bystander video was replayed on screens over and over again. Circulated around and around for days and weeks on end. The instantaneous outpouring of rage was felt across the globe. The anger that a Black man's life could be extinguished on a street, by a police officer casually kneeling on his neck, ignoring his cries to breathe, was not just traumatising for me, it was an affront for many. Hundreds and thousands, if not millions of people around the world were broken-hearted and resolved to demand that it never happened again. Anywhere in the world. Protests sprang up across the globe: from rural Gloucestershire (where some residents, the MP and the town council tried to block it[7]), metropolises like my home town of Birmingham, London, Leeds and Manchester, to Japan, Germany, Australia, New Zealand, across the US and even Antarctica. Around the world, people were being forced to acknowledge the injustices that Black people face on a daily basis.

As the Black Lives Matter movement grew here in the UK, so did the numbers of Black British people who began sharing their experiences. The images of George Floyd, and then Breonna Taylor, killed just two months before in March, imprinted upon the souls of Black people everywhere, were a catalyst for the outpouring of grief and trauma in the UK. We had heard anecdotal evidence before, but this was different. From unknown voices of students in drama and independent schools sharing their stories of anti-Black behaviour. Even celebrities and public figures like Black British singers Alexandra Burke, Misha B, and Keisha from the Sugababes, calling out the barrage of anti-Black behaviour they had faced from the media, journalists, reality-show contestants and the public alike. Who can forget ex-cricketer Michael Holding's tearful testimony on Sky Sports? A veteran of the game discussing the ill treatment he received because of his skin colour. And the pleas from Ebony Rainford-Brent, an English cricket commentator and former cricketer, who was the first Black woman to play for the England team. All of it so painful to watch.

There were common threads running across each person's experience: they were hated for no reason, or dubbed a bully; they were 'difficult' and 'moody', hard to get on with or even be understood. In some cases they were being seen as not worthy of any emotional support whatsoever, not deserving of any accolades, their achievements undervalued. I say 'They' but in 'They' I also include me. Because I've experienced all of that covert and overt racism. The weight you bear carrying that crushes you. Holding it in can warp your brain and distort your view of the world. Those brave enough to speak out were all in pain. Racism impacted their life chances, their physical and mental health. British people were saying, 'Hey, this is not just an American problem. Anti-Blackness is a global problem and it needs to be stopped.' With the true extent of the experiences of Black people from industries across the board on display, we saw that the abscess was deep in the psyche of the nation.

For me, the trauma was so painful that I turned down multiple invitations from mainstream media to discuss any of it. Newspapers, radio stations and TV news programmes wanted to know how I was feeling as a Black British woman and why these protests were happening all over the country in big numbers. But also the fact that so many people from a range of communities were involved in the protests was curious to them. At the time I was a senior lecturer and journalism educator in higher education, therefore being a media commentator was both an organic part of my role and expected of me. However, I knew this would be tougher than usual. Around the time of the Naga Munchetty–Trump saga, being on non-stop rotation for interviews about that was exhausting enough: 'Should Naga have said what she said?' 'Was she breaching Ofcom guidelines on impartiality?' How can anyone forget the way in which the *BBC Breakfast* presenter was accused of breaching 'what the guidelines allow for' after she criticised President Donald Trump for perceived racism. The George Floyd murder touched a deeper nerve for me. So I continued to turn down BLM requests, except for Gaydio. Dean, the breakfast show co-presenter at the time, reached out to me, wanting to help his audiences understand the movement and offer guidance on allyship. It was a pleasure to work with them on some shows and answer questions from their listeners.

However, I reserved my comments about my own experiences

for just two journalism publications.[8] I was interviewed about the challenges I've experienced throughout my career, about the lack of representation on TV and in the hugely elite journalism industry. I talked about how I had worked in newsrooms where I have been the only Black woman on shift, about the struggle to get where I was and how I have been forced out of several jobs due to what I perceived as racism. People in those organisations and audiences disliked me, for whatever reason, and worked hard to see me gone. Behind all of this is a culture that makes you feel you have no right to be in the role or as though you are a token 'diversity hire'. There isn't that immediate acceptance that you're there on merit, because you've worked hard and are competent at what you do. People are suspicious of you and make comments as though they're surprised you can do the job. I would be living in a bijou flat in Monaco on the riches collected if I had a pound for every time I heard 'Wow, Marv,' when I completed some standard, average task that's part of my job, like editing a package as a radio reporter. I worked hard, I didn't break sweat, but my colleagues seemed constantly amazed at me doing the work that my White counterparts simply took in their stride. Weird. I have a long list of times I recall being 'the other' in White spaces.

Once I did a screen test for a role as a breakfast presenter. The studio crew pulled me aside and told me I'd done a brilliant job, but the editor at the time told me plainly, 'You are not going on air with your hair like that.' My hair was straight, relaxed, with a light caramel brown colour running through it. It was not bright red nor a Mohican style. Is this racism? I don't know. What I do know is that there are a lot of Black journalists out there still having a lot of unpleasant things happening to them. I had countless conversations during those weeks with journalists who were being told by their bosses not to talk about Black Lives Matter at all, or they'd risk losing their jobs or not getting any more shifts. They thanked me for speaking up. I know journalists who want to leave the industry after just three or four years of qualifying because they've had enough of how they are treated in newsrooms. Black journalists who have been leapfrogged by White journalists who have not delivered the same level of impact with their work, or have been paid less despite working diligently and doing excellent work. I hear similar stories from peers who long left the industry, and from youngsters going through this situation right now. In 2021. It's perverse to me that some sectors of the industry I once loved continue to do all they can to browbeat Black journalists. When all they want to do is do their job: hold power to account and give a voice to the voiceless.

Living with the weight of racism

Still, some people saw a glimmer of hope behind the BLM campaigning. Was June 2020 a sign of change? Certainly, lots of brands and people were posting black squares – but where was the concrete action? I saw this as a missed opportunity to act on McKinsey data, which shows that profitability will come from diversity.[9] Businesses could have taken steps to embrace this alongside Covid-19 priorities to stay afloat. Instead, the agenda is more focused on maintaining the status quo. Some firms still see diversity as an add-on, positive discrimination as bad, the political right seeing it as 'woke'. The message is that being Black is to be constantly on the fringes of mainstream; that you can never be mainstream. It all stems from the same heart and spirit. The spirit of no one wants to hear us, we cannot be individual, we are othered, we are forced to conform to avoid being othered; yet when we do conform, we are still never good enough. Those in power – the hirers, the firers, the agenda-setters, the policymakers – still keep those doors locked. It's lots of talk, lots of lip service all these years while denying the reality that Black culture is British culture and you cannot get away from that.

The impact of weathering on Black people's mental health from living in a society where racism is so ingrained, sometimes denied, and frequently hard to call out, is exhausting. I am exhausted. All of the Black women I know – and those I see on social media platforms – use the same word. When we speak up about racism and injustice, our experiences are compounded by even more racism. Too often I was gaslighted into believing the behaviour is acceptable – that this was the way things were in a majority White country, and if you dare say otherwise, if you dare to stand up and show any notion of activism, you will be branded as loud, aggressive, confrontational, difficult to work with, foolish, putting your career in jeopardy. Our tendency to feel we must work twice as hard to prove ourselves and to support our families means we're more likely to pander to advice to 'Just get on with it,' 'Keep your head down,' or 'Don't speak up or you'll cause a problem.' We are in an impossible cycle.

After George Floyd died, I reached out to as many of my Black students as possible, as I understood how they would be feeling. A few understanding colleagues asked me how I was. I wished others had, but they did not. They did not realise the damaging effect George Floyd's death had on me and my ability to 'keep on keeping on' in our day jobs as we were all expected to do.

What's my position now on those forces in life that come to try us? I am completely selfless about my selfishness. Most days I am fighting to protect my brain. To strengthen its borders from attacks. With everything I am asked to do, I step back and evaluate it. I am a huge admirer of Shonda Rhimes and everything she has accomplished. Who isn't? *Scandal*? *How to Get Away with Murder*? *Bridgerton*? *B-R-I-D-G-E-R-T-O-N*?? But the 'Year of Yes' stance she adopted a few years ago is most definitely not for me. With every approach I receive as a freelance journalist and broadcaster, I only accept after I have evaluated how the job will work for me. Not what looks good to be 'seen' to be doing – which is what I used to do when I was younger. Now I judge every request for my time and skills against my 'Peace Barometer'. Can I do it? Do I really want to do it? Does it help me thrive creatively?

Dreadful data

The stats around Black women's mental health in the UK are a huge concern to me as someone who's been medically treated for depression in the past. There are clear disparities in the way we access health services: the horrifying data of Black maternal mortality rates is an example of this. But as the latest report has said, data alone cannot paint a clear enough picture of factors such as different levels of need for services.[10] Hands up. I am not a data journalist or a statistician. But it seems clear to me that ethnicity is itself a factor, given the consistency of disparity across different sectors of society, from education to Black people's experience of the criminal justice system.

A stark comparison is also evident in Black people's experience of working in the health sector itself, where many decisions about our needs are made. Eighteen per cent of the non-medical NHS workforce is from an ethnic minority group, yet only 7 per cent of very senior managers and 11 per cent of senior managers are from an ethnic minority background. NHS boards are 93 per cent White. Court judges are disproportionately White. Conviction ratios are highest among White defendants, but Black and Asian men receive longer prison sentences, and Black men are less likely to be remanded on bail. They are also more than three times more likely to be arrested than White men. And although Black women are most likely to have experienced common mental disorders and Black men are most likely to experience a psychotic disorder, it is White British adults who are more likely to receive treatment for a mental or emotional problem than adults in any other ethnic group. They also experience better outcomes from psychological therapies.

Does that demonstrate then that Black women's mental health doesn't matter? Clearly, there is a need for increased mental health service resources in areas with high proportions of Black people. However, while mental illness accounts for 28 per cent of the national disease burden in England, only 13 per cent of NHS spending is on mental health care.[11] For many, the biggest concern in the White Paper published in January 2021 was over a single line that says these changes would be 'subject to future funding decisions'. Is Black women's mental health being prioritised?

More sophisticated and nuanced resources and approaches to treatment are desperately needed if we are to provide adequate support for people going through crisis. But the 100 million dollar question is: does our government have the will to engage solutions like this, which are so desperately needed? Does it have the desire to do the right thing, and not be afraid of the reaction from right-leaning news and media organisations that enjoy crying 'Woke' at any attempts to redress the balance of systematic inequalities for Black people? I am not a health expert, but I believe we need culturally sensitive alternatives to hospital admissions, as well as to improve the conditions for people once they have been admitted. We need more alternatives in the community for serious cases, like crisis houses, and preventative support, like talking therapies. There needs to be more variety in the levels of support care, and more recognition of those grassroots voluntary and charitable organisations and faith establishments which carry much of the load when it comes to mental health help. Those frontline services should be supported by a long-term commitment to funding.

But we also need support shaped around our specific needs. When I went through my experience, I was conscious of a problem around the kind of care Black women receive. I tried sessions with a White male therapist to tackle my anger management – and I've nothing against White males (I married one, for goodness' sake, and he understands me). However, cultural sensitivity does matter. The health professionals and clinicians I've spoken to in the past have told me this too. Personally, I felt sure that if I could find a therapist who shared my culture and background, that would help, and it did. I worked with a Black female therapist, who I found through the Black, African and Asian Therapy Network, a database of private therapists. There's a shorthand there and a full appreciation of what I wake up to and have to handle every day. She is a joyful part of my week. It brings my husband joy too because – as much as he is my rock and my shoulder to cry on – when I get angry and rant to him, it is unfair that he bears the brunt of that most days. With my therapist I don't feel I am burdening her. She is there for me, and it's her life purpose to help. Of course, I have to pay for her services, and the reality is that not everyone can afford this. I realise I am extremely fortunate in that sense and I do not take that for granted.

It isn't to say that choosing a therapist from the exact same race, faith or ethnic background as you is going to be your cure-all. But more that opening up to someone who you feel understands you, and empathises with the inequalities and prejudices that you have faced, might clear a smoother path to personal peace. Otherwise, you could end up where I was: doing a lot of legwork to help your therapist understand and appreciate the fundamental forces which are against you. That could make the entire healing process you need to engage in a much tougher uphill battle. It might make you struggle to gain ground and cause more damage.

So what else is out there for us? Although we have Black therapists, we need more. African-centred therapies are available, but from what I can see, securing sustainable funding is a real barrier to widening access for all. There are excellent practitioners who prefer to work privately or apply for funding to provide what I believe is a fundamental basic for all ethnic minorities.

Again, I think shorthand is crucial. In my documentary I spent time with Dr Erica McInnis, an inspirational clinical psychologist and proud Mancunian from Nubia Wellness and Healing. She is doing outstanding work through groups like the Emotional Emancipation Circle to plug the gap. I visited one that she led in London. We all gathered in a bright, airy room at the Pan African Centre, and after presentations it was time for small group discussions and workshops, ending in some motivating chanting. I remember arriving wondering what on earth was going to happen. But the positive energies exuded from the group around me. You could feel the air fill with sighs of relief from everyone who was there. The ability to speak and be listened to was powerful. We all had shared experiences. We were all very used to not being heard, and being gaslighted or, worse still, castigated for actually speaking out about the racism we faced. An elephant in the room was addressed. That was a shock to me because I had never heard it uttered before. Erica revealed her perspective on the issue of post-traumatic slavery syndrome in people of African or Caribbean heritage. Whatever your view on this, the space for Black people to talk honestly about how they feel and be offered self-care solutions on how to deal with the onslaught felt hugely valuable to me, and I witnessed the effect on the others in that room around me. We removed our mask and any notion of the need to fit in. Thankfully, Dr McInnis offers some of these workshops online now. Believe you me, they are well worth investigating.

For my BBC Radio 4 documentary, I also spoke to Sandra Griffiths about this problem. A practitioner with over twenty-five years of experience in mental health, she founded Catalyst for Change, an organisation that helps Black women to access the help they need early on. She said that it is often women's organisations or faith organisations that pick up the mantle of support to these women. But many of those services are being delivered on low/no budget, without any sustainable financial support or wider recognition for the vital work they do.

So, while a multitude of examples of good practice exist, they are grossly under-resourced and ad hoc. What's needed is government commitment to creating a network of Black therapists on the NHS who are free to access for all. But I also agree with experts like Professor Kamaldeep Bhui that while there is an opportunity to embed it in the NHS, we also need much more of a mission and a will from the UK government not to overlook the underlying problems that undermine the effectiveness of these services.

There is hope. There are people fighting for us as Black people saying BLACK BRITISH LIVES DO MATTER. The Runnymede Trust, the UK's leading independent race equality think tank, works to challenge race inequality in Britain through research, network building, leading debate and policy engagement. And there are a wealth of new digital communities finding new ways to tell our stories, such as the Dope Black Mums and Dads networks, Black Ballad, Blakademik and *gal-dem*.

The only danger is, until everyone sees us, until we stop preaching only to the converted, there will always be a policy disconnect. The elite who rule, who hand out the funding, will continue to set the agenda for our mental health.

BLACK BRITISH POLITICIANS MATTER

Tackling institutional racism means challenging the most important institutions

DAWN BUTLER MP

Central to any discussion around Black lives in society must be the issue of where power lies and who wields it. It is for this reason we felt that it was vital to explore political power and the importance of Black British politicians.

Dawn Butler first became a Member of Parliament in 2005 and, at the time, was only the third Black woman ever to sit in the House of Commons. She was also the first elected African Caribbean woman to become a government minister in the UK.

I haven't watched the video of the death of George Floyd. Nor do I ever want to.

I know how it ends.

People have tried to tell me that I should watch it because it is an important piece of social history.

I should look at the bigger picture.

It was a tragic death, an inhuman crime committed in broad daylight by the very people who are meant to protect us against such crimes. But, so the argument goes, it has led to a global movement for change.

In the aftermath of the video, and the Black Lives Matter protests that followed it, multinational companies have promised to increase their racial diversity. Governments around the world have reviewed how they will address systemic racism. And millions of people of all races are now talking about the role race and racism plays in our society and want to see real change.

The argument goes, the killing of George Floyd was horrific but the fact it was recorded and the video went viral has contributed to a greater good. It is a good thing that people watched it.

This narrative concerns me.

If people need to watch a recording of a white police officer killing a Black man in front of their eyes to finally recognise that Black people are the victims of police brutality, despite all the evidence already out there, they have not been watching the news, listening to Black people's lived experiences or have seen the world through a different lens.

If people need to share a viral video of a Black man pleading for his life to understand that Black people's very reasonable demands for justice and fair treatment all too often go unheeded, they have clearly ignored the last 400 years of history.

Finally, if people need to see a Black man breathe his last breath while calling for his dead mother to help him, to accept that Black people are human too, something is deeply wrong, with them and society.

We all need to change society.

We should not need to watch Black men and women be killed to achieve this. And in not watching the video I am refusing to subscribe to the narrative that we needed George Floyd to die or sacrifice himself to achieve a greater good.

I want to create a new narrative. I want to put forward a new argument.

I believe that what we need is more Black people in positions of power.

What the video of George Floyd's death shows is a Black man pleading for his life and being ignored, a Black man being unheard. I do not want to simply change the situation so that when we plead for our lives or beg for change, we are heard and not ignored. I want to change the entire narrative, so that we no longer need to plead, beg or ask. So that society is changed to treat everyone fairly, with dignity and respect.

It is a concept at the very root of the Greek word 'democracy'. Democracy means 'rule by the people'. We do not want to live in a world ruled by the powerful, where the powerless or those in the minority are begging the powerful for rights and recognition. If we accept that this is not feasible and we must stick to the status quo and the rise of the racist, narcissist authoritarian then we need a new term to describe our society – an 'iketovocracy' – rule through begging. It is not enough to have to beg to live. If George Floyd had been listened to while he begged to breathe, he would have lived, but the world I want to live in is where he didn't need to beg.

I want us to live in a real democracy where we have power over our own lives – not where the people in power listen to us better when we beg. This power dynamic needs to change. And it is in everyone's interest to ensure there is a change. It will ensure that all lives indeed matter, and not just those at the very top.

We need more Black politicians making laws, helping to decide the direction of the country and, most importantly, understanding what real changes need to be made, listening to people before what they are saying becomes cries for help and definitely before they die on a viral video.

In many ways my motivation for change through politics came from a police brutality case. It wasn't as shocking as George

Floyd's, and in the days before social media and mobile phones recording everything it barely made a ripple in the fabric of the universe. But it had a profound and life-changing effect on me.

When I was just eighteen years old a white guy tried to stab my brother. The details are unimportant – what is important is my brother was the victim and his attacker was the criminal. When the police arrived on the scene of the crime, however, they grabbed my brother, a young Black man, threw him into the police van and arrested him.

When I first heard about the video of George Floyd's killing, my mind immediately went back to that incident more than three decades ago and I called my brother and asked him, 'Do you remember when the police arrested you? When the white guy tried to stab you with a knife?'

My brother's response was simple and to the point: 'Do I remember, sis? I've still got the scars.' And then he told me something he had never told me before, a detail that shocked me, even scared me, but unfortunately didn't surprise me.

He said, 'You know, sis, when I was in the back of that van the police all had their knees on my neck and on my back.' There is no need to go into the rest of the conversation I had with my brother but suffice to say the death of George Floyd brought that trauma of thirty years ago right back for him.

And the idea that I too could have lost my brother that day has created fresh trauma. Trauma that we, as Black people, carry with us, often buried only to surface decades later.

That is why I do not need to watch George Floyd being killed.

Because, at eighteen, my response to the police arresting my brother – the Black victim of a so-called white-on-Black-crime – was to organise. I wrote a formal letter of complaint to the police and I received an official letter of apology.

For my teenage self that was the biggest victory one could achieve. I remember receiving the letter and running to show it to my brother. I was like, 'I got a letter of apology from the police! Look, bro, we got a letter of apology from the police!'

The letter still exists somewhere, and the truth is, it was simply the first of many letters of apology I have received about racism, not just from the police but from numerous organisations and people in positions of power when it comes to the treatment of Black people.

But while that first letter of apology might have been enough for me at eighteen, we need to do more. Dealing with the one racist person, dealing with that one single act, getting a letter of apology really excited me. But I was excited because I didn't fully comprehend that if racism exists in the structures of those organisations, an apology isn't enough, especially if we are not dealing with a single act but a pattern of behaviour, or one racist person but a culture of racism; then, with one apology have we made any real progress?

The brutal answer is no. It almost feels like I was played because in reality there has been no progress when somebody else goes through the same discriminatory profiling. And because I did not pursue the issue, I don't know if those police officers were disciplined, so they could have gone on to terrorise other innocent Black men for years. So unless we deal with the structural racism that exists we're not going to make the changes that are necessary to have a fully functioning and fair police service that polices with intelligence and consent. And why the hell should another generation of young Black men and women like my brother go through being racialised and profiled because of the colour of their skin, why should another generation go through that?

So, we, all of us, have to stop this decline. We need to change society. We need to change the laws and we need to change the way Britain is run.

And that is why Black politicians' lives matter – you knew I had to get there at some point.

We need a critical mass of Black politicians who do not need to see the death of a Black man to realise the importance of fighting racism.

That is not to say that there are not politicians of every race and even every political hue who haven't fought racism and continue to do so, but there is something qualitatively different when you have a politician who has first-hand lived experience of the issue they are fighting for.

I do not need to see the George Floyd video because I had already lived it when I was eighteen. While I know it is important, I do not need to see a Black Lives Matter protest to prioritise the need to fight racism and understand that Black lives matter, because I instinctively know the lives of my friends, families and even my own life matter.

Black issues are not a policy brief that someone has prepared for me. Or a series of talking points I need to memorise before going on the news. I don't need to use language to shock people – I just need to tell my story, my lived experience, and some people are genuinely shocked and often appalled by the racism and injustice.

I understand police disproportionately targeting Black people when it comes to stop and search because I have been stopped and searched.

I understand the importance of tackling higher rates of Black unemployment because I have been unemployed and I have friends who are unemployed.

I do not want to address Black educational underachievement simply because I think it might win me votes – in fact it is often quite the opposite – but because I went through the British educational system as a Black girl. And while my brother might still carry the physical scars of the police arrest, I still carry the psychological scars – as does every Black British person who has survived the British schooling and police system.

Our lived experiences are important. They give us a unique insight that you cannot get any other way.

We need more Black politicians with real lived experience, but not just that.

We need Black politicians who are brave enough to talk about their lived experience knowing that others might not like it. Knowing that in order to make progress it might mean sacrificing personal progress in your party political careers. We need Black politicians who are strong enough to speak their truth irrespective of the abuse they know they will receive for speaking it.

When I first became a politician, people told me that I 'mustn't be too Black'. I had made it into the oldest democracy in the world but now to participate I should 'leave my Blackness at the door'. I was told I should be careful about people thinking I had a 'chip on my shoulder'.

I was told, you need to blend in, I shouldn't stand out, I shouldn't talk about race issues, I should talk about other issues.

The irony is even if I'd wanted to leave my Blackness at the door, so to speak, the Houses of Parliament have constantly found ways to remind me of my race from the time I became a politician.

I made headlines when I was talking once on a BBC radio programme and the presenter asked me if I had ever experienced racism at the Houses of Parliament.

My response was: 'Yes – God, there are so many incidents. There was a time when I was in the lift. It was a members' lift that is at times reserved for MPs' use when we are time-limited, like when we only have seven minutes to reach the voting lobbies. I was in the lift and some other MP said, "This lift really isn't for cleaners."'

The headline the next day was 'Black MP Dawn Butler reveals she was victim of racism in Parliament after fellow MP assumed she was a cleaner'.

On the same radio programme I talked about how a former minister had accused me of not being an MP, confronting me because I was sitting in an area on the terrace reserved for Members of Parliament.

'He actually said to me, "What are you doing here? This is for members only."'

And at least once a week I am mistaken for another Black female politician when I am walking around the Houses of Parliament. And if you are curious which one, the answer is – all of them.

Although again it only became headline news when the BBC confused me with my colleague Marsha de Cordova.

In some ways it is progress of sorts that when I speak out about this it makes headline news. But the reality is this is not headline news for Black people. It actually reveals the different life experiences between white people and people of colour.

I doubt there is a single Black person who works in a majority white environment, and that pretty much means 99 per cent of us, who does not encounter this on a regular basis.

It is exhausting to constantly fight this battle, or to constantly have to justify your presence in a space. But my Blackness 'follows' me wherever I go – I cannot leave it at the door, as some people suggested I should do.

These experiences also put paid to the lie which underpins a frequent question: 'Do you think you are Black first or a politician?'

I do not get that question so much any more but when I first entered politics I was asked that all the time. And my answer was there's lots of things that I'm interested in, there's lots of things that I'm passionate about, but the one thing that will be with me my whole life, when I wake up in the morning and when I go back to bed at night, is that I will always be Black.

So, when people ask me to leave my Blackness at the door, they are not really asking me to leave my Blackness at the door, because they invariably bring it through the door themselves as part of their own racism and prejudices.

What they are really asking for me to do is to ignore the racism I receive, ignore the prejudice I meet on a daily basis. In short, they want me to make them feel more comfortable in the room even though for me to deny who I am I wouldn't only feel uncomfortable, but I would be sacrificing myself to centre their feelings. It would defeat the very reason I went into politics, believing we need more people who look like me and have different lived experience sitting in the Houses of Parliament.

But what those voices telling me to tone down my Blackness made me realise is that simply being Black is not enough. This is not about simply measuring the level of melanin in the room. It's important that Black politicians feel confident with representing our lived experiences.

And I think this is an important point that is sometimes lost in the combative nature of British politics and the insidious nature that is sometimes hidden in questions around Blackness.

There is no one way to be Black. There is no one Black British experience. There may be commonalities in our experiences but we are not homogeneous. And so the criticism that I sometimes receive when I talk about the ideas of representation and the need for more Black politicians is that we all need to adhere to the same type of Blackness and support the same policies or else we are 'not really Black'.

Nothing could be further from the truth.

Instead it is a plea for Black politicians to be confident, to be themselves and talk about lived experiences without fear, and to represent the issues that are clearly influenced by our ethnicity.

Because if that doesn't happen, some will dismiss racism, and even if a Black person is lucky enough not to ever experience it, I find it hard to believe that anyone can deny that racism exists.

In society, and in every generation, some people of colour will take the advice to leave their Blackness at the door and some may even deny their lived experience. And in doing so they may get rewarded by being parachuted into the front to be the voice in important debates and issues around race; their voices will be elevated and carry weight because it suits the narrative of people in power. This is for me the reality that's being played out at the moment. I often wonder what the history books will say about this time of racial justice and progress.

And in our oppositional politics when I raise this it quickly becomes one Black person's word against another's. One Labour MP arguing against a Conservative MP and both are viewed as 'different but equal' positions for politicians of colour to take.

Of course I accept the lived experience of a Black person who has never experienced racism – I am happy for them that they have never faced the trauma of discrimination – but for one person of colour to argue for a policy that would deny their own parents entry into the UK versus another politician of colour arguing for policies that would benefit other people of colour is not an equal argument.

I do not believe it is 'different but equal' for Black politicians to argue for policies that will disproportionately hurt Black communities versus a Black politician who is actively attempting to help Black people.

One person is trying to give voice to their lived experience and the other person is actively trying to suppress that voice.

In my view there are two ways to combat this:

The first is recognising the importance and power of representation. A lot of people still seem to struggle with why representation matters when it comes to Black people and ask me, 'Why do we need more Black politicians?' It is complicated because just having Black politicians is not enough, especially if experiences differ so vastly, but that is why a critical mass is important.

To try and simplify the response I often respond with another question:

I say, 'Why do we need female politicians? Why can't we just have men?' And those same people who challenge the idea of Black representation say, 'You can't just have Parliament full of men! You've gotta have women!'

Not only do I agree with their position on female representation as a matter of principle, I also agree with them on a practical level. And one only has to look at the influx of women MPs in 1997 and how they changed politics and British society.

The increase in female politicians has been directly linked to how we approach issues such as cancer. Survival rates of people dying from cancer dramatically increased as a result of how we thought and spoke about cancer care. In the 1997 general election Labour said we had twenty-four hours to save the National Health Service (NHS), and the influx of female politicians improved the discussions and the outcomes. Overall satisfaction with the NHS rose from lows of 36 per cent in 1997 to highs of 71 per cent in 2010.

The Labour government, thanks to the amazing work of the late Tessa Jowell, took a holistic approach to poverty and child progress and invested in areas such as Sure Start to ensure every child had a good start in life. Women in power made a big difference in areas men would not necessarily consider. As a Labour politician I have obviously picked Labour examples but we do not have the luxury to see this through a party political prism.

Just as women politicians can shift how we approach some issues, Black people can do the same. I recall being in government and there was a discussion around giving the police more powers and how the message would be delivered. And as the conversation developed I felt more and more uncomfortable. Eventually I said something like, 'Giving the police more powers will only scare Black people as they are already over-policed with higher negative outcomes.' I remember the room falling silent. The way people were considering the issue changed; a Black perspective had to be taken on board.

A different type of politician will bring in different ways of looking at issues.

Things change when you have people who are different, with different lived experiences, different thought processes.

You find that even people who explicitly talk against the need for better representation implicitly recognise its value.

I remember the bizarre incident of one Black politician trying to argue against the importance of their own skin colour in politics by incorrectly channelling Martin Luther King Jr's famous

'I Have a Dream' speech, saying that he should be judged by the content of his character not by the colour of his skin and his race was irrelevant to his politics. And then at the end of the speech this person said, 'When I saw Adam Afriyie, the first Black Tory MP, he made me feel that I could do it,' and I was like, see! There you go! You've just undone your whole speech in that one sentence, you've just said that seeing a Black Conservative MP made you feel you can do it!

Representation matters.

It is not a binary choice between recognising the importance of your ethnicity and your lived experience versus being valued above and beyond our levels of melanin. Our racial experience informs our politics and does not detract from it. In our oppositional politics, getting these messages across can be difficult and the Black Conservative politician looked genuinely confused, perplexed, that I was so animated on the other side of the chamber trying to express this.

But while individual role models and representation matters, 1997 and the large influx of women MPs taught us something else, and this is the second thing we need.

What we need is critical mass.

We need critical mass for a number of reasons.

First, it is hard work being so isolated. It's tiring, and if you're the only one in the room, the pressure is on you. If you're not brave enough and strong enough to fight back, you just get buried by it all. I was scared to raise the police issue as the only Black person around the table.

Second, it changes the culture. And helps reset agendas.

It is not 'Dawn Butler MP saying she has one lived experience' versus 'another Black MP disagreeing, saying they had another lived experience'.

It is a critical mass of Black people saying we all know what it is like to be isolated, we all know what it is like to be on the receiving end of racism, we all know what it is like to be mistaken for the cleaner or the security guard or the taxi driver. Not that there is anything wrong with these jobs at all.

The Black politician who leaves their Blackness at the door or who has never suffered racism or discrimination is then not given equal credibility as the politician who is trying to express their traumatic lived experience. The Black politician who is fighting against an entire culture of other Black politicians saying the opposite is delaying progress, progress that would ensure that more Black people don't have to suffer from racist attacks or discrimination. The Black politician who pretends that structural discrimination and systemic racism does not exist is slowing the progress of everyone who wants to just be their authentic self and live their lives to the full, and that's everyone – women, the LGBT+ community, disabled people, you name it. The system needs to change for all, because all lives matter.

Ultimately that is the only way we will be able to change our politics and our policies and structures – if there is a Black person who has never experienced racism then they are unique and lucky. But that is not the experience of the majority. And that is far bigger than any single Black politician.

Which brings me to my conclusion of why Black politicians' lives matter.

We matter because in politics different policies can go out of fashion. Even the most important issues can be at the front of your party's manifesto one day and be relegated to the back pages at the following election.

We cannot afford for that to happen to us when it comes to combating racism and fighting for Black people's lives.

I started this essay stating that since George Floyd's death there is no doubt that there has been an increase in interest and progress in combating racism and the issues affecting Black people.

But my fear is that a change that started from something as ephemeral as a viral video could just as easily revert back.

We cannot just develop policies decided by social media interactions or TikTok videos.

I'm scared as we go forward that organisations will think, 'We've done it now, we've promoted a few more Black people, we've got a Black person around the decision-making table, we've ticked that unconscious bias training course box.' Job done.

But in truth that would be hardly any more progress than the first letter of apology I received from the police when I was eighteen.

The uncomfortable truth is while a white police officer killed George Floyd, a Black police officer stood by and did nothing. And by all accounts he may have joined the police force to combat police brutality against Black people. But the pressure of the system may have been the reason he didn't feel able to intervene? We will not know the reason until he decides to tell his story but it highlights that we cannot make a few appointments and then move on to the next issue.

It's like John Lewis, the great American civil rights leader, said, 'Ours is the struggle of not one president, you know, or one week, or one lifetime, you know it's a struggle over generations.'

It is what I have now learnt after I received my first letter of apology. It is about the structures.

And that is why Black politicians matter fundamentally. Because often it is only through the power of politicians and the law that we can change structures and systems.

We need to tackle the structures of the police that enable and embolden a white police officer to think he can kill with impunity and a Black police officer to feel that even if he wanted to he has no power to stop it.

We need to change systems which are built in such a way that they lead to racist outcomes even if the individuals in the system might not be racist and have the best of intentions.

We need to create systems and structures that create positive outcomes for Black people, that value Black lives and recognise our commonalities and differences.

That will not be achieved in a year or even through a few protests.

Systemic change happens through systemic action.

We need to empower the anti-racists, the good police officers for example, who want to speak out but are in fear that it will reflect badly on them, ruin their chances of promotion or, even worse, lead to them being victimised. We need diversity at the top of the police service. We don't need police officers to talk tough – we need them to be fair. If we can create a society where people feel comfortable speaking to the police, we will see safer streets, the police will gather more intelligence and this will result in more knives and criminals being taken off our streets.

I will give one last example. I was recently stopped by the police in London. It was an incident that was filmed and went viral. I didn't criticise the polite police officer who stopped me; I queried the system he was operating under because that is what needs to change. While I am pleased that the Metropolitan Police have agreed to work with me to address some of these issues, I am under no illusion that if I was not an MP, probably the best I could hope for is a letter of apology of the kind I received when I was eighteen.

Black politicians working day in, day out are one of the best ways to push through systemic change and to ensure that, no matter what the popular topic of the day, the quest to end structural racism doesn't slip back.

Black politicians' lives matter, but here is the rub – only if there are enough of us to actually change the culture of the very institutions we are part of.

There needs to be more of us. And if we strive to get this right all lives will eventually matter.

BLACK BRITISH TECHNOLOGISTS MATTER

A conversation between

LENNY HENRY AND DR ANNE-MARIE IMAFIDON

New innovations in the fields of science, technology, engineering and mathematics (STEM) affect every aspect of our lives both positively and negatively, and their importance is only growing. But while the scientific method might be based on the principle of objectivity, it is human beings that bring forth every breakthrough and decide what is and isn't researched.

STEM is also notoriously undiverse.

The UK has the lowest proportion of women in engineering of any European country, with females accounting for just 10 per cent of roles and 14 per cent of engineering university places. And when it comes to race, less than 4 per cent of Facebook's employees and less than 3 per cent of Google's employees in the US are Black, despite both companies being based in America, which has a Black popula-tion of over 13 per cent.

It is why it was vital for me to talk to Dr Anne-Marie Imafidon about why Black people in STEM matter.

She is the very definition of the word 'prodigy'. Aged eleven, she was the youngest girl ever to pass A-level computing – casually com-pleting her maths AS-level at the same time – and was just twenty years old when she received her master's degree in Mathematics and Computer Science from the University of Oxford.

But it is her continuing efforts to increase diversity in STEM

*that led me to talk with her. In 2013 she co-founded the Stemettes,
an award-winning social initiative dedicated to inspiring and pro-
moting the next generation of young women in the STEM sectors.
The organisation has worked with more than 50,000 young people
across Europe to try to fulfil Anne-Marie's vision for a more diverse
and balanced science and tech community.*

Here is an edited version of our conversation.

Lenny Henry: Dr Anne-Marie Imafidon, it is such a privilege
to speak to you about why Black British people in technology
matter. Now, in many ways since George Floyd's death we're all
living in a world of Black Lives Matter. It's very unremitting. It's
in everybody's faces. What does that phrase 'Black Lives Matter'
mean to you?

Anne-Marie Imafidon: Well, you know, you say it's in everyone's faces. I think for me it's a fact. First and foremost, before
it's a movement, or an organisation, I think for me Black Lives
Matter has ended up being a simple statement of fact.

Initially, for me, it was actually quite a fraught movement. In
the beginning, I didn't really want to say anything, didn't really
want to engage with it. Often in a professional setting, as a Black
woman you end up having to put up shields. Sometimes you
want to explore other attributes beyond your ethnicity. I didn't
want to suddenly start reliving traumas in public interviews or
on screen. I didn't want to become the 'rent-a-Black'.

Of course, I'm very much a Black woman. As 2020's Most
Influential Woman in UK Technology (according to *Computer
Weekly*), I sit near the top of certain technology circles. I am
also – sadly – the only Black person a lot of people know in that

space. Initially, I actually didn't want to engage because I didn't want to engage in that trauma with there being no promise of something actually being done to rectify it for others.

So although I now engage with Black Lives Matter and think it has become a move in the right direction, it still hasn't really come with as much action as I'd have wanted.

Lenny: I understand the burden of being the only Black person, or one of only a few, in your field. You become the go-to person for all things Black; it is a burden that distracts from what we are actually trying to achieve. You can spend all your time answering questions around 'What did you think of this?' or 'Oh my God, how do you respond to X?' Case in point is the George Floyd video and all the questions that come from it. So let me ask the most basic question: did you watch it? Have you seen it?

Anne-Marie: Why would I watch nine minutes of a man dying? I don't even watch horror for entertainment. It was never something I wanted to watch. It was not something I wanted to see, it was not something I wanted with a disclaimer on *Newsnight* of 'some people may find these images disturbing' – who doesn't find that disturbing or shocking or horrifying? And so I didn't watch the video. I still don't want to watch the video.

Lenny: True, Anne-Marie. I've seen him being led to the car. And I've seen a bit of it, but then I just stopped because, like you, I kept thinking: 'Hang on a second, this is our trauma and we're living it vicariously because you're choosing to put it on the news.' There's something twisted about that.

Anne-Marie: There's something twisted in the fact that people had to see that for everything to happen subsequently – which is the other thing I think about when I have any discussions about Black Lives Matter. I think someone had to die for you to know that maybe I have not been treated the same as others. I'm gonna have to die for you to realise that, 'Yeah, racism is still a thing.' You'll know this better than me, Lenny, it's something we've kind of run away from in Britain. We are almost in denial about racism in Britain.

'No, no, we don't have racism.'

'We didn't have slaves, we abolished slavery.'

I'm sure you've heard all of this nonsense before.

Did people need to see that video to acknowledge that there is racism; did it have to be shown for other people to realise we are human beings? I didn't want to watch it because I don't want to see him dying. I wouldn't even want to see a dog die like that.

I do think it speaks a lot to the fact that sometimes we – Black people – aren't seen as human. And if we are not seen as human, our potential as humans is not going to be recognised. And that goes to the heart of why I am fighting for more diversity in STEM.

Lenny: You've dedicated your life to Black people and Black women in STEM. Why does it matter to you so much?

Anne-Marie: I have dedicated my life to women in STEM, and now I'm also focusing on non-binary people in STEM. And it matters a lot because science matters, right?

When we think about innovations, I always say to people: think about what the future will look like in about five or twenty years' time. You might remember *Knight Rider*, the show from the 1980s? This guy would talk to his car and they'd fight crime together. And that's the thing that we now have. It's no longer science fiction. It's reality. You can talk to your car, ask it to change your radio station and do any number of things – maybe not necessarily to fight crime, but almost everything else.

Now, it's one of those opportunities but also challenges that if you think about the future, what happens next, we will be in the future – before you know it. But, if Black people, or women or non-binary people are not part of those decisions that shape the future, if we do not understand how our wifi fridge works, or whatever else might be the next innovation in the future – then not only will the future *not* be shaped by us, the specific problems that we face as women, or Black people or non-binary people won't be solved.

They won't be seen as important enough to dedicate time, effort and resources to solve, because middle-aged white men have different problems from younger Black women, let's say.

And that is deeply problematic not just at this point in time but because if we're not included now, we will be excluded from what's going on in the future.

For example, there is a girls' academy in Ghana, the African Science Academy, which has a focus on STEM subjects. It was set up by Tom Ilube CBE, a British entrepreneur and educational philanthropist and current non-executive director at the BBC. The perspective the girls in the academy have, the life they have, the way they see the world around them is very different even from me and we're all Black. We don't just need Black people in STEM subjects – we need the full range of different Black experiences.

The fact is if we are excluded, not only will our perspective not be included in what is created, these innovations or creations won't be able to serve us properly. The most basic example of this is facial ID technology. This technology is used to renew British passports, for instance. With the move towards e-government and digitalisation of government services, we now have algorithms that are meant to make all our lives easier and more efficient by checking through these images online before you upload them to make sure the photos are in the correct format. The problem is, as a Black woman, if I upload my photo, it will ask me why my lips are open, because it can't tell that my bottom lip is actually many shades lighter than my top lip. And that is because it won't have had enough people who look like me in the data that shaped and trained the algorithm.

This might be just a minor inconvenience when it comes to renewing my passport, but these are issues we in the tech community see being repeated in algorithm after algorithm, in the data being used to combat crime and even decide criminal sentences.

We also see the same issues cropping up in the medical arena. Here is another real-life example to illustrate. I happen to have a skin condition. The problem with my skin condition, however, is that as a Black woman I will never go red, but all the reference pictures that are used by the people building the technology to recognise this skin condition use pictures of red skin. A doctor or nurse using this tech – especially with online consultations being more popular – will never be able to diagnose that I've got this skin condition.

So the question is: how many more areas of our digital life am I – we – going to be written out of when it comes to the future, if we are not involved now? To go back to the *Knight Rider* example, the equivalent is only white men being allowed in future to drive and talk to their cars. Everyone else has to get the bus, or go in person to the government office or the doctor to line up to get services 'manually'. That's productive time lost, that's efficiency we are locked out of. It has unequal effects. So there's an agency and an equalising power that comes from being in the room when these decisions are made and this technology is created.

Lenny: So if we want to shape our future, to be part of society and have equal access to all parts of society, we need Black people in STEM.

Anne-Marie: Precisely.

Lenny: That makes sense. Now, the examples you gave of renewing your passport or recognising skin conditions, is that a case of who is deciding what images to feed the computers? And I am guessing the background of the person matters?

Anne-Marie: Absolutely. It is all about who owns the data, who gathers the data, who decides what data is fed into the algorithm, and who decides the parameters of that data. Or in other words, 'garbage in, garbage out'. Or to be a little more emotive, 'prejudiced data in, prejudiced data out'.

What it effectively means is if you're not being spoken about, if you're not part of that data set, or if you have no ownership of the data set, then that algorithm will never be able to understand your needs and serve you properly. Here are two examples which can be really helpful in explaining this.

One is from some case studies put together by the Institute for the Future of Work, where I'm a trustee. A company was using an algorithm for help with hiring decisions. Its explanation went something like this.

At our company there are the people we already have in our organisation. There are the people that we know do well. And there are the people that we know don't do well. And we know this by going through customer feedback, and all other kinds of data. Next, we are going to see if there is a way to see if there is a link between the successful employees and their social media profiles. If there is, it will be really simple. We will be able to spot a prospective successful employee simply by looking at their social media profile, and if it matches our successful workers we will employ them.

The company even patted itself on the back because they felt this was not just innovative, they took the extra ethical step to ask for permission from the employees for access to their social media profiles, and they said no problem.

But this is where it got interesting. The company fed all this social media profile data into an algorithm and it turned out there was definitely a certain type of person that fitted the social media profiles of the already successful workers. But the algorithm ended up only hiring white men.

Why? The reason was simple. This was a telecoms company and didn't have any Black people at all. They had no examples of Black social media profiles to even compare against white people's social media profiles, let alone successful Black profiles. So when the algorithm was fed the data of what a successful candidate looks like it was literally given profile after profile of white men.

We weren't part of that data set, we weren't reflected there.

The second example of 'bad data in, bad outcome out' is one that is even closer to my heart: what does a scientist look like?

If you go through Google or Wikipedia, you'll find a huge number of images of scientists. And if you take all of those images, if you take the average of them, you won't find a Black face. That's not because there are no Black scientists. But because if you look at the selection processes for Google or Wikipedia, if you look at how they did that, if you look at people that were recognised as successful innovators in the past, or perhaps didn't even want to be documented as Black because of discrimination, then it means our search engines effectively have a bias towards dead white dudes. And so therefore, in these online definitions, as a Black woman, I'm not a scientist. I don't fit the image.

Lenny: But is it just a case of needing more data? If we just start collecting Black people's data, put better data in and more data of more scientists or more social media profiles, will the problem be solved? We are feeding all this data into algorithms, and algorithms aren't prejudiced, right? Oh and, confession time, even though we've been having this conversation and we've been talking about algorithms, what exactly is an algorithm? Hashtag asking for a friend.

Anne-Marie: OK, so to help your 'friend' this is what I would say: an algorithm is a series of instructions.

As you know, I founded Stemettes to support young women into STEM subjects and we use a special exercise to explain algorithms with the girls when we're teaching them to code. It's called 'jam sandwiches'. To make a jam sandwich you've got two slices of bread, you've got a knife, you've got a plate and a filling – in this case, jam. The algorithm is essentially the recipe to allow a computer to make the jam sandwich. But in that set of instructions, you can tell the computer that it can switch out the jam and replace it with Nutella or Marmite. Whatever you'd like.

That's the simple version. It's what an algorithm was before. But then we had this big bang and disruption called Artificial Intelligence (AI). With AI, the computer can essentially learn and change what it does. It can make ten sandwiches with different fillings and, if it sees that the one with honey always gets sent back and the one with jam is never returned, it learns to make more jam sandwiches and to stop making honey sandwiches.

Lenny: So why do we need more Black people or more diversity in who is making the original algorithm? If you can get the right initial 'diverse' data to put in, and use that over and over, that doesn't seem inherently biased to me.

Anne-Marie: Well, no – it is deeper than that.

When we talk about algorithms being biased, there are two sides to it.

One side is: what is that data that you're feeding in? As in – to continue the sandwiches analogy – are you just taking the data from sandwich orders from one shop or many? Are you taking sandwich orders from your entire chain? Are you taking sandwich orders from the whole world? And the complicated part is that more data is not always better. If the computer is making sandwiches for a shop in your local neighbourhood, it might make the 'wrong' sandwiches if you feed in the sandwich preferences of the entire world. But less data is also not always better. If I only feed in the data of what my current local customers like, that might exclude all the tastes of people who have moved into the neighbourhood more recently. So deciding your data set is subjective and will be influenced by who decides the algorithm.

So that's the first type of possible bias. The second way it can be biased is what is the reason that you're telling the computer to make sandwiches in the first place? There are other things that people can and do have for lunch. Why did you limit the algorithm to making sandwiches? Why didn't you allow fish and chips to be part of the algorithm? Or noodles? Or jerk chicken?

The bias can easily be – excuse the pun – baked in at the very start and is heavily influenced by the type of people making those decisions.

Lenny: Let me just make sure I've got this right. What you're saying is that there's the bad data – the garbage in/garbage out issue. But even if we have good data, we need Black people to be involved in deciding what good data we use; we need Black people deciding what the algorithms should be focused on. Otherwise, we're not going to actually set or create the right algorithms to solve the issues which are affecting us. They won't be addressing our problems and that will exclude us from society from the get-go.

Anne-Marie: Exactly. It's for these reasons that we need to be in the room – even just to avoid such algorithms or other technology actually doing Black people, women or non-binary people some harm.

However, beyond getting more women and Black people into STEM and design and delivery, you have to also look at what is financed and what the people who finance tech look like.

Here is one very simple example. A couple of years ago there was a start-up trying to launch an app called Yo. Tech start-ups are like a microcosm of the business world. You have venture capitalists (VCs) and investors, who have lots of money to put into ideas that they like the look of and that they believe in.

Think of it like the programme *Dragons' Den*. If someone goes on *Dragons' Den* with a business idea for afro hair, they often don't get anywhere because no one there understands that the afro hair market is worth billions. Extend this to other aspects of Black life, and potentially multi-million ideas one after the other are not getting financed. The tech world is sometimes like *Dragons' Den*. In fact, it's worse than *Dragons' Den* because on *Dragons' Den* two out of five dragons are women, I think, whereas in tech, only 3 per cent of tech VCs are women.

So, getting back to the Yo example. All the Yo app did was send a 'Yo' from one phone to another – that was it. And it received $1.5 million in funding, giving it a valuation of $10 million. Bear in mind, there's WhatsApp, there's texts, there's all these things, but an app that enables you to send a 'Yo' to your friend gets over a million dollars in funding. At the same time, other ideas that we don't even hear about – an idea, let's say, for Black hair – can't get any funding. This means tech ideas are being funded to the high heavens that do not solve any of our problems. We get completely ignored.

Lenny: But what about you? You are getting in the room. Is that good enough?

Anne-Marie: I am in the room, yes, but my experience is not the experience of a typical Black woman – or man for that matter! I'm Oxbridge-educated, I have this whole history behind me – child prodigy, master's by twenty and so on. I know that the experience I have is so different from the experience that other Black people in STEM might have – despite my own efforts to place a ladder behind me. For example, I regularly get called on to do media appearances. And it'll be: 'We want Anne-Marie as that Black woman or no one at all.' If I send a long list of all the other Black women who could talk on the issue – which I usually do if I'm busy, and there are quite a lot of us – you see other people aren't picked and they are more than qualified.

Lenny: Are you saying you haven't experienced racism or sexism then?

Anne-Marie: There is no doubt that I have experienced racism or sexism. But what I've struggled with – and I think others recognise this too – is to be able to pinpoint on my own the specific occasions and instances that it has happened to me because I'm Black, and/or I'm female. It's only when I'm in a circumstance that allows me to compare notes with someone else, such as at a Black Lives Matter roundtable, or a women's leadership discussion, that you can really unpick these experiences. I've been in a room of all Black women, and over our conversation we realise we all have applied for a particular non-executive director role in a STEM-related organisation. And it's not gone to any one of us. None of us were called for interviews. Then it's easier to say 'huh', and really understand what has happened. So often as Black people we experience these instances behind the scenes, never talk about them and internalise them as if they were to do with us specifically, when really they are systemic.

Lenny: You've convinced me that Black people in tech matter. I understand you can't be the only one. But why aren't there more Black people in STEM?

Anne-Marie: We actually need to be more precise with how we answer that question. Black people are actually over-represented at some STEM-related university courses compared to the wider population. Engineering courses are a good example. But it's the next step up that then shifts the balance. We are not hired, because our potential is not acknowledged or recognised. It's the racism I've talked about through our interview. If I don't 'look like an engineer', and I turn up to your engineering interview, you're less likely to put me through because I don't look like an engineer. So despite us being more, we are often starting from points of disadvantage, having to prove that we are better than all the other white candidates and whatever candidates that have been shortlisted.

Then there is the step beyond hiring. If we are hired, we are also often not promoted. So there is an additional challenge of not just having to prove ourselves, we end up being over-worked and under-credited a lot of the time. And then there's the kind of 'death by a thousand cuts' that Black people get from micro-aggressions. I know a number of Black women who have entered women-only spaces which are meant, in principle, to be safe spaces, who've been treated awfully.

And there is only so much someone can take before they're like, 'You know what, I'm out of here, I'm going to go and either set up my own organisation, or I'm going to leave the field entirely.' Or worse. It does a lot to human beings to be subject to death by a thousand cuts. Eventually you can die, right?

Lenny: We have an entire other essay in this book about Black mental health – that is what I think about when you talk about 'or worse' or 'death by a thousand cuts'.

Anne-Marie: Exactly. But I don't want to end this conversation on a negative note. For me it all comes back to thinking about the future. That's what motivates me to keep working on increasing diversity in STEM. You can either have a utopian view of the future or a *Black Mirror* dystopian view of it all. I have a far more utopian view because that makes it much easier to say I'm going to carry on going, despite everything that I see around me. I'm going to continue to push.

I want to continue to create intersectional spaces, where Black people can co-exist alongside other people. I want to continue to be inclusive and have non-binary folks, as well as girls and boys, in what I'm doing. Across Stemettes, my podcast, my books, on stage and in media appearances, I want to continue to create the safe spaces for folks to explore and to understand their options uninhibited by what's going on already outside. For me, that is the motivator – we need different people in those STEM rooms. We need them influencing and making decisions. We need them to be fully comfortable with what's going on, technically; we need them to be fully confident, no matter what's going on in those environments, and have the perspective that they bring to be valued.

It's not inevitable that things have to be the way they are. We can make fish and chips or jollof rice or noodles. We don't have to stick with sandwiches. Together we can make and fund the tech to make a tastier world; we just need to be in the room.

Lenny: Thank you so much, Anne-Marie. You have definitely given me food for thought – and now . . . I'm off to get that jerk sandwich.

BLACK BRITISH MOTHERS MATTER

Without us there would be no we

BARONESS DOREEN LAWRENCE

When George Floyd was murdered by a White police officer the words that resonated across the world and were emblazoned on countless placards were 'I cannot breathe'. But these were not his only words; tellingly he also called out to his mother, who had died two years earlier, saying 'Momma!' followed by 'Momma! I'm through.'

Mothers play a central and unique role in Black communities across the world. That is why we were honoured when Baroness Doreen Lawrence of Clarendon agreed to contribute to the book. The mother of Stephen Lawrence, the Black British teenager who was murdered in a racist attack in South-East London in 1993, Doreen has campaigned tirelessly for racial equality and has been central to how we view racism in the UK.

I don't cry in public.

I fight in public.

But make no mistake about it, I do cry – I need to say that because some people seem to think I honestly do not cry. People show their emotions in different ways and I've learnt that people grieve in different ways, but I believe the different outward appearances of emotions belie the fact that we all feel the same emotions. It is only in children's drawings, and silly emoticons that my granddaughter loves to send me, that happiness is always portrayed with an upward turn of the mouth and sadness has tears streaming down your face. But the truth is we can be happy when we are crying and grieving through clenched teeth and dry eyes.

My eldest son Stephen died on the 22nd of April 1993. Murdered by a gang of racist thugs. He was eighteen and a half. I had not long turned forty. I mention my age because sometimes, I could even say 'most of the time', I am aware that to many people I am ageless. I am ageless in the way that people in the public eye often are frozen in time by a single event when they come to public prominence. I am also ageless because people don't always see me as human.

I am the Black woman who fought against the racist system. To some I am a hero who exposed the institutional racism that runs deep throughout our public institutions. To others I am the 'angry Black woman' who fought the police and the justice system in order to bring my son's killers to justice. Occasionally, I am the Black woman who carried the Union Jack in the 2012 London Olympics opening ceremony in a sign of multiculturalism.

I went to a school the other day and the children had to draw pictures of important Black people in history. My picture was there, eyes slightly too high up on my face and my lips just a little too red, but I recognised myself and underneath written in neat joined-up pencil was a description of who I was.

I try not to think about it too much, but when I do it feels strange; it is hard to see myself through the eyes of others. I recognise the fact that I am a sign, a symbol of something greater than myself. My very public struggle to bring justice for Stephen may have been very personal for me but I also realise it has become a struggle that represents every Black person's struggle against racism. It is rare that I can go for a walk or visit a restaurant without somebody, usually a Black person, coming up to me and saying 'thank you'. I normally just respond with a smile and say 'thank you' back. What they are thanking me for is rarely fully articulated, but I know it is not for the fact that at least some of Stephen's killers have been brought to justice – after all, they never even knew Stephen. It is obviously for something far greater than both of us.

I was told the other day by my granddaughter that I am what they call an 'avatar'. She was at pains to explain to me that she didn't mean I was in a computer game or that I was one of the blue people in the movie. An avatar, she explained, is defined in Webster's Dictionary as 'an embodiment (as of a concept or philosophy) often in a person'.

I can't fight the fact of what I have become but I can add to it.

I am possibly one of the most formidable things society has ever created. And I say that in all modesty because I know I am not the only one. I am a Black mother. I am a Black mother who gave birth to three children, lost one, and loves my surviving daughter and son in ways I find difficult to express to them and have grandchildren who they think I spoil rotten.

I am telling you about my love for my children and grand-children, because Black mothers are not avatars, we cannot be reduced to symbols, we are not ageless. We go to work, we make our children's breakfasts, we pay our bills, we cry, we laugh, we get frustrated, we have our favourite movies, and we are all too often trying to eat a little bit healthier because the doctor told us we are prone to high blood pressure. We are flesh and blood.

I mentioned my age at the beginning because ideas and sym-bols do not age and I do not want to be reduced to a symbol – I do age. I am not the same person I was when Stephen died twenty-eight years ago, and I am definitely not the same person I was when he was born forty-seven years ago. I am human. And I want my humanity and the humanity of all Black mothers to be recognised.

I gave birth to Stephen when I was only twenty-one. I was a young mother. I took on the full power of the British state when I was forty. Once you know those two facts it often brings back my humanity to people who see me as merely a symbol. I can reclaim my humanness. For everyone reading this who is in their forties and older, can you imagine what it must have felt like to meet Nelson Mandela just a few weeks after your son has died, hoping, aged forty, that meeting him might somehow bring attention to your situation and bring your son's killers to justice? Once you think about doing that yourself, think about how you would feel the night before, preparing for the meeting, how you would feel taking pictures with a world leader that most people dream of meeting. But I had to do it in the depth of my grief. I challenge anyone to think about these things and think of me as just a symbol.

And I need you to remember my essential humanness and the essential humanness of all Black mothers when you read the next few pages.

Because in celebrating them, in celebrating us, I do not want to strip Black mothers of the very part of them that makes them (or should that be 'us') so special. We achieve everything not because we are superhuman. We achieve the things we achieve because we are human. Our strength does not come from not having any weaknesses, our strength comes from overcoming them.

When I first saw the video of George Floyd's death I didn't watch it as a campaigner. My first thoughts were not to go to the streets and protest. When I saw the video I watched it as a Black mother who had lost her son at the age of forty and still grieves for him daily.

I saw a Black man being brutalised, killed by a white person who never thought he would be held accountable for his actions. A policeman who, because of white privilege, thought he was above the law. Most people who have watched the video remember George Floyd saying that he could not breathe. The words 'I can't breathe' were emblazoned on placards and T-shirts all over the summer of 2020. When I watched the video I too saw a Black man plead with his killer, telling him he couldn't breathe, but those were not the words that resonated with me – that struck me to my very core. As he was dying I heard him call out for his mother.

When I saw that video it was impossible not to think of my son. Stephen's killers might not have been in uniform but they too, because of their skin colour and the skin colour of my son, they thought they were above the law. And here is the strange thing I felt when I watched the video, the thing I am still grappling with. I felt jealousy. Although I am not sure if 'jealousy' is the right word.

There is no video of my son's death, and I've always wanted to know: when Stephen was hurt, did he call out for me? Like George, did he call out for his mother? Lying on the ground left to die, who did he need there to comfort him? And nearly thirty years later I still can't get it out of my head – I can't let go of the fact that if he did call out for me I was not there for him. I was not able to protect him.

I wasn't there.

I wasn't there when he was crying.

I wasn't there when he was in pain.

And that's something I can't, I can't get over. I can't get it out
of my head. That's possibly the worst aspect for me. This is not
the pain of a symbol, or the questions an avatar asks lying awake
at night in their bed. These are not even the thoughts that a
child's painting of a 'name a famous person for Black History
Month' provokes. These are the painful emotions, questions and
thoughts of a very human Black mother who still thinks about
her son.

But, not being there, I will never know the answers to any of
these questions and my grief will persist. I would love to at least
know his last words. I'm not sure if it would give me comfort
but it's something I'd like to know.

We all know George Floyd is not the first Black person to be
killed by white police, nor will he be the last. We all know that
Stephen was not the first young Black man murdered by racists,
and he will not be the last. Like an itch that you know will not
be cured by scratching it but not being able to scratch it only
makes it worse.

So, while the cry goes out to remember the names of the
murdered victims, with sporting stars like Naomi Osaka wearing their names on her face masks at the 2020 US Open, I want
to add to that plea. Please do not forget their Black mothers,
because our pain is real and we must comfort the living just as
much as we remember the dead.

I do not think it was insignificant that George Floyd called
out for his mother, Larcenia Floyd, who had actually died two
years earlier. Black mothers are special and hold a special place
in our communities. For every Black death I think about their
mothers. Breonna Taylor, who was shot and killed by police,
her mother's name is Tamika Palmer. Elijah McClain, who
died in police custody, his mother's name is Sheneen McClain.

Ahmaud Arbery, who was shot and killed when simply jogging, his mother's name is Wanda Cooper-Jones. Trayvon Martin, whose death sparked the Black Lives Matter movement in 2012, his mother's name is Sybrina Fulton. And along with George Floyd I have simply mentioned the names on Naomi's face masks. I think about how, like me, these mothers – all with names – were not there to help them. I always think about the victims' mothers, that's the first thought that always comes to mind.

I think about their pain.

I think about the mothers who, like me, do not know what the final moments of their children's lives were like. Haunted by the unknown. But I also think about the mothers whose children's deaths were caught on film, usually on a mobile phone or a police body camera, and are tortured by knowing what the last moments of their child's life were like.

For those parents, some of whom I have already named, I can only imagine what it is like to go through watching that. Seeing the events leading up to your child's death knowing exactly how it will end and then watching your son or daughter being killed in front of your eyes – possibly time and time again. Not being able to stop the killer. Not being able to protect your child. Not being able to even comfort your child in their final moments. And every time a mother watches a video of her child being killed she is watching her own impotence and complete lack of power being played out time and time again.

And writing as someone whose son was killed on the 22nd of April 1993, I can say with confidence to all the mothers: the pain will never get any easier. The best I can describe it is like a permanent injury. If you lose both your legs, you do not learn how to walk again; you learn different ways to get from one place to another. But it is not as if over time your legs grow back and you find yourself walking. It is the same with losing your son. You find ways to get through the day with the pain and live with the grief but it does not go away. The pain no more vanishes than legs can grow back if they are amputated.

At the same time as recognising that the pain never disappears, what I can advise the Black mothers to do is always talk about their children. Just talk about them. Bring your child back to life every day through words and actions. Bring them to life within you, and within your family, and within your communities. That is what I try to do with Stephen.

In my bedroom is a painting of Stephen and his eyes always follow me. The painting is on the wall and every time I look at him I see him looking back at me. When I'm in bed I can see his eyes looking at me; on the other side of the room I can see his eyes looking at me. So, he is always there, he's always there physically and in my heart. Stephen never leaves me and I'm sure the mothers of all the murdered Black people feel the same way. Their children will never leave them and it is the living memory of your child who comforts you when you need that comfort.

I saw the wounds that killed Stephen, although I never saw them being inflicted. And I recognise that being able to see that must be another level of pain. Those are images that will never leave those mothers. Those are memories that will never leave them and there's nothing they can do. There is nothing they can do except cry. Cry for them every day and bring them to life. Remember all the things you can about their lives from the time you gave birth to them, to the time they were taken away from you too soon.

Remember and celebrate their whole lives, not just the two-minute news clips that the world sees and remembers of their death. Their lives matter and that should not be overshadowed by their deaths.

People are constantly surprised by the things I remember about Stephen as a baby.

I remember walking to Woolwich one day in South-East London, and Stephen as a baby in his pram. As I was walking, I noticed another parent; her child was a little older than Stephen and wasn't in a pram and was holding his mother's hand. The two of them were walking along the street and while the mother walked on the pavement her child was walking along a slightly raised wall next to the pavement. As I caught up with the mother and child I said to the other mother, 'I can't wait until Stephen can do that,' and all she said to me was something like, 'The best time is when he's in his pram!'

I remember loving what people commonly call the 'terrible twos' because he was growing and developing at such a fast pace and learning new things almost every day. I couldn't wait for him to be a 'wall walker' like that other child.

I remember every doctor's visit, every mundane check-up and every injection. I had Stephen when I was twenty-one – I was a young mother – and as Stephen grew older I remember people sometimes thinking I was his older sister rather than his mother. And I remember one time when he was a teenager walking in the rain with him and he had his arms in mine as we shared an umbrella, and as we walked people gave us funny looks as they tried to figure out our relationship to one another.

In many ways these are all inconsequential memories bordering on the mundane, and if Stephen was alive today I doubt I would share these memories with anyone; the fact of the matter is that I might not even remember them myself.

But I share these memories. I tell you my age. I tell you that

I think about Stephen every day to impress on you that I am human. Black mothers who lose their sons and daughters are human.

Black Lives Matter is not just some kind of political slogan for us. My son's life mattered. And for every Black life that is taken you are destroying the life of a Black mother. You are creating pain and anguish that can never be extinguished, only managed.

We are not what we are portrayed on the news.

I was very aware, from early on, how the media wanted to reduce me to a two-dimensional stereotype, in the same way they want to reduce the mothers of all the Black people who have been killed – the 'grieving mother'. The truth is I'm as vulnerable as anybody. I don't find it difficult to cry. I can cry at the drop of a hat. If I am watching something on TV it doesn't take a lot for tears to start flowing, whether that is a sad movie or my favourite contestant being voted off *Great British Bake Off*.

But I never allow myself to cry in public, all through my struggles to bring Stephen's murderers to justice. Through all the frustration of fighting against the entire UK establishment to expose the racism inherent in the system. Through to the most personal and intrusive questions by reporters and journalists, I never cried.

Refusing to cry in public did not start off as a deliberate policy – and I think crying is healthy for any grieving mother to do – and I am still not 100 per cent sure why I have taken this position. I've thought about it and I believe it is for a number of reasons. It is partly because I do not want to give any more of myself than I have already. I have already given the world my son; they do not deserve my tears as well. Those are for me and Stephen.

But the other reason may be because deep down I still view

tears as a sign of weakness, a sign of vulnerability. The killing of our children has already exposed how weak and vulnerable we can be as Black people. Our weakness is on full display when George Floyd begs for his life and in his final breaths calls out for his mother. Our weakness is on full display every time a video goes viral of a police officer approaching a car of a Black person and we know the outcome of the interaction is completely in the hands of the police officer and not in the power of the Black person to decide.

I do not need to add to those displays of weakness that the media loves to show. I may be a victim – I am a victim because I am a mother who has lost her son. But I am a fighter. I do have power. We encountered far more losses when fighting for justice for Stephen than we experienced victories. But I never allowed myself to be defeated. And most of all I never wanted to appear defeated in front of either the people who wanted to see me give up, or the people who were cheering me on.

I am very conscious of the fact that by taking this position people often think I am a hard-nosed person who not only doesn't show emotions, but doesn't even have emotions. Or, if they are kind they say 'Oh you're so strong.' And my answer to that is 'Not really, not really.' But at the same time I cannot be a symbol of weakness because Black mothers are not weak. Which is why for me Black mothers must be a sign of strength, because throughout history we have always been a sign of strength. Even when we lose we are undefeated.

Now at this point I expect some readers may be asking why I have been talking about mothers and not fathers or brothers or sisters or aunts or uncles. Because there is no denying we all feel pain.

I focus on Black mothers because I believe Black women and

Black mothers in particular hold a special place in our communities and history. We carry the joys and burdens of motherhood, womanhood and our Blackness.

Make no mistake about it, it is not easy being a Black mother. In 2020, statistics showed Black women in the UK were four times more likely to die in pregnancy or childbirth. And that is a sign of things getting better! In 2019 a report showed we were five times at higher risk than the rest of the population.

And raising Black children in the UK is challenging to say the least. Children of Caribbean heritage are twice as likely to be excluded from school as their white counterparts: in 2020 one out of every ten children of Caribbean heritage in a British school was excluded at some point. Our children are more likely to suffer unemployment and more likely to fall foul of the criminal justice system.

Is it any wonder that a 2017 report showed that Black women in the UK, more than any other group, are more likely to have experienced a common mental health disorder?

But despite the challenges our bond to our children is unbreakable.

I remember I went to Jamaica one year when Stephen was still quite young. My aunt asked if I would like to send the boys to her to look after them, to 'grow them up', as they say in Jamaica. It was a kind and generous offer but it didn't matter because as a mother I could not be parted from my children.

There is in Black mothers a feeling of responsibility that can transcend death. It creates a bond between a mother and child that can be unbreakable, ironically even when that bond can feel painful. Being a Black mother is a gift that, if you are lucky, is bestowed on you, but it is a gift that is impossible to understand before you receive it.

Before being a mother I was an aunt, a big cousin and an older sister. I looked after other people's children and loved them. But when you become a mother there is a depth of love that cannot be expressed and only felt. Your child's pain is your pain. Their joy is your joy. And for me an injustice against them is an injustice brought against you. Black mothering is a tireless, all-encompassing love and giving for your own children.

In a time of social media, when 'likes' seem to be more valuable than love, and individual achievement is celebrated and even deified, motherhood forces you to push against this. Motherhood forces you to realise that you are greater than yourself, whether you like it or not.

The process of caring and fighting for someone other than yourself with the same amount of strength and love that you would for yourself immediately creates a fight for a wider community. It may start off as a fight for just one person (your child) or even just your immediate family, but it soon becomes a fight for your Black community because it is a fight that is bigger than your immediate self. And it is a fight that you take on because you have no idea how you could live your life without taking it on.

Before writing this piece I wanted to make sure that this wasn't just my personal experience and that I was right to think this was a special feature of Black mothers. And I was introduced to the infamous case of Emmett Till. The fourteen-year-old Black boy who was murdered by racists in 1955 in America for allegedly just looking at a white woman.

Emmett was far from the first Black boy to be murdered for supposedly transgressing a racist set of rules and beliefs. But echoing the more recent killing of George Floyd, his death took on international significance because of technology. In the case of George Floyd it is the ability for these recent examples of brutality against Black people to be caught on mobile phones. In the case of Emmett Till it was because his mutilated body was photographed in an open casket.

Photographs of Emmett Till's brutalised body were seen around the whole world and so people could once and for all fully get a glimpse of the horrors inflicted on a Black person that caused his death. They were photographs that in many ways were instrumental to the civil rights movement in the US, both in terms of galvanising Black people and in creating white allies who seemed to finally understand what they were fighting for. It destroyed the argument and myth that America was a separate but equal society.

While the story of Emmett Till is well known in America, and throughout much of the Black diaspora in the Caribbean and even Europe, what is less well known is that it was his mother, Mamie Elizabeth Till-Mobley, who showed the forti- tude, strength and wisdom to insist that his casket was open.

She famously said, 'I wanted the world to see what they did to my baby.'

It was a Black mother who went against the social norms of supposed decency and let the world see the pain. It was a sup- posed decency that protected racists and had previously pulled a veil over their crimes. It was the suffering of a Black mother that was able to articulate the grievances and full grief of the Black community.

When I think of Emmet Till's mother, again I do not merely think of a two-dimensional person whose only act in life was to decide to have an open casket when her son was murdered. I think of a woman who raised her son. Who loved her son. Who grieved for her son and whose fight for justice for her son is inseparable from her fight for justice for her entire Black community.

And she refused to be reduced to a single moment, she refused to be reduced to 'just' a grieving mother. She gave speeches all over the country, fighting for civil rights and against racism right up until 2000.

Her greatness comes not because of one act. Her greatness comes because of everything in her life. And the importance of mothers for pushing the boundaries of social change do not stop with Emmett Till's mother.

In Mexico, Mother's Day has become a day of resistance, as mothers march annually to demand answers about the disappearance of their children who have gone missing, killed or abducted since the government declared a war on drugs. To my knowledge there is no similar outpouring for any social activity and protest anywhere in the world centred around Father's Day. That is not by accident.

And yet despite our central role in defining and fighting for justice, Black mothers and Black women are all too often erased.

While the power of the mother to have an open casket is one reason Emmett Till's death became such an important moment in Black civil rights history, it is striking that we seem to remember the names of male victims before we remember the names of female victims.

Similarly, the Black male leaders in the struggle to achieve better racial justice are championed and remembered, while the mothers who have been central to the struggle are relegated to single acts of defiance or providing the emotional background. Men are the main protagonists, women are the supporting cast.

I primarily fought for justice for Stephen because Stephen didn't have his voice and there was no one else to speak up for him. There was no one else who could tell his story – I needed to be his voice. I knew there were many other Black boys who had died before Stephen, and just the other day it came back to me that I vowed when he died that Stephen's name was never going to be a statistic. I was determined that everybody would remember him, not just as a victim but as a human being who had dreams and ambitions. Which is why I have also concentrated on the fact he wanted to be an architect. I set up initiatives not to address knife crime – that should be the police's job if they are doing it well – but to promote young Black talent.

But just as I have fought for my son not to be a single statistic or simply a victim, we must make sure our Black mothers are recognised in the same way. We must remember their struggles and their fights. And we must remember that they too are not just two-dimensional figures and strip them of their humanity.

We must champion them – because without us there would be no we.

Black mothers matter.

BLACK BRITISH FATHERS MATTER

No more Mr Babyfather

COLIN GRANT

After asking Baroness Doreen Lawrence to contribute to this book on why Black British mothers matter, commissioning an essay on Black British fathers was essential. Colin Grant was an obvious choice, with his semi-autobiographical book Bageye at the Wheel *lovingly detailing the complex role fathers often play in Black families.*

The importance of fathers was further underlined in the murder of George Floyd, himself a father, as he called out for his children when he was being murdered, saying 'Tell my kids I love them.'

'Either I can beat him or the police [can].' Challenged by his wife, Ta-Nehisi Coates's father defended his belief in the urgent, necessary and violent disciplining of their son. At the time, the young Coates was dismayed and aggrieved by his father's extreme behaviour, but when he became a father himself, he better understood how violence could be misconstrued as an act of love; the kind of love that would propel a father to kill a son himself 'before seeing [him] killed by the streets that America made'.

Coates's reflections on the obsessional love that some Black fathers show towards their children, found in his memoir *Between the World and Me*, also resonate with many Black British children and their fathers. Growing up in 1960s Luton, the archetypal West Indian father appeared to me to be a man who best expressed himself, not with words, but physically. Before the apparently reluctant beating began, as he undid the belt from his waist, the parent might issue the words: 'If you can't hear, then you will feel.'

Black fathers may have failed in other areas of parenthood, but they excelled as world-class beaters; some even took pride in the quality of their beatings.

My parents, Ethlyn and Bageye, arrived in Britain from Jamaica in 1959. Their attitudes towards parenting differed – Ethlyn was far more nurturing – but both had been shaped by their lives in Jamaica. Bageye never darkened the doorstep of a church but his method of parenting seemed drawn from the fire and brimstone of the New Testament. 'My papa didn't bring me up to be no rogue, and there'll be no rogues in my house,' was one of his more memorable admonitions.

Only later in life would I learn that Bageye's father *was* a rogue who took no responsibility for him (on Bageye's birth certificate the box for the father's name was left blank).

I conducted no survey, as a child; I simply paid attention to the stories told to me by my West Indian friends, and recalled closer to home the 'bitchlicks' I received from Bageye's hand before Ethlyn wisely showed him the door.

But, looking back now, maybe it was the same fear articulated by Ta-Nehisi Coates's father that unleashed the violence that arguably in the 1960s and '70s, with a few exceptions, was a dominant characteristic of Black British fatherhood.

But corporal punishment was in line with the school of thought that equated respect for your father with fear of him. The logic of Coates senior's argument chimed with the West Indian admonition about a failure to learn; if you didn't absorb the lessons of the proportionate 'licks' meted out by your father, then you were liable to suffer the lasting consequences of a far more punitive State.

From the 1960s onwards, if not before, the framing of the Black father's role has been imagined as much through the dominant culture of African America as through Black Britain. To reach Black British or Caribbean writers like George Lamming, V.S. Naipaul and Andrea Levy, I first immersed myself in the work of Ralph Ellison, James Baldwin and Toni Morrison. There appeared to be a more substantive and established tradition of interrogating race, family and society to draw on among African American authors. Peculiarly, though the Black American discourse of fatherhood in the public sphere was more sophisticated than anything on offer here, it didn't put the USA's Black population at an advantage; there was always more jeopardy over there. The hip-hop group the Fugees called it right in 'Family Business': 'Just walkin' the streets, death can take you away.' Of course, the dangers were within and outwith. And as the tragedy of Stephen Lawrence's murder and today's preponderance of knife crime among Black youths has shown, that description by the Fugees also, if not equally, applies to this country.

On both sides of the Atlantic, Black lives continue to be shaped by attitudes towards the Black body. But the attention given in the USA to reflections such as those of Ta-Nehisi Coates illustrates the dilemma we face as Black Britons, and particularly as Black fathers. Apart from politicians such as David Lammy and journalists such as the former *Guardian* columnist Gary Younge, there are too few Black British public intellectuals given a platform to speak with the force, clarity and influence that Coates and his myriad peers command in the USA. Here we must settle for circular partisan discussions, sniping in newspapers and the kind of Groundhog Day-like posturing that posits that Black children have been failed by the shortcomings of their absent Black fathers. End of story!

Times are, of course, a-changing, and with it so too are our cultural references. If you'd typed the phrase 'Black British fathers' into the search engine of your choice in the early days of the internet you'd have been inundated with references to *Babyfather*, the novel by Patrick Augustus, and the furore in some quarters over its BBC TV adaptation, broadcast from 2001 to 2002. Insights from *Babyfather* hardly moved the dial along. It was not a high mark in political, personal and social engagement but it did, perhaps, reflect the persistence of the stereotype of feckless and promiscuous Black fathers ('bless them, they just can't help it').

At an upwardly mobile Black middle-class party around that time, I remember talking about Augustus's book with a small group of earnest, tertiary-educated women, including a thirty-something designer called Marsha. When I mentioned that I had three children of my own, without skipping a beat, Marsha asked, 'Really? All with the same woman?' It wasn't said as a joke, but when I protested, Marsha simply laughed: 'C'mon, let's be honest, you Black men like to dip your pen into more than one inkwell.'

The bitterness of such an assertion is understandable. The consequences of promiscuity have scarred Black families down the ages. But they have not gone unnoticed. Recently, the Royal Society of Literature asked me to select a memorable line from a book that has stayed with me the longest. The choice was easy.

In the great Caribbean novelist George Lamming's autobiographical coming-of-age novel *In the Castle of My Skin*, the nine-year-old protagonist explains: 'My father who had only fathered the idea of me had left me the sole liability of my mother who really fathered me.'

The sentiment expressed in that 1953 publication resonates with me as it does with so many Black kids who were raised, and continue to grow up, with absent fathers, adult males who were missing in the action of parenthood, or who just never showed up, having laid down with a woman and planted their seed; they judged their work to be done.

Lamming's praise of his mother (to whom the novel is dedicated) and criticism of his father piqued the interest of the Jamaican social anthropologist Edith Clarke when she came to publish *My Mother Who Fathered Me: A Study of the Families in Three Selected Communities of Jamaica* a few years later in 1957. Writing up her research as a participating observer in the rural communities where she was embedded, Clarke argued that:

> Stability in families arose in households where parents cohabited even if they were not legally married; households where this was not the set-up, where the mothers had to 'father' their children, led to faults and fissures in family dynamics. But even when fathers were present, children's relationship with them was 'often ambivalent'.

The not so ambivalent view that Black fathers get a hard time and an unfair press is often a lament of my Black male peers, but hell, don't they deserve to be given a hard time? Growing up in a West Indian household and being forced to attend Sunday school at a Black Pentecostal church, which served as a kind of village for us in the 1960s and '70s, I'd often overhear women complain that their men used them as warming pans for the bed; that their 'partners' had no plan beyond their conjugal rights; that they paid as much attention to the result of their procreation as someone blowing his snot into a handkerchief.

And yet it is too easy to repeat the trope, almost a mantra, of the good-for-nothing Black father. The notion becomes an uninterrogated cliché which abounds throughout the continents.

In 2007, British Prime Minister Tony Blair sparked fury among Black parents when he pointed the finger at them for the lack of control they exerted over their 'feral' sons. Blair argued that economic inequality was not producing the most violent expression of this social alienation. Rather, he maintained that it was 'to do with the fact that particular youngsters are being brought up in a setting that has no rules, no discipline, no proper framework around them'. Blair was alluding to absentee fathers. His sentiments echoed across the Atlantic.

Months before Blair's outburst, and just ahead of President Barack Obama's election in 2008, Black America's number-one daddy assailed the 'brothers' who had reneged on responsibilities that ought not 'to end at conception'. Where had all the Black fathers gone? Obama wondered (to a chorus of Amens from his Black audience). Too many were missing-in-action. But as Michelle Alexander points out in *The New Jim Crow: Mass Incarceration in the Age of Colorblindness*, the answer to their whereabouts was simple: they'd gone to jail. In Chicago, for instance, 55 per cent of the adult Black male population has a felony record. And today a young Black man in the USA is far more likely to go to prison than to university.

As for the USA so too for Britain. In this country Black men and youths are over-represented in prisons, four times relative to their percentage of the overall population. In 2016, Prime Minister David Cameron commissioned the prominent Black

Labour MP David Lammy to conduct an independent review of the judicial system's treatment of Black people and other ethnic minorities. Cameron could have been quoting from a brief about the USA's penal system when he wrote: 'If you're black, you're more likely to be in a prison cell than studying at a top university. And if you're black, it seems you're more likely to be sentenced to custody for a crime than if you're white.' When the Lammy Review was published it revealed that there is 'greater disproportionality in the number of Black people in prisons here than in the United States'.

It's difficult to be a father when you're behind bars. But even those statistics hardly account for the huge numbers of Black fathers absent from Black households.

Figures from the Office for National Statistics (based on the 2011 census) reveal that, more than any other ethnic group, Black parents with dependent children are likely to be in single-parent households. Fifty per cent of Black children in Britain have no father living with them at home.

In her response to the Lammy Review, Baroness Lola Young acknowledged that family breakdowns, a lack of male role models and struggling single parents were of grave concern but 'institutions should be careful not to pathologise black family life as inherently dysfunctional'.

I'd agree. So where do we go from here? A significant number of Black fathers are in jail, but a larger number are not; are they out there fathering babies and conforming nicely to the stereotype? If so, why are Black fathers the way that they are? What made them? As far as the late Jamaican scholar Professor Freddie Hickling was concerned, the answer is simple: the transatlantic slave trade.

I'm not used to overly emotional and performative psychiatrists but when I visited Jamaica's leading specialist in mental ill health (or 'the biggest Obeah man on the island', as he styled himself) in his office in the capital a decade ago, Hickling was incensed. He was most vexed, it seemed, by the phrasing of my question about whether the received notions of Black paternal fecklessness were without merit.

Didn't I know my history? Hickling wondered, his voice high with sarcasm. 'During slavery days enslaved men were kept apart from women in barracks. They were allowed visiting rights! . . . They could only visit for the purpose of procreation.' Hickling argued that the same pattern of behaviour was evident with young men today. 'But the pathology was introduced in the eighteenth century! Let's get the history right,' barked Hickling. 'If we can't get the history right, we won't get the diagnosis right.' Fair point, professor, I'd say today. But if we agree on the diagnosis, what about the prognosis or treatment?

What is the way forward? Step one surely, and unfashionably, must come through education, through the cultivation of empathy and an understanding that, as the Bible says, 'as you sow so shall you reap'. Elders such as Franklin Jackson, a revered community and 'race' man in Manchester, have long ago come to that conclusion. Their voices need to be amplified.

'In Jamaica a lot of us grow up backward,' says Jackson, 'because, take my father for instance, the fundamental things like making facial expressions we wouldn't learn from my father because it was considered ill-mannered to look up into his face; we were supposed to look down just like the slave master would have teach our forebears. My father taught us how to have manners, to expect one or two "licks" if you didn't show manners and how to be clean, and that's it.'

Cleanliness and violence can only take you so far. Patterns of behaviour are memes passed from generation to generation. At its root always is slavery and the psychological condition that mental health professionals have taken to calling 'post-traumatic slavery syndrome'.

Another Jamaican, Bert Williams, recalled from his childhood in the village of Ticky Ticky that when he was in line for a beating, his father would send people to catch him: 'They'd tie me up to the house post until he was ready. If I escaped, he wouldn't worry 'cause he knew I'd have to come back for my food, and he'd give me a few licks then.'

Corporal punishment was not just a feature of fatherhood; mothers defaulted to it, too. But there was a difference between them and the Black fathers. Edith Clarke found that the subjects who 'regaled us with stories of their mother's floggings would, in the same breath, enlarge upon her devotion to them and theirs to her. One reason for this was to be found in the intimacy and stability of the relationship . . . often the only stable relationship in the child's life.'

Tough love? Beatings as socialisation, as preparation for what the child can expect in the future if they are not sensitised to fear? The burden of responsibility for bequeathing a life of suffering to your children must lay heavily on the soul. But, beyond a subliminal embrace of the codified practices of slavery and its perpetuation more than a century after emancipation, what other tools might be at the Black father's disposal?

There comes a time when the father hangs up his belt and sits his child down for 'the talk'. In the absence of a father, the talk will be delivered by the 'fathering' mother. Gary Younge recalls, 'My main reaction to the "talks" when my mother gave them was like, here we go again . . . "If a woman comes in here and says she's pregnant with your child, she's coming in and you're going out." And I'd be like, I'm thirteen!'

In literature, the letter from father to son has been a version of 'the talk'. It didn't start with Ta-Nehisi Coates in *Between the World and Me* or even earlier in 1963 with James Baldwin's 'My Dungeon Shook: Letter to My Nephew on the One Hundredth Anniversary of the Emancipation'. Those works are direct appeals to young relatives – a nephew (in Baldwin's case) and a son (when it comes to Coates) – that are intimate in their detail but public in their design to illuminate the great calamity perpetrated on the souls of Black folk. Such literary interventions didn't begin with twentieth-century Black American public intellectuals; the narrative is not linear, but the publication of personal epistles from writers of the African diaspora stretches back to the eighteenth century.

Ignatius Sancho, born aboard a slave ship and later a protégé of the Duke of Montagu in London, was a portly bon viveur of great energy who lived at a time when the Black population in Britain was estimated at just 10,000. He was celebrated as a great 'African Man of Letters'. And on 11 October 1772, Sancho took it upon himself, almost as a surrogate father, to counsel Julius Soubise, a former slave who in the late eighteenth century had become a foppish darling of British high society: 'Happy, happy lad! What a misfortune is thine! – Look round upon the miserable fate of almost all of our unfortunate colour – superadded to ignorance – see slavery, and the contempt of those very wretches who roll in affluence from our labours.' Sancho counselled: 'You, Soubise, tread as cautiously as the strictest rectitude can guide ye . . . but armed with truth, honesty and conscious integrity, you will be sure of the plaudit and countenance of the good.'

By 1963, one hundred years on from emancipation in America, James Baldwin was not sure that humility or magnanimity was the answer. His essay 'A Letter to My Nephew' opens with a warning to his fifteen-year-old nephew, urging him not to pay attention to what white people think of him. That was the mistake of Baldwin's father, such that 'he was defeated long before he died', he writes.

Baldwin's tone is both despairing and defiant. Published with an accompanying 'Letter from a Region in My Mind', the essay was a searing indictment of America and a prediction of the terrible price that would be paid for the continued denial of Black civil rights, spelled out in the book's title, *The Fire Next Time*.

Just over five decades later, Ta-Nehisi Coates's perspective on the evil that lurks in the heart of the white man matches Baldwin's bleak assessment. Early on in *Between the World and Me*, he recounts his paralysing dread on reading the news that an amiable college friend has been killed by a policeman, allegedly in self-defence. The dread gives way to rage and the sober reminder to himself and his son that Black people are never in the clear. His friend's death – 'haloed by all that was possible, all that was plundered' – is evidence of the constant threat faced by young Black men.

Coates's conclusion to his son is chilling in its clarity: 'All you need to understand is that the [police] officer carries with him the power of the American State and the weight of an American legacy, and they necessitate that of the bodies destroyed every year, some wild and disproportionate number of them will be black.'

A life of watchfulness, of living on amber alert, can be wearing. The deficits are many but the letters by Baldwin and Coates both signal at least one advantage: a unique way of seeing through writing. Each generation seeks to protect those who follow. But battle-hardened by the brutality of America, Coates feels duty-bound not to soften the lesson for his son. 'I am sorry that I cannot save you,' he writes, while adding that he's not *that* sorry, for 'part of me thinks that your very vulnerability brings you closer to the meaning of life'.

The perils that threaten Coates's son's despised Black body stretch back to slavery, but they are still woven into the narratives of Black Britons and African Americans today. Stephen Lawrence's death was a sobering wake-up call, a reminder to us of what our parents used to say about the threats that we were likely to encounter as Black children, every day in Britain. The stats were not in our favour, though nowhere near as bad as the existential threats faced by African Americans. When Trayvon Martin, an unarmed youth, was shot and killed in 2012, Barack Obama, then president, understood, like all Black parents, that he had 'skin in the game': 'If I had a son, he'd look like Trayvon.'

Parental advice on how to come of age and stay alive as a Black American has become a sadly recurring theme. African Americans make up over 13 per cent of the country's population, but in 2018 they accounted for more than a quarter of the 1,165 people killed by the US police. Our father also believed there were risks to Black children in the UK. We were fools if we thought that white Britons did not fear and despise us and would do everything in their power to rid society of the threat they perceived that we posed. It was a sentiment echoed in every West Indian household I visited.

I believe some Black fathers regarded silence as a form of protection. Saying them out loud would make many ugly truths manifest. But the fathers' strategy of maintaining ignorance was also a means of protecting themselves. There are some things you shouldn't be party to, you shouldn't see or be exposed to. My father never spoke about his past. That silence may have been explained as the result of 'bad blood', of family feuds and squabbles, but clearly the roots of the phrase continually heard in West Indian households ('me don't like people chat my business') are to be found, once more, in the stigma of slavery. In the larger community, our little village of partisans in Luton, slavery was hardly ever mentioned. There could be no pride in the admission that you were the descendant of despised enslaved Africans. It was why so many of Bageye's peers proudly claimed a lineage with the Maroons who'd resisted the British during the days of slavery and achieved a degree of autonomy, albeit one which included the return to the British of any runaway to their territory.

The abducted Africans endured a lifetime of humiliation on slave plantations in the West Indies; that degradation of men and women in front of their children was meant to achieve anything but a settled and loving family unit. The only surety was a lifetime of humiliation. 'Overseers, paid on a commission basis, had little interest in the welfare of the enslaved other than in preserving the slave "stock"', writes the historian James Walvin. Worse still, the West Indian islands seemed to attract sociopaths such as Thomas Thistlewood. In his innovative history text *The Trader, The Owner, The Slave*, Walvin explored the depths of the overseer's pathology. As well as keeping a diary, 'annotated in simple schoolboy Latin', of the scores of women he raped, Thistlewood also recorded how certain recalcitrant enslaved men were broken. Of one captured runaway he wrote: 'Gave him a moderate whipping, pickled him well, made [the slave] Hector shit in his mouth, immediately put a gag whilst his mouth was full & made him wear it 4 or 5 hours'.

That sense of humiliation was written into the DNA of many of the Black fathers I encountered in the 1960s. It is possible to see now that which was obscured (for me) in my childhood. I was always perplexed by how the larger-than-life West Indian characters who were Bageye's spars seemed to shrink somewhat in the company of white people. It was pitiable and disappointing; and, whether acknowledged or not, these Black fathers, at quiet moments of reflection, must have felt that sentiment, too, and the difficulty of maintaining respect in the eyes of your children when they have witnessed your daily degradation.

Often it felt, growing up, that Black fathers were embarrassed that they could do little more than prepare their children for expected humiliations. Sometimes it was framed coldly as 'the world is as it is' and you have to make your peace with that; at other times, fathers couched their warning almost as an apology for having brought their children into the world in the first place; a world where, notwithstanding their salutary lessons, their children would be largely unprotected.

Ethlyn, like so many mothers who were petrified for their children, counselled that we should avoid conflict. Similarly, to find a way through the prejudice that was inevitably coming his way, Gary Younge's mother offered practical advice of 'avoiding that teacher, staying away from that place, being polite to that person that you don't like'. Younge now finds himself in the position of administering 'the talk' to his son about how to live and adapt to racism in a racist society. 'That upsets me, [but] it doesn't upset me as much as if I had to visit him in prison or if I had to bury him before me.'

Do Black fathers have a different role to play from any other group of fathers? Surely the limits of parenthood, as described cogently by the poet Philip Larkin, apply to the Black man as well as the white: 'They fuck you up, your mum and dad. / They may not mean to, but they do.'

The shortfalls of Black fatherhood have been highlighted in recent years in Inua Ellams's insightful stage play *Barber Shop Chronicles*, a multi-voiced drama of Black lives intersecting at barbershops; the key drama and spine of the play centres on a young man 'coming to terms with his absent father's less-than-perfection'. Of course, only imperfection is possible. But the biggest failure is the failure of the imagination. It's a failure that shouldn't be underestimated.

'The Bible say,' Ethlyn would always remind us, 'without a vision the people perish.' Marvyn Harrison, a Black father of two children, had a vision when, three years ago, he started an organisation called Dope Black Dads to try to change the negative narrative usually trotted out about Black fathers. Harrison was motivated by his own experience of his father: 'My father was a horrible excuse for a human being. But I didn't want that to be the legacy. I wanted to stop that being the end of the conversation,' he says. 'What ends up happening is that hurt people hurt people. I've had a bad experience with my father so I then transfer that energy into my kids out of frustration, out of my lack of knowing of self. I didn't want that to happen.'

And here, then, is a valuable and vital lesson: there are inspiring and engaged people such as Marvyn Harrison attempting to turn the argument and change the narrative. Let's pay attention to these individuals and families; even if they are exceptional, they inspire and change the model of the dysfunctional Black family that is rolled out routinely in the media. Families in Britain comprise on average two children and no prodigies; few, if any, bear resemblance to the Kanneh-Masons. Their Black household includes seven children, all of whom are prodigiously gifted in classical music; their father, Stuart, has been key to their development and well-being. The Kanneh-Masons are not a fantasy; they're as real as those real-life characters who inspired the writing of *Babyfather* and *Top Boy*.

All human beings only have one set of experiences but they experience them to different degrees according to their circumstances. What lesson is to be learned about Black fatherhood? Clearly the answer is to be careful about the degree of attention you pay to your father; he, too, may have experienced in the past what you are suffering from today, and is a likely candidate for compassion.

Notwithstanding his failures as a father, I often think Bageye did me a favour, in seeding my determination not to repeat his mistakes, and for underscoring the inevitability of a lifetime of vulnerability I'd experience as a Black person in Britain. But even as you stack the cards (of well-being) in your favour, it doesn't seem possible to fully legislate for the future. The fable of the two brothers who have led widely disparate lives comes to mind. One of the brothers is content and settled, a caring, loving parent; the other brother is a failed absentee father, in and out of prison, and rehab. The brothers are asked individually to account for how they turned out as adults, and each in turn answers: 'Well, with a father like mine what would you expect?'

BLACK BRITISH JOURNALISM MATTERS

We must bear witness to our own reality

CHARLIE BRINKHURST-CUFF

In 2016 a survey of 700 news professionals conducted by City University London found only 0.2 per cent of British journalists are Black. Another study by Women in Journalism found that only 25 per cent of stories on national newspaper front pages between 5 June and 22 July 2017 were written by women. This means we disproportionately receive our news through a White male perspective.

It was important for us to hear from a leading Black woman journalist what this means to her and the work she does. Charlie Brinkhurst-Cuff is the former editor-in-chief of gal-dem magazine, an award-winning digital and print publication that prioritises the perspectives of people of colour from marginalised genders.

I decided to become a journalist when I turned seventeen. My decision wasn't based on anything particularly profound. I didn't idolise any news broadcasters (I grew up in a house without live TV) or even imagine myself to be the next Anna Wintour (I was hugely disdainful of glossy magazines) – though I did have the 1990s children's show *Press Gang* on videotape, and was essentially in love with both Lynda Day (Julia Sawalha) and Spike Thomson (Dexter Fletcher), two of the main characters who helped to run the student newspaper *Junior Gazette*. But my logic was that it would, quite simply, be a way to feel like I was putting good out into the world – alongside learning new things, meeting new people and telling stories. It wasn't until a couple of years in that I realised to achieve this ambition – to put good out into the world – the industry I was existing within needed to be primed to accept people like me and the stories I wanted to tell. And, very clearly, it wasn't.

I began my journalism training in 2017, the same year that the National Council for the Training of Journalists revealed that just 8 per cent of Black journalism students were working as journalists six months after graduating compared to 26 per cent of white journalism students. A separate study in 2016 by City University London revealed that British journalism was 94 per cent white, and only 0.2 per cent of journalists were Black. In the years since, there have been countless discussions, panels and comment articles written in an attempt to address this, fever-ishly picking up pace after the resurgence of the Black Lives Matter movement in the summer of 2020. On a personal level, in this time I became a child of multiple diversity schemes; des-perately lapping up every scrap the industry would offer me in an attempt to dig my heels into the dirt, skirting around racist micro-aggressions in industry spaces – and very early on realis-ing that part of my role was going to centre around advocacy as much as it would on telling stories.

What I've come to realise recently is that this trajectory that many young Black British journalists seem to go through – joining the industry with hopes of improving it and then being caught up in the never-ending cycle of diversity discussions – often works to overshadow the immensity of Black British journalists' achievements throughout history. That's not to say we shouldn't continue to talk about the racism we experience in the industry, the impacts of under-representation and the importance of Black British stories being told. But, by necessity, Black British journalism has been driven by resistance and activism and it should be more widely known that the current generation striving to improve the mainstream media, or create their own spaces in response to it, are part of a lineage; part of a radical tradition. A lot could be gained if we were to focus more on taking learnings from our elders than repeatedly answering the questions of beleaguered senior white journalists who put the burden of representation firmly on our young shoulders.

It is only through understanding the struggles and history of Black journalists and Black media organisations in the UK that we can begin to understand their importance both to the Black community and wider society. If we believe Black journalism matters, it is important to document our successes and setbacks. Which is why, when I was asked to write this piece, I realised that this had to be bigger than just my own personal experience; I had to talk to my journalistic peers, people who have studied this subject, as well as the people who came before me.

'I don't know if it's been lost, as much as it hasn't been shown yet,' muses Zakiya McKenzie, a journalist currently studying towards a PhD in literature on the tradition of Black British journalism. 'We haven't put it on record and said: Look, here it is, right? And made it a body of knowledge or study. And so we don't know [things like] how few Black journalists there are now, whereas back in the day, through the community, there were hundreds of journalists that ended up [working on titles like] the *West Indian World*, *West Indian Gazette*, all kinds of small journals.'

Noting that, unlike creative writers, journalists tend not to be 'egotistical' – which means that they don't 'scream about themselves' – over the past few years, Zakiya believes her work has helped to lead to the re-emergence of figures such as Barbara Blake-Hannah, the first Black female reporter on British TV whose achievement was overshadowed for many years by names such as Moira Stuart and Trevor McDonald. Another Black journalist who has dedicated the early years of her career to spotlighting Blake-Hannah's name is Bree Johnson-Obeng. In 2019 she spoke to Blake-Hannah for Sky News, covering her experiences interviewing Prime Minister Harold Wilson and the actor Michael Caine, as well as the virulent racism the broadcaster experienced from viewers.

'She's a force, so gentle but so authoritative,' Bree tells me of their communication. 'She's really spiritual yet really grounded. The amazing thing about her is that she doesn't feel like she's the person she was back in the 1960s. She's completely reinvented herself. She's now Rastafarian. She's just a rebel. She went back to Jamaica. She was friends with Bob Marley. She talks about how she would smoke and how she would write and how no one liked it but she was true to herself.'

Bree also successfully pitched to have Blake-Hannah recognised at the 2020 British Journalism Awards. 'I just knew her name was special and I knew it was something that shouldn't be neglected,' she says. 'There's an agenda to erase our history, if you don't mind me saying, and that's why I pushed so heavily for the Barbara Blake-Hannah award with the help of the BBC journalist Megha Mohan.' The inaugural award was won by the journalist Kuba Shand-Baptiste, a startlingly talented comment writer (and my friend) who had written incisively in the past year on topics ranging from the Windrush scandal to her obsession with *The Real Housewives of Beverly Hills*.

'It is important that we remember and recognise the work of Black British journalists who have helped to pave the way because of their tenacity, the audaciousness it must've taken to exist in spaces that can often be hostile for us. Of course, we must rate them too for the stories they told,' says journalist Nadine White, who, at the time of writing, recently accepted a role as the *Independent*'s first-ever race correspondent, reporting on issues affecting the lives of people of colour and exposing stories of racial injustice.

'[Black British journalism is] something that everyone, regardless of background, colour or creed, can draw inspiration from. In order to know where you're going and move forward with a true sense of direction, you have to know where you're coming from and, especially as a Black reporter, have reverence for who came before you.'

Nadine cites names including Val McCalla, the founder of the *Voice*, as her journalism heroes, someone 'whose work moved me long before I knew his name'.

Another, in my opinion, undersung Black British journalist of years past is the delightfully interviewable Juliet Alexander. Juliet, who swears like a trooper and has had an illustrious career that scattered her around the world in pursuit of stories, came to my attention as the lead presenter on the UK's first Black news and current affairs TV show, *Ebony*, which first broadcast in 1982.

Juliet became a journalist with the help of a pseudonym. As a teen growing up in East London in the 1970s, she started sending off articles to be published in the local paper, the *Hackney Gazette*.

'They had no idea I was either Black or female, as I didn't use my real name,' she explains. Describing herself as 'bookish', by the mid-1970s she had decided to study publishing at university as there were no journalism courses yet available. 'I suddenly thought, "Bloody hell, I don't know what a newspaper office looks like, and they might ask me stupid questions."' She wrote to the *Gazette* and asked if she could take a look around the office, which they agreed to. 'My mother, being my mother, escorted me. When I got there the editor looked at me and realised I was Black, because it was quite obvious, and female, which he didn't know before. And he offered me a job. I said, "I don't know about that, I'm going to university, my mother would kill me!"' But, in the end, after being offered the job on the spot on the strength of her previous articles, she accepted.

'He said, "Did I see an older woman escort you in?" And I said, "My bloody mother is outside." He said, "Can I speak to her?" And then Mummy went in and said, "Well as long as you send her to university, she has to have a degree." So that's what they did.'

When I ask if it was common for Black British journalists to enter the industry through the local papers at that time she says, 'Not at all.' Her experiences at the paper were rough. When Juliet had been at the *Gazette* for around a week, the phrase 'N*gger-loving Commie' was daubed on the entrance.

'I'd cycled up from home and saw the proprietor doing something very strange, which was washing down the front of the *Gazette*. He was trying to hold me at bay. I was one of the early ones, I always made sure I [arrived at work] early, and he said, "No no no, go round the back, don't come this way." And then when I peeked around his arm I could see that the lovely National Front lot, from Excalibur House in Hoxton, which was opposite us, had realised I was there and painted the building.'

This wasn't Juliet's last encounter with the National Front (NF), a fascist political party at its peak popularity in the 1970s, whose headquarters were in Hackney. Alongside her other articles, some of her earliest assignments included reporting on NF meetings. When I react in shock to the fact that she used to attend, Juliet responds with characteristic insouciance, saying, 'Of course! I'm a journalist,' before continuing. 'They refused to allow me access so I said, I'm a member of the NUJ [National Union of Journalists], I'm the mother of the chapel, blah-di-blah-di-blah. As such, if I'm not allowed in, nobody's allowed in . . . And then I'd have to sit there and listen to some arse behind me going, "N*gger, n*gger, n*gger", and all sorts of crap.'

These kinds of stories can be so shocking that it is easy to forget the fundamental point that without Juliet we might not have had anybody reporting on the National Front from a Black perspective; who could understand on a personal level just how damaging their presence was. In 1978, according to one survey, a quarter of the UK thought the NF expressed the views of 'ordinary working people', and 21 per cent thought that it would be 'good for Britain' if NF candidates occupied seats in the House of Commons. Without Black journalists like Juliet, our entire understanding of the NF would have been mediated through a white lens. While I don't know if I am quite as brave as Juliet, as a Black journalist more than thirty years later it makes me incredibly grateful for her tenacity.

By the 1980s Juliet, who had aspirations of reading the *News at Ten*, landed the groundbreaking BBC show *Ebony*. 'It nearly didn't happen,' she explains, 'because I'd had a run-in with the director of the BBC News beforehand where he'd physically tried to basically throw me out of my own office. Then when my name came up as the presenter of *Ebony*, he said he wouldn't have that "dangerous interfering bitch" involved in anything he had overall control over.'

It is hard to find footage of *Ebony* – Juliet has been told that much of the archive has been misplaced by the BBC – but from some video footage published by the BBC Archive and audio recordings stored by the Bernie Grant Centre, I know that it covered fascinating topics which feel as relevant today as they did forty years ago; from reflections on the death of 'A Change Is Gonna Come' crooner Sam Cooke to the specific needs of Black children in school and the changing fortunes of the Black British haircare industry, which gave me a gleeful insight into the wet-look curly perms of my mum's generation.

'I think getting the BBC to allow us to interview [Pan-African activist] Stokely Carmichael was one of my proudest and happiest moments. They were dead against that,' says Juliet. Like many Black journalists of her time, her career is dotted with these small pockets of rebellion, which speak deeply to the fundamental political principles that have driven Black British journalism for over a century.

As argued convincingly by Lionel Morrison in his 2003 book *A Century of Black Journalism in Britain: A Kaleidoscopic View of Race and the Media (1893–2003)*, underpinning the historic publications by and for Black people in the UK and the journalists who worked both for them and for the mainstream has been a clear crusade. 'Many black editors saw themselves as educators as well as journalists and the black press served a vital political function,' he wrote. 'Whether they were and still are fighting for integration into the political system or equal economic opportunity, black journalists informed, inspired, unified and mobilised their readers.'

Morrison practised what he preached throughout his whole journalistic career. He died in 2016, but his obituaries detail in brief what sounds like a remarkably rich life, and one stuffed to the brim with activism. Born in South Africa in 1935, he grew up to become a newspaper reporter during apartheid. Due to his activism, he was put on trial with Nelson Mandela at the age of twenty-one for treason but thankfully was acquitted. After being exiled from South Africa following the Sharpeville massacre of 1960, in 1968 he moved to the UK.

He had a rocky entrance into Fleet Street ('I wrote to nearly 100 editors in newspapers and magazines for a job,' he told the *Voice* in 2014), but after gaining a foothold in the industry, he eventually became the first Black president of the National Union of Journalists. He helped to put into place the George Viner Memorial Fund to broaden the diversity of journalists and the NUJ's first code of conduct around reporting race, which detailed how members should not 'originate material which encourages discrimination on the grounds of race, colour, creed, gender or sexual orientation'. An NUJ race reporting guide still exists in an updated format today, a testament to the essential legacy of Black journalists' work within the industry.

One of the remarkable things about *A Century of Black Journalism in Britain* is that it is one of very few texts (the second I've found being *The Black Press in Britain*, written by Ionie Benjamin in 1995) which map out the trajectory of Black journalists in this country. Morrison notes that the first Black British magazine was the *African Times and Orient Review*, launched in 1912 as a 'monthly devoted to the interests of the coloured races of the world'. You can find archived copies of it online in all its faded, sepia glory – with issues covering themes such as the downsides and brutality of colonisation. Claude McKay is named as Britain's first Black reporter; while the legendary communist organiser Claudia Jones receives a nod for her co-creation of the *West Indian Gazette* in 1958.

When it comes to the radical nature of Black journalism, this has often been led by campaigning Black newspapers rather than individual actors. The twentieth century saw the rise and sometime fall of some impressive publications, including *Afro-Asian Caribbean News* (1958), *Flamingo* (1961), *West Indian World* (1971), *Root* (1979), the *Voice* (1982), *Black Briton* (1991) and *Weekly Journal* (1992).

'There is definitely something to admire about the radical history of Black newspapers,' explains Lester Holloway, the former editor of the Black newspaper *New Nation*, which was in print from 1996 to 2009. 'They were political organs with a political point; they were very much alive with the anti-racism movement, which itself was infused with internationalism and intersectionality, before the word really came about. Those things have gone. I don't think they can come back.'

At its launch in the mid-1990s, *New Nation* was pitched as an alternative to the *Voice*, with the editor at the time, Richard Adeshiyan, telling the *Independent*, 'We know about all the problems for blacks in Britain, and the *Voice* tends to be just a doom-and-gloom sheet. We are not in the business of protest journalism.'

'It was a radical paper, to an extent,' he says. 'It had a lot of entertainment. And even the news was treated as entertainment to a large extent, but it was also very serious as well. You did have serious columnists who were given space, but more than that, have a campaigning edge.' Lester, who now works for a trade union, got into journalism back in the late 1990s, 'around the time of the Stephen Lawrence Inquiry', because he wanted to make a difference. In his editor role, the paper campaigned around asylum cases and the bicentenary of the 'so-called abolition' of slavery in 2007. 'The mainstream in general commentary and media were just fixated on the fact that Britain abolished slavery, and not that they were actually doing it in the first place,' he notes.

In contrast, he reflects on his time at the *Voice* with some scepticism, deeming it a 'cash cow'. 'I think that it had lost its politics by the time I got there,' he says. 'They became comfortable, didn't invest in the future, and yeah, it became timid . . . Racism stories were aplenty but they were all single stories; there was no campaign, there was no follow-through. And all it does is it serves to depress the community and feel more hopeless. Just a never-ending barrage or reminder of how structurally and institutionally and individually racist that society is.'

Of course, like many other Black journalists, Lester has respect for the *Voice*, which is now the lone Black British newspaper and, at the time of writing, seems to be pushing forward with a new digital strategy. Many of the Black journalists I admire today have spent time at the *Voice*, with Nadine White, who worked for the paper between 2016 and 2018, speaking fondly of a team 'able to relate to my lived experiences, empathise with my struggle and accept me exactly as I was'.

'The team was very small and intimate – a family-like atmosphere . . . I'm talking about both bonds and beef too! People would laugh together, banter, cry sometimes and cuss two time. It felt like home. The experience was grounded in love and a sense of camaraderie in facing the unique struggles that come with being Black and British. We didn't just work at the *Voice*; it wasn't just about collecting salaries or wages,' she explains. 'The team was driven by a resounding sense of purpose, an obligation to raise our people's voices up from within our communities and create harmonies with it, week in and week out. Sometimes the tunes were sweet, other times not pleasing to the ear

– pain-filled. But always our communities', always our truths.'

For new Black media, the ambition isn't to replace the old guard but to fill natural gaps that have emerged. Jendella Benson is the head of editorial at Black Ballad, an online Black women's publication founded in 2014 by Tobi Oredein and steered by her alongside husband Bola Awoniyi. 'Growing up, I read *Pride* magazine, there was the *Voice*. I think there was one called the *Calabash*. There's always been small publications, community grassroots. But there was never enough. I've always been like, if you see a gap, and no one else is doing it, you are the person to do it.' Black Ballad has become well known among young Black Brits for its gentle but firm Black feminist tone, and its iconic reveal of the *Keisha the Sket* writer (if you know, you know).

In a complementary vein *gal-dem*, a digital and print publication launched by Liv Little in 2015, aims its coverage at people of colour including and beyond the Black community, but still fits into the blessed tradition of Black-led British media in the stories that it tells. I volunteered and then subsequently worked for *gal-dem* since its inception and it has provided me, and many others I hope, with an invaluable platform for exploration, expression and, in more recent years, serious journalistic investigation. There is also a brilliant and buzzy collection of newer Black-led zines and publications (AZ Mag, Onyx, Sweet Thang), but few others which are currently operating under a business structure and bringing in anywhere near the audience of the mainstream media.

With this in mind, how does the Black British press correspond with the mainstream media? And how do Black British journalists find their place within it?

'Certainly, there's always been a relationship between the Black press and the mainstream,' says Lester. 'Despite continual levels of Black under-representation in mainstream media, it has clearly moved a significant way from where it was.' But Lester, like all of the other journalists I spoke to for this piece, holds an ideologically pure concept of the purpose of Black-specific outlets. 'I think that the role of the Black press if you like, using that concept very loosely, still very much exists when it comes to having conversations amongst ourselves,' he explains.

Jendella has always believed this too. 'The mainstream media don't have the resources to cover all the stories that need to be covered with the kind of nuance, expertise or insider perspectives that make these stories rich and wholesome. They don't have the will. And they don't really have the range if we're being honest,' she says firmly. 'We need to be the guardians of our own history. And the only way we can do it is by doing it ourselves and not waiting for such and such organisation to suddenly find the TV series that they say was burned down. We can't be waiting for them to all of a sudden realise, "Oh, yeah, Black people matter, and they have stories that are interesting that other people . . ." We just can't, we can't afford to.'

Black press has always been synonymous with struggle, on the basis of the stories it covers but also on how hard it is to keep it alive. There is a reason why the *Voice* is the only Black British newspaper of its kind left, and that is very much bound up in how advertising revenues have been as much ensnared in racist proprietary as any other institution in this country. This has meant that, moving further into the twenty-first century, while all of the press has struggled – shedding thousands of jobs in some instances – the Black press has found things even trickier. Alongside generalised, infectious anti-Blackness, the lack of resource has helped to lead to a dismissive attitude towards the Black press, even exuded by many Black journalists who would be far keener, and more able, to break a story in media outlets that have traditionally excluded us than bring them to the Black British media.

'I think there is a factor there, or at least there used to be, that working for the Black press was not respected enough by the mainstream when it came to trying to get a job in the mainstream media. And I think that's something which is really, really disappointing. But obviously other people did cut their teeth and go on to bigger and better things,' says Lester. Nadine adds that the 'general perception is that Black media spaces are somehow lacking in validity and unimportant when, in actual fact, that couldn't be farther from the truth'. In 2017 she landed an exclusive interview with Shereen Jones, the mother of Terrell Jones-Burton – a Black teenager who sustained horrific, life-changing injuries after being detained by Metropolitan Police officers. The piece led to worldwide news coverage and was shortlisted for the Hugh Cudlipp Award for Student Journalism.

Nadine believes that she might not have longevity in the mainstream media. 'As a Black woman from "the ends" who carries herself in a particular way, has experienced life in a particular way and so thinks in a particular way, staying true to yourself while navigating white-dominated spaces that can often demand that the "other" conforms solely for the purpose of fitting in . . . is a damn skill.'

However, across 2020–21, the mainstream media started to take up more space in the arena of Black journalism. In early 2020, we saw the launch of Unbothered, digital women's magazine Refinery29's 'celebration of Black women', the *Guardian* pivoting two reporter and correspondent roles to focus on community affairs – 'with a particular focus on black, Asian and minority ethnic communities' (currently Nazia Parveen and Aamna Mohdin) – and, of course, the *Independent* hiring Nadine as their race correspondent.

Naturally, there is some scepticism surrounding these roles and platforms. While some of them pre-date the Black Lives Matter movement of summer 2020, on a personal level I have never been contacted by so many news editors with speculative job offers as I have in the period after that fractious, lonely time where I watched Black people who looked like family murdered, arrested and brutalised by forces beyond my control and skirted the edges of protest marches that weren't quite Covid-safe but felt too important not to attend.

'I'm very aware that these roles or spaces in mainstream media are contingent on popularity, on budget, on the priorities of the wider organisation, which are always up for change as the market changes, as economics change,' says Jendella.

Zakiya, echoing my own thoughts, asks, 'We are still holding our breath, because a lot of it is coming off of last year. How long are you going to keep it up?'

Juliet points out that this behaviour by the mainstream media has been cyclical. *Ebony*, she explains, only really came about due to the aftermath of the New Cross Massacre, a fire which killed thirteen young Black partygoers in a suspected racially motivated arson attack, and led to the mobilisation of the National Black People's Day of Action. 'We'd been pushing for a Black news and current affairs programme for years,' she says bluntly. The BBC no longer has a Black news and current affairs programme – despite there being a growing population of Black Brits. 'It's all knee-jerk crap,' adds Juliet on the current push for diversity and representation. 'I'm old and cynical, but it happens every twenty fudging years!' More broadly, it feels as though there simply isn't a critical mass of Black journalists – there are not enough of us who are Black and politically driven embedded within institutions to drastically change the culture in a way that means that small changes have true longevity.

Despite this, it has to be said that throughout history, Black journalists who have penetrated the mainstream media, including Juliet, have managed to work on important Black stories – like Lionel Morrison's work around Notting Hill in which he and two colleagues at the *Sunday People* investigated a particularly racist policeman in 1970, and Richard Adeshiyan being sent to South Africa to report on the first-ever 'all race' elections following the end of apartheid in 1994. In more recent years we've seen journalists such as Gary Younge documenting knife crime in the UK, Rianna Croxford investigating the death of Belly Mujinga for the BBC's *Panorama* and Nadine White's laborious research into the corrupt church SPAC Nation for HuffPost.

Outside of explicitly Black stories, political journalist Anne Alexander, who currently works for *Good Morning Britain*, tells me the story she's proudest of breaking is that 'the leader of the 7/7 London bombers had been given a tour of Parliament by an MP', while Symeon Brown, a reporter for Channel 4, highlights a fascinating Long Read he wrote for the *Guardian* on self-styled traders who market their 'super-rich' lifestyles on Instagram. 'It was a piece that captured the precarious economic life of young minorities and how it can be exploited by billion-dollar industries,' he says.

Sunday Times journalist Shingi Mararike tells me that his proudest story is an investigation he did about children as young as twelve carrying acid into school in drinks bottles to use as a weapon. The tip came from his younger brother, who was a student at a state school in Newham, East London, where the pair live. He then stood up the story by interviewing case studies who carried the corrosive substances to protect themselves and also youth workers aware of the issue. 'The piece kickstarted a *Sunday Times* campaign that ultimately led to a ban on the sale of corrosive substances to under-eighteens,' he says. 'It's also proof that being from a totally different background to your standard Fleet Street journalist gives you access to stories that otherwise wouldn't make it into the national press, let alone become campaigning issues.'

One of my own proudest journalistic achievements was helping bring attention to the case of Joy Morgan. In 2019, the young Black midwife (who was part of a Hebrew Israelite church) was reported missing and, as I wrote at the time, our 'systemically racist media didn't investigate her case or platform her family's pleas for information in the way they should have'. In a piece for *gal-dem*, I pointed out discrepancies in coverage between Joy's case and that of another missing student, Libby Squire. While this piece wasn't for the mainstream media, it signifies how the Black press can spread influence. A few months after *gal-dem*'s piece was published, the journalist Cherry Wilson was able to publish a significant story and brilliant podcast for the BBC on Morgan's case, and really uplifted the voices of her family.

What all these examples highlight are stories that simply wouldn't have been covered if it wasn't for individual Black journalists or Black media organisations, or, at best, if they had been covered, it is highly likely they would have been covered radically differently. When it comes to Black journalism, considering there are so few of us, the question that haunts all of us is how many important stories are not being broken. How many important aspects of our lives are going unrecorded? How many injustices are not being exposed because there simply aren't enough of us or we lack the resources to cover all the leads we come across? I always think back to an interview Jon Snow gave after the Grenfell Fire tragedy (in which mainly working-class people of colour died), where he said that just possibly if the media had been more diverse, we would have reported on the dangerous cladding long before the building was burned up.

A less-explored phenomenon, but one that needs to be spoken about openly by established Black British journalists, is how we can continue to create space for journalists who are not interested in writing predominantly about race issues or Blackness. Although I am thankfully someone who enjoys doing those things, as I find the nuances of identity fascinating and believe it's an area in which I can make a difference, when I started out in the industry I did worry about how quickly I was being boxed in as a journalist who could be rolled out as a commentator on race. I often reflect on the fact that I am hardly ever commissioned to interview non-Black people, despite having the ability to turn out a solid interview profile for the nationals.

As much as it's often important to have Black journalists interviewing Black public figures, white editors, who are still majority gatekeepers (especially when it comes to hiring freelancers to write prestigious longform pieces), need to be mindful of not limiting their commissions and creating more opportunities for exploration. Black journalists can be 'generalists' and, early in their career, need support to progress and freedom to expand beyond trauma and tackling inequality. Having the Black perspective – any marginalised perspective – on a variety of topics is always going to be valuable for readers who are looking to the press for inquiry, education and representation. The questions and topics I might want to interrogate because of my lived racialised experience may bring fresh tea and cake to eat. And, from the perspective of opportunity, they would open up a world for Black journalists to explore that might not be so overtly mired in pain.

'There is great content that is from the point of view of Black people. But Black people don't always have to be writing about "Black stuff", we don't have to always be writing about a racial issue. We have to allow Black writers to write other shit too . . . Hire them on the motoring pages or other areas,' says Zakiya McKenzie.

Gary Younge has spoken about the fears he hears from young Black British journalists on being pigeonholed into writing about race. Speaking to Journalists on Truth, his advice was thus: 'You don't control how you're seen; what you control is what you do. Pursue the things you enjoy, because they're the things you'll do best. And trust that you will bring your perspective with you. I'm not just a black journalist when I'm writing about race issues – I'm a black journalist when I'm writing about Muncie, about food, whatever.'

Black journalists who do cover explicitly race-related beats need support to progress and freedom to expand beyond knee-jerk reactions led by manufactured culture wars – space I'm hopeful will be given to Nadine in her new role. 'I would say that I strive to live in a world where such a role is not necessary. Unfortunately, we're a long way away from that sort of utopia and the playing field is not level,' she says in response to critics who question the purpose of a race correspondent. 'Racism and inequalities have plagued Black people for centuries and yet this race correspondent role is the first of its kind to exist in the history of UK journalism. What does that say? There's a lot of work to do.'

And overall, embedded into all organisations, there needs to be a commitment and investment in our stories even when they're not 'fashionable', trauma and tackling inequality.

◆

I cannot explain how inspiring it is as someone coming up in the industry to speak to people who have come before me and changed the world for the better with their stories. Though we could do better at taking learnings from history, always, there is undeniably a spider network across the mainstream and Black press of both informal and formalised connections; Black journalists willing to speak up and advocate for each other not on the basis of nepotism, but on the basis of a shared understanding of anti-racist politics. My career wouldn't be where it is today without the support of Black journalists such as Joseph Harker, Gary Younge, Elizabeth Pears, Kesewa Hennessy and Maya Wolfe-Robinson; alongside many other unseen champions, I'm sure.

Black British journalism matters to me because it's given me a community. It matters to the world because, as articulated by so many brilliant Black British journalists, we are the only people who can tell our stories. And, man, our stories. They deserve to be told.

BLACK BRITISH CHARITIES MATTER

Why Black lives will reinvent
the concept of charity

DEREK A. BARDOWELL

Charities play a key role in addressing society's ills and are often at the forefront of confronting issues around inequality. The reality is that in Britain they are overwhelmingly White, with 95 per cent of management positions being held by White people.

Derek A. Bardowell is a central voice looking at the position of Black people in the charity sector, having had key positions at the Stephen Lawrence Charitable Trust and the National Lottery Community Fund and now as CEO of Ten Years' Time. He is also the author of the memoir No Win Race, *a* Sunday Times *and* Financial Times *Book of the Year.*

Broken glass everywhere, as members of the police survey emblems of their deceitful behaviour, crooked investigations and negligence. Some clustered, others scattered, the shards are sitting outside the Stephen Lawrence Centre in Deptford. It's the morning after a group of young men had vandalised the windows of the building. Artist Chris Ofili's ecclesiastical moiré pattern on the entrance façade dances no more. As I arrive on the scene, the thought of the windows' demise is as vivid as a ballet dancer mauled in mid-air by a muddied rugby player. To this day, I cannot imagine what the glass sounded like as it cried.

The damage occurred in February 2008, a week after the centre's official launch. Situated in the rusty, winding Brookmill Road in South-East London, the building, honouring murdered teenager Stephen Lawrence, is sharp, metallic and spaceship-like. Stephen's story lies heavy on Britain's conscience. After his murder allegedly by five white racists on 22 April 1993, corrupt police actions perverted the course of justice. Doreen Lawrence and her family's campaigning led to partial justice. Two of the attackers were eventually jailed in 2012. The Lawrence case changed race relations legislation. The police were branded institutionally racist, while institutions and public authorities were required to combat racial discrimination and promote equal opportunities. Yet, the majority of Stephen's alleged murderers still have not been convicted for this crime.

In 2020, the UK government's response to the Covid-19 pandemic and the protests following George Floyd's lynching in the United States made me think back to that morning. As the centre's director of education, I was one of the few allowed onto the site. I remember feeling punctured and shuffling around aimlessly. I didn't know what to do or how to help. Seeing Doreen Lawrence, her lips pursed in defiance, told me to carry on. I knew she had been through more. I knew that the damage would not, could not stop her. I also knew that she would rather have her son back than have a building. But I was nervous too. Police always made me anxious. They had harassed me on too many occasions in the past. But it wasn't only the police that had put me on edge, and it wasn't the vandalism or the prospect of further harm either.

The centre's senior leaders were aware that we might face problems upon moving into the building because we had received threats. But we had other concerns. There were rumours that the police appeared more intent on spying on us than protecting us. Local authority personnel seemed eager to use the facility as their pupil referral unit, opposing our desire to inspire a new generation of architects and designers. The press was always sniffing around, waiting for us to make any mistake. And our funding agreements had us responding more to the funders' requirements than the community's needs. As a charitable organisation, it felt as if we continually had to dull our ambitions to deliver our work.

After the vandalism, the centre was boarded up for over a year. We couldn't afford to pay for the repairs. We couldn't mask the grief or hide the scars. The brown panels became a permanent reminder that we, as Black people, were still targets, that little had changed since Stephen's death. For the latter half of 2020, I had similar deflating feelings to those I had that morning. It was difficult knowing that our sources of hope may also be our potential foes.

Britain has historically tried to dehumanise Black people. To some degree, it still does. Since 2008, we have seen that with the coalition government's austerity measures and the political sentiments lying behind Brexit. We have seen it with Grenfell, the Windrush scandal, and the Tory government's colour-blind response to Covid-19, which had a disproportionately negative impact on Black people. Britain was largely built from the exploitation of Black bodies and the extraction of natural resources from our land. The system has been killing us, literally. Racism, for many, is a daily occurrence, not something we switch off. Every breath a 'relatively conscious' Black-Briton takes renders us activist. As with that morning, services aiming to help can harm as much as the racists who try to brutalise us.

Charity, the institution, not the act, is a culprit. It frames

Black people through our pain, with scant acknowledgement of Britain's complicity and often at the expense of our dignity. It institutionalises and reduces our protests, maintaining control through regulation and funding arrangements. It elevates and entices charismatic individuals, co-opting them into its systems and away from our communities. More than anything, charity eases white people's guilt more than it harnesses Black people's innovation and light.

If Black lives really matter, then charity must evolve or expire.

◆

You hate me, don't you? You can't denigrate charities unless it's about child protection, poverty porn or financial scams. The headlines. Primary criticisms of charities. These problems exist, but they are symptoms of a far deeper issue. It is a sector controlled by the elite and the government, predominantly benefitting a small percentage of mainstream organisations at the expense of the grassroots groups. It views people's circumstances through a lens of individual blame. The sector exists to change lives through services, not by altering systems; therefore, it is a tool for maintaining social order. It lacks diversity and, at its core, rejects cultural differences. And it is governed by officials with little understanding of the lived experiences of ordinary people. That's the institution.

The coronavirus exacerbated existing economic and social disparities. Black people were more likely than white people to live in run-down environments. Our children were more likely to be living in poverty; high numbers of us tend to be in precarious or frontline work, in debt or suffering from respiratory illnesses. Our vulnerability had everything to do with

socially constructed conditions, a consequence of white supremacy. A decade of austerity measures had already widened historical inequalities. The Runnymede Trust's *Intersecting Inequalities:
The Impact of Austerity on Black and Minority Ethnic Women in
the UK* report in 2017 highlighted that the most impoverished
families would have had an average drop in living standards of
17 per cent by 2020. It also found that Black households in the
lowest fifth of incomes would experience an average decline in
living standards of 19.2 per cent.

George Floyd's death at the hands of the police in May 2020
highlighted that state violence and the disposability of Black
bodies were universal and enduring, even in the wealthiest and
most technologically advanced democracies in the world. Over
200,000 people in the UK responded by joining Black Lives
Matter protests in 260 towns and cities.[1] During a demonstration in Bristol, marchers toppled the statue of enslaver Edward
Colston. Over five million people signed some 1,500 petitions
on Change.org in support of racial justice campaigns,[2] and the
Black Lives Matter UK movement raised £1.2 million from the
public. Never had the UK witnessed anti-racism protests of this
scale. Britain was woke. Well, it was finally lifting its eyelids.

In 2020 Bernardine Evaristo, who in 2019 became the first
Black woman and first Black-Briton to win the Booker Prize,
topped the paperback fiction charts with *Girl, Woman, Other*.
Reni Eddo-Lodge's *Why I'm No Longer Talking to White People
About Race* occupied the paperback non-fiction chart's top pos-
ition. The image of Patrick Hutchinson carrying and saving the
life of a white male opponent of Black Lives Matter went viral.
Grime artist Stormzy pledged £10 million over ten years towards
Black causes. Manchester United and England footballer
Marcus Rashford twice overturned government policy through

his campaign against holiday hunger, securing free school meals for low-income families during school holidays. After the tireless campaigning of Rosamund Adoo-Kissi-Debrah, a UK coroner declared that 'excessive air pollution' contributed to the death of her nine-year-old daughter Ella Kissi-Debrah in 2013. This groundbreaking case has created the legal impetus to ensure that local and national governments clean up the air.

Yvonne Field, the founder of social enterprise Ubele Initiative, flagged that nine out of ten BAME charities faced closure by the end of the first Covid-19 lockdown without financial assistance. Her campaigning led to more funds going towards Black causes. Motor racing champion Lewis Hamilton finally received a knighthood. He became a staunch Black Lives Matter advocate while securing his position as the UK's greatest ever sportsperson and Formula 1's most successful driver, equalling Michael Schumacher's record of seven championships and setting the record for wins (ninety-five). The Black Writers' Guild was launched, tackling inequity in publishing, and campaigner Patrick Vernon ensured that we did not forget Windrush victims' plight (only 17 per cent had received compensation by the end of January 2021). Lavinya Stennett's Black Curriculum campaigned to get Black history on the national curriculum. Dr Nicola Rollock's photographic exhibition *Phenomenal Women* celebrated the talent and experiences of Black female professors, while photographer Misan Harriman created a stunning visual narrative of the Black Lives Matter movement. British *Vogue* editor-in-chief Edward Enninful continued to bring diversity to the fashion bible. These were not deeds motivated solely by profit or bound by law. They were acts of boldness and brilliance, all, I suspect, inspired by these people's experiences of structural racism and being Black in Britain. They connected us to something bigger than ourselves, something that touched on our everyday realities. Their work was abundant and activist, not defined by the intensity of a white gaze.

It was also clear that the Conservatives would attempt to crush any possibility of Black power. When the Tories launched the *Beyond the Data: Understanding the Impact of COVID-19 on BAME Groups* report in May 2020, it allegedly omitted or compressed evidence from community groups linking the disproportionate effects of Covid-19 on people of colour to structural racism. Dame Cressida Dick, the Commissioner of the Metropolitan Police Service, denied that the police were still institutionally racist (despite over 20,000 stops of Black men aged fifteen to twenty-four in London during the first lockdown, only 20 per cent resulting in further action) and closed the Stephen Lawrence case. The Department for Education issued guidance to schools warning against anti-capitalist resources in teaching; a not-so-subtle attempt to censor anti-racist and climate justice literature from schools.

Minister for Equalities Kemi Badenoch reinforced the government's view that teaching white privilege in schools would be illegal. She also implied that writers such as Eddo-Lodge want a 'segregated society', a flawed and inaccurate assertion contested by the bestselling author. Liz Truss, the International Trade Secretary and Minister for Women and Equalities, set out her vision for fairness by essentially dismissing the experiences of people with protected characteristics. The Charity Commission's chair, Baroness Stowell of Beeston, warned charities 'to leave party politics and the culture wars' out of their work, her views reflecting the Conservative Common Sense Group's opinions while failing, as a regulator, to provide the political impartiality she seeks from charities. Then the widely condemned Commission on Race and Ethnic Disparities report, led by Dr Tony Sewell, asserted in March 2021 that institutional racism does not exist.

The Tory government's response to anti-racism was typical divide and rule tactics. They pitted racial justice campaigners against the 'white working class'. They implied that anti-racism equals victimising Black communities, segregation, thuggery, extremism, personal gripes instead of evidence. The government suggested that racism was a fantasy while stirring up a moral panic about anti-racist protesting. They used regulation, policy-based evidence, the press and smear tactics to present anti-racism as the threat and white supremacy as an illusion, framing the survivors as the perpetrators. In 1995, author Toni Morrison said, 'Racism may wear a new dress, buy a new pair of boots, but neither it nor its succubus twin fascism is new or can make anything new. It can only reproduce the environment that supports its own health: fear, denial, and an atmosphere in which its victims have lost the will to fight.'[3]

While the wider public sympathised with Black Lives Matter, there was little desire for fundamental change underneath. According to a study by charities Runnymede Trust and Voice4Change, campaigners and the public agree that racism matters and is an institutional problem.[4] They also believe that education is a good way to start ending racism. In contrast, campaigners see racism as a systemic problem; the public views it as an individual issue related to personal prejudice. Dr Sanjiv Lingayah, a founder of the Reframing Race programme, said, 'a significant line in public thinking pits anti-racism against other equalities issues, such as poverty, and considers these other problems more pressing'. He went on to say, 'The research also reveals that although members of the public largely avoid explicitly saying that one "race" is better than another, a key strand of public thinking accepts that there are coherent genetic differences between "races" and that these can explain people's physical and even intellectual capabilities.'[5] As writer and broadcaster Afua Hirsch said in her piece for the *Guardian*, 'in 2020, we took a step forward – from minus 10 to zero'.[6]

If being a bridge between the public and decision-makers and a voice for ordinary people are two of charities' main functions, they were primarily a bystander during the post-Floyd protests. There were some exceptions. The National Trust's research linked some of its historical places to colonialism and slavery, and the UK's largest children's charity Barnardo's issued a guide to white privilege for parents. But the real resistance came from grassroots charities, individuals, citizens, collectives, mutual aid groups and movements. There is no major national, Black-led body. We did not see a significant mobilisation among the mainstream charities to take up this fight. Charity is an institution rooted within a racist system; therefore, it cannot hold the weight of Black people's truths; it could never do justice to our pain; it would never fully appreciate our joy. This moment could have been charities' North Star. It wasn't. If there's racism, there will be charity, not because it is an antidote but because it pacifies our resistance.

◆

Charity, as an institution in Britain, looks something like this. It is white, male and privileged. On the surface, he's incredibly generous and compassionate enough to acknowledge Black people's issues. But he finds it hard to get out of the way of himself – his reality, his lens, his understanding of the world – long enough to be a faithful ally. He cannot stand beside us, and he can't quite stand with us without the desire to own our narrative because ownership is all he knows. Being a saviour is his tonic, and his status and legacy mean everything to him. He has seen our suffering from up close, perhaps because he spent time with us during a gap year. Still, he assumes that he knows best. He has been preconditioned to believe that our situation is the result of inferior genes. He *can* use the term 'white privilege' but does not know what that means for him or how this could influence every breath he takes. So, he will only tend to do something about racism when *he* realises that something is wrong or poses a threat to his business, not when we tell him.

He likes to pick our brains, unaware he is extractive but aware enough to know how vital our narrative is to his livelihood. He cannot help but try to monetise us. He's a quick, shrewd talker; he can embezzle our pain and make it his own. When he's unsure of himself, insecure about his relationship with Black folks, he'll call on people of colour within his circle to fortify his beliefs, to alleviate his neurosis. His tonic drives him to restrict the access we need to gain power within the system. He doesn't let us know the game. He fears displacement. Underneath, he fears us. At times, he becomes passive-aggressive, quietly undermines us. But then he'll nominate us for an award. We're unique, magical. We win, we soften.

His actions have served to uplift a few, without ever really shifting power. His efforts have dimmed the public's imagination about us, and the support he gives rarely takes heed of what we culturally need or what we are doing to help ourselves. As he maintains control, he realises it's not wise to rock the boat too much; he has a consistent revenue stream from our sorrow. Not wise to bring up the past. Not smart to talk about colonialism or structural issues. His governors agree.

But he takes great offence to anyone who criticises his work. He is so focused on doing good and being generous on his terms; he cannot see how he might be contributing to doing more harm. He's taking resources away from those who are more effective. He is complicit in maintaining the conditions where only he, and people like him, can own this agenda.

He gets an OBE. It's written into history now, and he is responsible for *that* social change. Those on the ground go unacknowledged. He moves on. He moves up. He has other people to save. The cycle starts again, for him and us. He realises that he cannot live without us. He has never learned how to live beside us.

◆

We are not only fighting white supremacy; we are also fighting ourselves. Black-Britain is treated, at times, by Black folks in other countries as if we are the only sibling that was not abused. For many years, our activism was imported. We were a by-product of struggles abroad or activists who found a home on our soil. Our experience is immersed in the soul of foreign lands.

There has never been a UK movement with the global impact of the Civil Rights Movement, the Haitian Revolution, Black Lives Matter, the Green Belt Movement, the First Maroon War, the Mau Mau Uprising or the Anti-Apartheid Movement. They transcended, impacted deeply. They gave us a universal sense of belonging, opened the doors to our liberation. But we have never had anything in Britain on that scale. Sheer lack of numbers, too great a distance from the plantations, perhaps, has got us thinking that – because we are better off than most Black people in other nations – better is good enough.

In much the same way that the influence of slave revolts has been diminished or erased from British history, so has Black people's history of protest in Britain. For example, as far back as 1773, before the release of the abolitionist, author and former slave Olaudah Equiano's famous slave narrative, *The Interesting Narrative of the Life of Olaudah Equiano*, in 1789, around 300 Black protesters opposed the imprisonment of two Black men in London's Bridewell jail for begging. The abolition of slavery in 1833 did not end the oppression of Black people. The UK government paid enslavers £20 million, the equivalent of £2.4 billion today. It was the biggest payoff from the Treasury until the bank bailout after the financial crisis in 2008. We (as taxpayers) didn't pay off this debt until 2015. The perpetrators prospered, the survivors were poorer, which is the root of today's economic disparities.

Writer Kimberly Jones's *How can we win??* speech in 2020 springs to mind when she said, 'for 400 rounds of Monopoly, you don't get to play at all. Not only do you not get to play, you have to play on behalf of the person that you're playing against. You have to play and make money and earn wealth for them and then you have to turn it over to them.'[7] And when you finally get to play, your opponent gets all the money from the bank and the properties, and he sets the rules and questions why we cannot win.

Black people have been on the back foot ever since, which is why activism runs through the veins of many of us. Progress has not been easy – most of it was achieved against the odds. Even though we may not define ourselves by race, we are being judged by it. And this is inescapable, inexcusable – often the defining factor in our life and death chances.

Throughout the late nineteenth and early twentieth

centuries, resistance came in many forms. This included Barbadian-Trinidadian law student Henry Sylvester Williams's African Association in 1897, drawing attention to the struggles of people of African descent; Dr Harold Moody, a Jamaican GP, who formed the League of Coloured Peoples in 1931 to tackle racial discrimination; Trinidadian historian and writer C.L.R. James, whose anti-colonial writings influenced a generation of activists; and Amy Ashwood Garvey, an entrepreneur, publisher, director of the Black Star Line Steamship Corporation, and ex-wife of Marcus Garvey.

Black activism, in its many forms, changed or influenced the law. Kidnapped by slavers in the Kingdom of Benin (now part of Nigeria), Equiano's literature helped incite the 1807 British Slave Trade Act. The Bristol Bus Boycott led by social worker Paul Stephenson in 1963 led the way to the first Race Relations Act in 1965. When the Black Panthers protested against the Metropolitan Police's harassment of Frank Crichlow and his Mangrove restaurant in Notting Hill, writer and campaigner Darcus Howe turned the trial against the Mangrove Nine, accused of inciting a riot, into an examination of the police, and won. It was the first time the UK's judicial system recognised racism in policing. Doreen Lawrence's campaigning led to changes in race relations law, while Rosamund Adoo-Kissi-Debrah's efforts will unquestionably save many lives.

Black people pioneered credit unions. Ten Caribbean members of a Baptist church founded Britain's first one in 1964. The Hornsey Co-operative Credit Union started as a savings club based on the Caribbean *pardner* or West African *susu* circular monetary schemes. The Hornsey Co-operative commenced because Black people had trouble accessing financial support. By the time Hornsey celebrated its fiftieth anniversary in 2014, there were 371 credit unions with some 1.3 million people benefitting from them. Approximately 38 per cent of people of Caribbean heritage were investing in credit unions.

The Notting Hill Carnival, founded by Trinidadian activist and journalist Claudia Jones, remains one of the largest and most iconic festivals globally. Although the first official Carnival in Notting Hill did not take place until 1966, its roots originated from Jones's Caribbean Carnival at St Pancras Town Hall in 1959. Around one million people attend the Carnival each year, contributing close to £100 million to London's economy.

When Stokely Carmichael, leader of the Student Nonviolent Coordinating Committee (SNCC), spoke at the Dialectics of Liberation Conference at the Roundhouse in London in July 1967, his speech added impetus to a growing movement of Black activists in Britain. The British Black Panthers was formed in 1968. Writer Obi Egbuna, Darcus Howe, Linton Kwesi Johnson and Olive Morris led the party. They were joined later by Altheia Jones-LeCointe, Farrukh Dhondy and Mala Sen. Black was a political term encompassing all people of colour in Britain likely to experience racial discrimination. Besides the Mangrove trial, Panther members were responsible for documenting Black politics through the *Race Today* journal (1973–88). Howe, alongside others, organised the Black People's Day of Action (2 March 1981), where close to 20,000 people marched for justice for the victims and survivors of the New Cross Fire. Linton Kwesi Johnson's poetry (*Dread Beat an' Blood, Inglan Is a Bitch*) became a voice for the Black-British experience. Olive Morris co-founded the Brixton Black Women's Group, the Manchester Black Women's Co-operative, Black Women's Mutual Aid Group and Organisation of Women of African and Asian Descent (OWAAD).

Writer and activist John La Rose's New Beacon Books was central to many movements, events, protests and institutions from the 1960s onwards. After La Rose opened his bookshop in Finsbury Park in 1966, New Beacon started publishing Black literature that wasn't seeing the light of day in Britain. 'There was also a discontinuity of information from generation to generation. Publishing, therefore, was a vehicle to give an independent validation to one's own culture, history and politics – a sense of self – and to make a break with discontinuity.'[8] La Rose helped establish the International Book Fair of Radical Black and Third World Books (1982–95) with the Race Today collective, Bogle-L'Ouverture Publications and Walter Rodney Bookshop. He also chaired the New Cross Massacre Action Committee, mobilising Black People's Day of Action.

After Bernard Coard's seminal text *How the West Indian Child Is Made Educationally Sub-normal in the British School System* (1971) exposed racism in the education system, La Rose co-founded the Black Parents Movement in 1975. Before that, he founded the George Padmore Supplementary School in 1969. Indeed, the Black supplementary school movement from the 1960s onwards combatted racial discrimination in schools, providing thousands of children with cultural learning and critical maths and literacy skills. La Rose would go on to set up the National Association of Supplementary Schools in 1987.

The breadth of Black-British culture and activism is too vast to fully capture on these pages. I think back to the first wave of Black politicians in the eighties – Bernie Grant, Paul Boateng and Diane Abbott – the Lovers Rock sound, Saxon Studio's fast-style chatting, Soul II Soul, Jungle, UK Garage and Grime. I think of the works by Stuart Hall, Paul Gilroy, Nicola Rollock and David Olusoga, documenting Black lives and experiences while supplying research that would be prophetic. I think about Dr Debbie Weekes-Bernard becoming the first Black woman to become Deputy Mayor of London and Marcia Willis Stewart QC, who represented seventy-seven of the ninety-six families of the Hillsborough Disaster as well as the family of Mark Duggan. Kwame Kwei-Armah, the second Black-Briton to have a play staged in the West End and now the artistic director of the Young Vic, the *Voice* newspaper, which provided a platform to the mainstream media for so many Black journalists, Voices that Shake! and Ruth Ibegbuna's RECLAIM, groups that revitalised youth activism, all spring to mind. I think about comedian Sir Lenny Henry and executive producer Marcus Ryder, providing a vision of what a diverse British media could look like. There's also artist Sonia Boyce, architect Elsie Owusu, journalist and broadcaster Afua Hirsch, the Black Cultural Archives and Irish academic and author Emma Dabiri. There's artist and director Steve McQueen, Black well-being charity Black Thrive, novelist Zadie Smith, writer and photographer Johny Pitts, model Munroe Bergdorf, mayor of Bristol Marvin Rees, Women's Equality Party leader Mandu Reid, *The Real McCoy*, Dope Black Dads, and Black Police Association co-founder Leroy Logan. *galdem* founder Liv Little, charity leader and activist Shane Ryan, film-maker and Media Diversified founder Samantha Asumadu, journalist Gary Younge and Lord Woolley's Operation Black Vote. I think of the nurses, mothers and fathers, caseworkers, youth workers, legal aid solicitors, key workers, and the many people who housed their people when others wouldn't accommodate our people.

We have continued to thrive despite the state and the establishment, not because of it. Take the charitable sector, for example. Rarely have Black-led charities received significant or proportionate funding from the state or independent funders. There has been a drive to legislate advocacy and campaigning out of the sector. We have faced two decades of sustained opposition to anything resembling Black self-determination. Mainstreaming has diluted many aspects of Black culture and compromised our independence. By 2018, there was a lower percentage of BAME trustees in the top 500 charities than in FTSE 100 companies.[9]

Yet, the achievements of Black people in Britain are immeasurable. We have often succeeded against a hostile environment that views us through the constricted lens of slavery (subhuman), colonisation (a need to be governed), crime (folk devils) and entertainment (magical, naturally gifted). We have seen many of our leading voices leave these shores because of this. But also because we, at times, have fallen into the trap of narrowing ourselves – our quest for status or credit dividing us, making us more vulnerable to Britain's frequent attempts to erase us.

It's messy. An impossibility, some may say. Expansive. A gift and a curse. We struggle to define ourselves. Unsure whether there really is an us. Black-British. Black. Should I capitalise? Global majority people. People of colour. Minoritised racial groups. Many of these achievements arose not because of status or for selfish reasons. Much of it surfaced because of who and what we are. And while we may admire those braver than ourselves, those who take a public stand, there is an unrealised beauty in the fluidity of our hybridity that is often dulled by institutions like charity. We cannot surrender to a system that reduces us. If status and superiority underpin our culture and how we define ourselves, then true liberation will be unobtainable.

◆

American comedian Richard Pryor is in an interview on the set of *Stir Crazy* in 1980. Pryor wears tanned trousers, a buttoned-down white shirt with what looks like Venetian-coloured rectangular lines on it, brown socks and casual turmeric-tinted shoes. He seems more like a corner store owner than a Hollywood star. Pryor's eyes lack focus. He is high and appears on the verge of hysteria as he stares into the camera, ignoring the man to his left, interviewing him.

Pryor, by 1980, has already bagged an Emmy and three Grammy awards. He is one of Hollywood's biggest stars, the most famous Black actor of the day, and the man most likely to replace Muhammad Ali as the voice for African Americans. But in December 1978, his beloved grandmother, former brothel owner Marie, dies, sending Pryor into a drug-fuelled descent.

In one segment of the interview, Pryor, still inspecting the camera, says, 'They paid me $2 million to do this movie.' He leans forward, 'Do you believe it?' His arms go up, and then they come down. He claps his right hand onto his flaccid left palm twice as he says, 'My grandmother didn't make that [in] all her life.' He points to the camera as he says, 'She's a better woman than you are a man.' He's laughing now. Momentarily. He falls back into his seat and covers his mouth with his shaky right hand. Pryor looks like he's about to cry. He suddenly turns his face off. Shuts emotions down. He crosses his leg. Right arm drops into his lap as if, for a moment, he wants to end it, the interview, the film, life, something, right there and then. Pryor snaps out of it. He looks at the presenter, who's trying to maintain some control of this scene. The interviewer wants Pryor to move on. He wants the movie star to talk about the film. 'Sure,' Pryor says, 'what do you want to know about this movie?' He looks exasperated, as if he cannot believe that all the interviewer wants to discuss is this frivolous flick. Pryor shouts, 'It sucks.'

I keep watching this sequence, over and over. Causes me pain every time I see it. It's that moment – the hysterical laughter, near weeping, then shutting down – so familiar, all too frequent, a permanent crease in our souls. Such moments likely inspired Pryor's genius as a comedian. When you think about the people who helped you, did not give up on you, the person you do not want to let down because you know that society likely let them down, it's heart-breaking. When I hear politicians or anyone who tries to deny or diminish my experiences, my truths, observing and preserving through their narrow lens, I think of that Pryor Moment, and the audacity of Britishness becomes too much to bear.

A deep, untouchable melancholy comes over me, akin to when the only tone you hear from a loved one is bitterness or annoyance, even in moments of joy. A melancholy many of us arrive at when we realise that the life we invested so much in prevented us from devoting time to things that mattered. The despair of a father slowly drifting to the periphery of a home he thought he'd built. A melancholy when your head is always too heavy for your pillow. A melancholy when you understand that your fate is in the hands of institutions you just can't trust.

Much of British charities' fate should lie in the hands of the Black-British experience. The inventions, the creativity, the breakthroughs mentioned earlier liberated all, not just Black people. We are the canaries in the coal mine. Our experiences provide a warning for all; our responses offer answers for everyone. That is why Black activism, not Black charities, matters.

Us and our truths will never be something Britain is comfortable with until it can reconcile its past. Right now, it is in no fit state to do so. Humility does not arrive from a desire to own. What we as Black-British people have achieved, less than sixty years after the first Race Relations Act outlawed racial discrimination, after '400 rounds of Monopoly', despite comprising less than 4 per cent of the population, must be troubling for those in power. Our ability to transform and regenerate is as boundless as a UK government's thirst to extract. As such, they meet our movements with silent violence, the unseen, the policies, the practices, while upholding the fallacy of fairness by any means necessary. They will conceal George Floyd moments with all their might because they do not want any martyrs, and they do not wish for Black-British activism to transcend. They understand and fear how the public's opinion of culturally accepted norms can change swiftly due to narrative power, particularly during crisis points.

At some point, charity will not look like how we see it today. It will not be white, male and privileged. In the future, she/they will build a society and institutions through the lens of the most marginalised. She/they will have lived experiences of anti-Black racism. Her/their work will recognise how our struggles are interconnected and how race, gender, class, ability and sexual preference intersect. She/they will be fair, compassionate but with a warrior spirit. She/they will not fear a community's right to self-define. Her/their work will cause no harm to people or the planet and will not exclude or ignore. She/they will be transparent and accountable to her/their communities, and she/they will decolonise and then reimagine our systems. She/they will envision a society where money is evenly distributed, recirculated, where everyone has universal basic income, so we do not fear time. Good deeds will not require mediation; it will be a society where our multiple identities are celebrated, not reduced. She/they will not diminish other people to own or extract from them. She/they will create a powerful space beside the private and public sectors, but she/they will never run away from the past or the uncomfortable truths. She/they will be guided by her/their ancestral past and will strive, always, to create visions of a fertile future. She/they will not let money or ideology stand in the way of humanity.

This image may sound idealistic. But I've seen large elements of this. I've seen it in the work of Ruth Ibegbuna and cultural producers Sade Banks and Amahra Spence. I've seen it in the work of Black feminist activist Marai Larasi, contextual safeguarding pioneer Carlene Firmin, Yvonne Field, and many others. Black people's solutions are as real and essential to our humanity as the breath we breathe. When Britain fully wakes up, an image like that of Patrick Hutchinson will shine brighter than the fallen ballet dancer.

BLACK BRITISH ARTISTS MATTER

A conversation between

LENNY HENRY AND KWAME KWEI-ARMAH

Art plays an intrinsic role in any society, community and country. Marcus and I knew we could not do a book covering the importance of Black British lives without tackling the place of the Black British artist head-on.

In talking about why Black British artists matter, our fear was that we were trying to put a value on two things which, by their very nature, are impossible to put a value on: Black lives and art. Which is why we approached the subject not only with excitement, but also with a large dose of trepidation.

For both of us there was literally only one person who we thought could tackle this incredibly important issue, but who would do it in a way that would make it accessible to everyone . . . Finlay.

For those of you who are too young to remember watching the BBC's best-known medical drama before Grey's Anatomy *took over the world, Finlay Newton was the screen name for Kwame Kwei-Armah, who played a paramedic in the weekly prime-time drama* Casualty.

Beyond this role, he was also the second Black Briton to have a play staged in London's West End.

We then 'lost' him to the US, where he took up the position of Artistic Director of Baltimore's Center Stage theatre for seven years. He triumphantly returned to these shores in 2018 to become the Artistic Director of the Young Vic in London, one of the most important artistic institutions in the UK.

So if anyone can articulate the answer to why Black British artists matter, Kwame can.

He agreed to chat to us over Zoom in a conversation which covered everything from Black Nationalism to Soul II Soul.

We are proud to present this edited version, which starts with Lenny's own reflections on watching George Floyd's death.

Lenny Henry: Kwame, it is so good to talk to you on such an important issue – why do Black British artists matter. Now, in many ways the recent incarnation of Black Lives Matter was triggered by George Floyd's death.

I remember watching the video of his death . . . well, a little bit of it, I didn't watch all of it because it made me cry every time – I just thought, I feel like I'm watching myself. Because if I shaved my head and grew a goatee, that's me or my brother, or my cousin or my nephew.

And I felt powerlessness. I felt the powerlessness for all Black men. How did you react to the video and the news surrounding it? And indeed, before you go into that I should ask – did you watch it?

Kwame Kwei-Armah: So first of all, I should say I have not watched it.

Deliberately. I do not wish to see an execution. I wouldn't watch a lawful execution, so why would I watch an extrajudicial execution? So I have refused to watch it. I also haven't watched it because I don't wish to be triggered.

Interestingly, I was triggered by another video just a few days before the George Floyd killing.

I watched Amy Cooper weaponise her white woman-ness. [*For readers not aware of this, this was a viral video of a white woman who falsely reported an incident to the police after she told them Christian Cooper, a Black man who was birdwatching in New York's Central Park, and who is not related to her, had threatened her and her dog. He did not.*]

And that triggered me. And as we know, that was probably just, like, the weekend before George Floyd. [*The date of Amy Cooper's 911 call was 25 May 2020, the same day as George Floyd's death.*]

And that's the kind of micro-aggression – well, actually it's not even micro – that's the kind of aggression, the kind of naked racism, that as a Black middle-class executive male I receive on a daily basis.

And so by the time we got to George Floyd, it felt like a one/two. [*Kwame mimics a boxing combination for our Zoom viewing pleasure.*] You have the jab of Amy Cooper, weaponising her white woman-ness that could have brought death to an innocent Black man due to the structural racism of the police, followed by the uppercut of the killing of George Floyd. In fact, it wasn't just a one/two. You also had the body blow of Ahmaud Arbery being killed in an old-fashioned racist style. [*Ahmaud was an unarmed twenty-five-year-old Black man shot by two white people while jogging, on 23 February 2020, in the US state of Georgia.*] So, by the time we got to George Floyd, I couldn't look at the video.

Lenny: I agree. It is just awful. Do you remember the famous picture of the naked little girl in Vietnam running after a napalm attack? I know there are differences but, for me, it feels like that – our pain and suffering on display for the whole world to see. It was both triggering and very uncomfortable.

Kwame: What I thought was interesting is that if you look at all the Black Lives Matter marches that followed George Floyd's killing, artists and actors were often at the centre.

When we think about those marches in the UK in 2020, the image that is often conjured up is of the actor John Boyega speaking his truth and articulating what so many of us felt. I cried when I saw John give up his soul. He was strong. He was real. And what was magnificent about it for me is that what John was doing was being a beacon for what many artists call themselves today. They don't just call themselves 'actors'. They don't just call themselves 'writers', they call themselves '*actor-vists*'.

There was a time, when I was growing up, when actors shied away from politics, and musicians would say, 'Yeah, I talk about politics in the corner. I never do that on my records.'

The establishment would love us not to question the status quo, or dare to bring politics into our art. But what John did, and what so many Black artists do, is right in the DNA of their work. They were using that art as activism.

They aren't the first. It has always been part of being a Black artist. Personally, I looked at the film directors and writers Spike Lee and Robert Townsend in the 1980s. Through their films *Do the Right Thing* and *Hollywood Shuffle* they showed me that the Black artist can lead the way when it comes to articulating our pain – either through pathos or through comedy – and then activate us to use our art politically, and to be of service.

John and other artists are following in that tradition.

Lenny: When I was starting off my career I was actually told by an older white comedian, 'Don't do politics on stage, son. We're on stage to entertain, not to do politics.' And years later

– particularly when I was talking to people like Norman Beaton and, in more recent times, yourself – I keep thinking, everything we do as Black artists is political, everything; that act of choosing to draw a line around something and not talk about it is a political act. Because people are sitting there going, 'Oh, that's interesting. Why isn't that character talking about that?' It is a political statement to decide what you don't think of as 'political'.

Kwame: I would like to think I would have pushed back against what that older comedian told you but, to reference *Eddie Murphy Delirious*, it's easy to say 'F*** you, massa' when you're not in the situation.

But what comedians, and not just comedians but artists of our generation, were being told was to separate yourself from your politics, or you will lose – that was the implicit threat, your career will not succeed.

But there is actually no such thing as being apolitical; the absence of the overt politic is a political statement. The very moment that a human being puts themselves in front of other human beings and begins to create a narrative, it is a political act – from the way you dress to the actions you use to tell your stories, every single word you choose. All of that is total politics.

I would argue that most of the art you see in the public sphere is politically leaning to the right because it says: 'I'm here and, by not challenging, by not being progressive, I'm supporting the status quo.' The act of supporting the status quo is an act of conservatism.

That is why I always push back when I hear the government or someone say, 'Oh my God, why is so much art left-wing activism?' Well, actually, we're quite small in the subsidised sector; the overwhelming majority of work in the commercial sector is conservative work if you think of it in terms of the status quo.

Lenny: When you're writing, when you're doing your thing at the Young Vic, what are you hoping to achieve when it comes to Black British people? I mean, is there an agenda? Are you focusing on work that captures the Black British experience, figuring out our reality, giving credibility to our existence? What's your role as a Black creator, and director of a major theatre?

Kwame: I think it's really easy to sit in binaries or do singular things but, in reality, we're always doing multiple things. My favourite title is *Two Trains Running* – a play by African American playwright August Wilson – because for us, as artists who are Black or of the global majority, there are always two or three trains running – and some trains running that we're not even in control of.

So I would say this: first of all, I see myself as part of the global majority. And if I were creating work in Nigeria, it wouldn't be seen as Black and political, it would just be judged on its quality. Fundamentally, I begin as a generative, interpretive and curatorial artist and ask myself: 'What do I want to do?' 'What do I want to say?' 'Who am I trying to serve?' In asking those three simple questions, there are always at least three trains running at the same time.

And while those trains are running, I can say that in my position as a gatekeeper of a major international theatre, what I choose to curate is, first and foremost, an act of service to my audience and my community. How I choose to speak universal truths will change in time but my Blackness will always be in it, whether I'm doing a Nordic European classic, or an Egyptian play from 4,500 years ago.

So what I'm trying to say is, in a really odd, rather long-winded way, that I'm trying to do it all. I can and do serve multiple masters. But at my core, what I never wish to do is create, generate or curate work that will be a hindrance to the next Black British artist.

Lenny: But even with multiple trains running, can your focus on not wanting to be a hindrance to the next Black British artist ever limit you? Or, to put it more broadly, can our Blackness ever limit what parts you can play or what you write about?

Kwame: Let me speak to the 'I'. I am 'tri-cultural'. I'm African. I'm Caribbean. I'm British. I hold the keys to all of those cultures. I am European. I'm pan-African. As an actor I can play any and everything and have ownership of any and everything. Why? Because I am intrinsically part of those three cultures. So there's no European text that I can't play. And if someone tries to limit me because of my Blackness, I just use my British and my European card and say it's part of my history.

Lenny: So do you disagree with August Wilson's treatise that Black actors should not play European roles? When I read *The Ground on Which I Stand* – which is a seminal work on the role of the Black actor in society – I always think he's telling me that I can't play King Lear. I can't do the Scottish play. What's going on, August? I want to be able to do everything!

Kwame: Like you, I am a child of August, without a shadow of a doubt. I mean, literally, [*Kwame reaches off screen on the Zoom* *chat*] here are my first editions of the ten August Wilson plays. They are within an arm's length – I am literally in their shadow.

Lenny: Oh, you think you're bad?

[*Now Lenny walks out of frame and comes back holding his first editions of the ten August Wilson plays.*]

Kwame: Yeah – but you had to walk to get them, I just reached. [*Both laugh.*]

Kwame: I think this is important to unpack. I won't even say that August is a man of his time, but he was a nationalist. And he said the thing that a nationalist should say, which is *privilege your own culture* (Black culture). And he makes you question the culture of those who deemed you an inferior, and forces you to ask, why do you want to have a place in their work and, in wanting that place, are you placing their culture above yours?

And so I think August was absolutely right, to lay that challenge down to the Black artist and say *privilege your own work*. Produce some work that is of a standard where we can go this is our Scottish play. This is our *Romeo and Juliet*.

So the truth is, everything that August wrote in *The Ground on Which I Stand* was particular to that moment in history, and is a challenge to everyone who comes after that.

Lenny: I agree with you. It makes you question your political standing. Basically, August Wilson is saying: This is the Black artist's agenda. This is my mission statement. This is what we should be doing. We should not be indulging in European culture, we should be fostering African American culture.

Kwame: Absolutely. And I might augment that by saying that *The Ground on Which I Stand* is a clarion call to Black artists to be their best self. The race is almost secondary. He's saying: Artists, be your best proudest selves! I think it was Harry Belafonte who said that the problem that we face as Black artists is that we are trying to put on Afrocentric stories on Eurocentric stages.

And when you do that, if you don't know who the f*** you be, it can f*** you up.

As Black artists, we don't just have to bow down to Ibsen when it comes to understanding the psychology of human beings. When it comes to verse, you don't just have to bow to Shakespeare, but you can look at yourself and say, I'm not an interloper. I'm not a stranger in a foreigner's land. This is my land.

August Wilson is standing on the shoulders of Malcolm X and the Black Panthers. And saying I'm going to determine my future, not have the world determine me.

Lenny: But here is the contradiction – if you can see an August Wilson show on Broadway, the audience will be predominantly white. And when a Black play gets hot in the UK, you see something similar happening. As Jazzie B [*from the Black British band Soul II Soul*] once said to me: 'We started off underground – now we're overground. Now it resonates with everybody.' But does the audience matter?

Kwame: My favourite experience ever was at a Broadway theatre seeing an August Wilson play. I was sitting in the gods and sat directly in front of me and behind me were four rows of Black women. It was a Sunday matinee performance, and I found myself actually in a Black majority audience. There were lots of chants and historic songs embedded in the narrative that I did not know – and what the audience did was they sang along. When the actor on stage started to sing a song, it didn't just stay on stage, it went into the audience. And they educated me – this Englishman, for want of a better term in a modern cultural sense – they educated me about what August was triggering, who he was triggering when he was telling these stories.

The audience transforms the art, so it is a different piece of art depending on who is viewing it.

My other story about the importance of the Black audience was when I saw a Tyler Perry piece of work. It was in DC in a thousand-seater theatre and tickets were like two hundred and fifty dollars apiece for the bad seats. So people were spending big money to be in the audience – and it was almost exclusively Black.

An African American woman was sitting behind me, and there's a bit of dialogue that we would call in the profession a 'handbrake turn'. I was thinking: 'Oh boy, I don't know how you got from that subject to that next bit of dialogue.' And I couldn't help myself, I actually said out loud 'Jesus!' in exasperation. And the woman behind me simply exhaled 'Jesus', but it was one of appreciation.

Why? Because she understood.

I was sitting there with my Eurocentric critical mind, looking at the construction of the sentence in the way that I've been taught to appreciate theatre, whereas the woman was watching it in the moment. While I was sitting in the cerebral, she was sitting in the spiritual.

So to answer your point about audiences – while the Black artists can speak to the general and universally to everyone, you can also tap into the spirit and you pass into the spirit more easily when enough Black people come. It might not even specifically be about race but how audiences choose to consume your art.

Lenny: A lot of our references have been about African American art and experiences. These are all very relevant for explaining the importance of the Black artist, but is there anything specific about the Black British experience when it comes to art?

Kwame: For me, being Black British, talking about our lives – in juxtaposition to the African American life – it's easy for Britain to hide as if there is no racism, but as artists we should *shine a light in those hiding places*. In many ways, only the Black British artist can shine a light on what pains Black British people, but also what brings us joy, as well as everything in between.

We also need Black British artists, in particular, because we are documentarians of our experience.

And I worry some of those experiences are being lost. I went to a Black Lives Matter event in London recently and I overheard a young Black woman saying: 'We need to do this because no one did this stuff before.' And I wanted to sit with that young queen and say: 'This is magnificent what you're doing, but you do know about the New Cross fire? You do know about the Brixton uprisings? You do know about Stephen Lawrence?'

Good art passes down knowledge, it holds knowledge. Otherwise, we are in a constant state of ignorance and reinventing the wheel.

Lenny: One last question. This conversation is going into a book about why Black British lives matter in different areas of life. We've got essays about why Black British policing matters, and why Black British health matters, and why Black British politicians matter. To play devil's advocate for a second: the lack of Black police could lead to more police brutality against Black people; the lack of Black doctors can cause more Black people actually dying early. Why do you think Black British artists are important? It's not as if anyone is going to die if there are fewer Black British artists.

Kwame: I think that that is a brilliantly framed question that hopefully can catalyse an argument against the mechanical way we have been trained to put a value against output. The artist should not be measured in those terms. Civilisations are judged and remembered through the lens of their artists, not their accountants.

If I say Egypt, what is the image that pops into your head? If I say Ancient Greece, what pops into your head? It is the art they produced – be that the architecture or hieroglyphics or paintings. They record, they reflect, they translate.

So if you wish only to create a Milton Keynes circa 1980s human being, which had many roundabouts but little art, then I say you don't need the artist.

But if you wish to look at the economic powerhouse that is London, the economic powerhouse that is New York, you can't extract the art from it. If you do, you reduce not only its economic, but its spiritual viability. Why does the Black British artist matter? We matter because we are more than the sum of our parts, and we need to see it reflected and refracted. It is a small mind that can only see the mechanical and not the spiritual.

Lenny: I knew we were going to cover some ground in this conversation and – just like the plays you write and the performances you curate – you have given me a lot to think about. As always it has been a pleasure.

Kwame: The pleasure, my brother, is all mine. Now I'm looking forward to reading the other essays in this book. I understand there's one about why Black fathers matter? My children definitely need to read that one!

BLACK BRITISH BUSINESS MATTERS

Show me Black pounds and I'll show you Black power

NELS ABBEY

The role of Black businesses in addressing economic inequality in the UK has gained increased importance with the first 'Black Pound Day' announced in 2020, encouraging people to spend money with Black-owned businesses. Government statistics indicate that approximately 90 per cent of small businesses in the UK are majority-led by a White person.

Nels Abbey is a British-Nigerian writer, media executive and satirist, and author of Think Like a White Man: A Satirical Guide to Conquering the World . . . While Black. *But most importantly for us, before moving into the media industry he was a banker. With his incisive perspective on race in the UK, he was the ideal person to examine why Black British business matters.*

Close your eyes and visualise the last time you placed your hard-earned money into a business owned by a Black person.

How did it feel? How normal did it feel? How often do you do it? Did it feel good? Did it feel like a political act?

Well, it was a political act. A revolutionary act even.

In Britain today one of the greater acts of anti-racism anyone can perform is simply shopping, spending or doing business with a Black-owned company . . . on a regular basis.

It may not feel as empowering and oppositional to racism as,

say, going out on a demonstration, tweeting in support of Black
Lives Matter or even offering a Black person a post-stop and
search back rub – although all back rubs gratefully received. But
the fact is, simply spending your money with a Black-owned
business is revolutionary. It really is.

In Britain anti-Black racism is such a uniquely ingrained and
normalised concept that it is taken for granted. It doesn't just
pass the dinner-party test. It's often pudding. Britain seems to
find it entirely digestible and acceptable that:

- Black unemployment is ~~double~~ triple the white unemployment rate and is the joint highest among ethnic groups in the
  UK;
- Black women die in pregnancy or childbirth at four times
  the rate of white women;
- 17 per cent of Black victims of crime were seventeen or
  younger, compared to an average of 11 per cent across all
  ethnicities;
- 40 per cent of prisoners under the age of eighteen are Black
  or mixed race;
- Young Black Caribbean boys are nearly four times more
  likely to receive a permanent school exclusion and twice
  as likely to receive a fixed-period exclusion as the school
  population as a whole.

To jolt society out of acceptance of anti-Black racism and
into recognising it to be a problem often takes an extreme act
such as: the death (and not 'mere' serious injury) of a Black person in police custody and the subsequent declaration that the
killing was lawful despite the evidence; the deportation of Black
British African Caribbean elders, etc.

Anything that doesn't meet this very high threshold of Black pain and suffering struggles to garner empathy, headlines or serious state intervention. 'Oh dear' tends to be the response. And on we move with our days. Well, some of us can.

As a result of this threshold, this racial empathy bias, the day-to-day deprivation of Black people is swept under the rug. Sadly, this deprivation is at its most damaging in the economic realm. This is where Black British people are at our most vulnerable and where deprivation is at its most normalised.

The great Toni Morrison once famously said:

> The function, the very serious function of racism is distraction. It keeps you from doing your work. It keeps you explaining, over and over again, your reason for being. Somebody says you have no language, and you spend twenty years proving that you do. Somebody says your head isn't shaped properly so you have scientists working on the fact that it is. Somebody says you have no art, so you dredge that up. Somebody says you have no kingdoms, so you dredge that up. None of this is necessary. There will always be one more thing. [1]

I have long struggled with this statement. And I have decided to do something very controversial: I am going to publicly disagree with Toni Morrison. I believe that the primary function of racism is not to distract but to exploit.

Racism exploits Black people significantly more than it distracts. And significantly more than it does anyone else. We can, to some degree, ignore and avoid distraction; we cannot, however, ignore and avoid exploitation.

In the British context, going back centuries, the basis of

widespread anti-Black racism at its core has for the most part been a matter of ruthless exploitation.

From the plantation, to the colony, to the world wars, to post-war reconstruction, to huge employment disparities, pay gaps and more: Black people living under direct or indirect British rule (wherever we were in the empire), i.e. the burden bearers of the empire, have always been uniquely susceptible to the more horrendous (and profitable) areas of exploitation that permeate from British racism. And without a strong economic base, that will continue in perpetuity.

Without a strong economic base, we're effectively powerless.

Without a strong economic base, we'll have opinions but we'll never truly have a voice.

Without a strong economic base, we're defenceless in the face of any form of exploitation.

The historically (and sadly still too current) brutal nature of the relationship between Africans and Britain is one that has for the most part been predicated upon race-based exploit-ation. This arrangement has helped make Britain eye-wateringly rich and helped make Africans (everywhere) extremely poor by almost any measure.

Nothing lasts forever. And this racism-driven deficit cannot be allowed to go on in perpetuity. There has to be a way out. And there is.

Black businesses matter.

As a result, every single penny anyone spends with a Black business funds some degree of Black liberation. For the root of our plight is economic, is poverty. The overwhelming majority of our problems are, at the core, economic in nature.

The root causes of the over-representation of Black Britons on unemployment lines, illicit trades and therefore prison cells are economic in nature. Each of these elements has a serious multiplier effect for other forms of crime – which are all most likely to be carried out within predominantly Black communities and against Black people.

The wholesale main impact of anti-Black racism has been the economic debasement and decimation of Black people. This, in turn, has had spiralling social, cultural, political and economic impacts.

Take London, for example: every major immigrant group in Britain has a geographical area (or areas) in which their cultures, businesses and, especially, their cuisine can be experienced, patronised and consumed.

The Turks own Green Lanes, the Arabs have Edgware Road (and a lot more), Brick Lane is pre-1947 (pre-partition) India, the Vietnamese have Shoreditch. The Polish? Everywhere and everything (possibly even your well-maintained home). Chinatown? It's somewhere in the name.

But what about the first immigrant group to arrive here in large numbers after the Second World War? What about Black people? West Indians? Africans? *What about us?*

Our areas are owned and controlled largely by anyone other than us. Where the hell is the Black high street in Britain? It doesn't exist.

It gets worse.

For ages Brixton has been synonymous with Black Britain. In every corner of the world I have been to, from the United States to the Middle East to the Far East to Eastern Europe, all over Africa and beyond: I am always asked about Brixton (even though I am from West London) or 'Bricks-town' as it is often accidentally called.

Brixton was considered to be our mecca and our spiritual

home – considered so both by Black people and everyone else. In reality we were just keeping it warm while simultaneously making it a cool place for moneyed property developers to exploit.

Not long ago I went for lunch with an associate in Brixton village and to my amazement I would have received fewer 'what are you doing here?' looks in the poshest of West End restaurants. The most impressive private members' club in London I have ever been to is in Brixton. And in there too Black people stood out like we would at a Pall Mall private members' club.

Self-preservation is the first law of nature. And in our kind of societies, a strong economic base underwrites self-preservation and, indeed, basic safety.

The killing of George Floyd triggered the second wave of the Black Lives Matter movement. But, other than the murderous nature of the wretched police officer Derek Chauvin, what triggered the killing of George Floyd? What was the root cause of the atrocity?

An allegedly lousy fake $20 note.

George Floyd was literally killed for a worthless piece of paper. But even before that moment, George Floyd's life was blighted by intergenerational poverty, economic insecurity and perilous employment. A very familiar story in Black communities.

The lack of private sector entrepreneurial activity renders Black people disproportionately employed by local and central government. This, in turn, places Black people at the whims of political spending – and never controlling our destiny and fate. In this age where the two main political parties are tearing chunks out of each other to see who can best offer a lower tax, lower spending and smaller state government, it will of course contribute to the already fantastically high unemployment and underemployment rates among Black people. Equally, we cannot wait for the right liberal (-presenting) person to get into a position of power or influence in order to diversify organisations (for they never do).

In one of the most lucrative parts of the economy, the City of London (i.e. financial services), where I once worked, Black people were appallingly under-represented (especially in key front office roles and senior leadership). When I moved to work in media, I quickly realised that financial services were a Benetton advert by comparison.

Nevertheless, in both realms – media and banking (and far beyond) – there is a dearth of Black enterprise. There is certainly no such thing as a major Black contender. When you glance across most sectors, you'll notice we are yet to really capture one area in order to provide opportunities and build an economic base from which we can grow and help each other. This includes areas that exclusively cater to the cuisine habits and hair texture of African people.

Reducing the disparity in Black and white unemployment rates (8 per cent and 4 per cent respectively), turning the tide on increasing Black British youth incarceration, reducing crime in our communities, improving Black academic attainment, substantially and substantively enhancing Black political representation, bolstering Black prosperity and excellence, etc. – all start at the same place and with the same thing. It starts with the economy, stupid; it starts with business. Black businesses. Black enterprise. The normalisation of Black people owning and dominating commercial activity in several areas.

There are, of course, countless strong anti-capitalist or capital abolitionist arguments to counter everything I have said. Once upon a time I'd have been making those arguments myself. I would be a fool not to listen humbly to any theory posed. But I have one issue with each of those theories: it's an inconvenient concept known as reality.

As appealing as the idea of Britain somehow morphing into a socialist paradise may be, it is, by all indications, little more than a time-wasting, wild fantasy – at least in any time frame I can foresee. Let the exit polls of the 2019 election serve as a wake-up call: this is an unforgiving, cutthroat, unashamedly capitalist nation. That is the game: play or be played, the choice is ours. It is critical that we focus on reality, on what is, and not on what should be, not on fantasy. Unfortunately, flying-pig solutions don't remedy swine flu.

Imagine the transformative impact it would have on the minds, lives and ambitions of young Black people if they walked through, say, the City of London, and were able to point to several skyscrapers knowing that the buildings and the institutions within them were owned and controlled by Black people – people just like them? Knowing that these companies were sources of wealth as opposed to exploitation for us? Imagine a competent, credible and wide-reaching Black media organisation competing with the BBC, ITV and Sky? Imagine walking into a Black British supermarket – one that was a reflection of our tastes, personalities and vast range of cuisine? Imagine walking into 'Diane', a hair and beauty product retailer (named after Diane Abbott) owned and controlled by Black women? Imagine a Black-owned electric car company? Imagine if the next hot social media app were not inadvertently marketed and promoted for free by Black people but owned and controlled by Black people?

Imagine the power and influence we would get from all of the above.

Well, we don't have to imagine it. We have to work towards it. We have to work together to get there . . . to make Black Britishness a globally admired, respected, loved and feared force to contend with. For centuries, through our ingenuity, blood, sweat and tears, we have made other people's wildest dreams come true. It is time to realise our own dreams. Dreams for our children.

Without breaking the cycle of economic disadvantage, all other cycles of anti-Blackness keep spinning furiously. As happened with the Mangrove restaurant in 1960s Notting Hill and many other places, we will face stumbling blocks, crippling doubt and sabotage, but somehow, someway, we will make it work. We have to.

There are so many amazing Black British businesses already doing the work. Through the pain and plight of Mangrove, today we have businesses like Uncle John's Bakery, Cinnamon Leaf Foodhall, New Beacon Books, Afrocenchix, Fish, Wings & Tings, Zoe's Ghana Kitchen, Uptown Yardie, Wales Bonner and many more. It is absolutely critical we support and spend our money with establishments like these.

When boiled down to the bones, Black Lives Matter is an economic empowerment movement. It just has to be. Anything and everything else are just condiments. The main course is economics, is the economic empowerment of Black people. And it starts with the embedding, spreading, supporting and normalising of Black businesses.

Black businesses matter.

BLACK BRITISH ATHLETES MATTER

Why Black British lives in sport matter

MICHELLE MOORE

Michelle Moore is a leading figure in the campaign for equality in sport in the UK. In 2015 she was named by the Independent *as one of the '50 Most Influential Women in Sport'. In 2016 she was the winner of the UK PRECIOUS Award for 'Outstanding Woman in Sport', and in 2017 she was recognised for her community and grass-roots work by appearing on the prestigious Football Black List.*

The importance of sport to British society, and the central role Black people play, meant that any collection of essays that examined the importance of Black British lives without looking at the Black athlete would have been incomplete.

Sport should be leading the way in fighting racial inequality, but it's not. Instead, all too often it presents a false image of racial progress and damages Black athletes in the process. The Black Lives Matter movement offers a rare opportunity for society and Black athletes to push back against the way society views Black sporting achievements and recognise that their Black identity and communities are central to who they are as opposed to a side issue.

I love sport and know first-hand what it can do to transform lives both individually and collectively. The part of my leadership work from which I get most joy and reward is when

I'm mentoring and advising athletes, because I learn so much about the world through their eyes and because we are bound together by our passion and lived experiences in sport. I'm a sportswoman, having been a track and field athlete in my younger days and now a netball player; sport has and continues to play a massive part in my personal and professional identity. I talk about sport a lot. I use sport to explain life. Above all I am inspired by sport. Sport is my elixir; it wipes the slate clean on one side of the coin and on the other holds up an almost blinding light to injustice.

Because of my work I naturally view world events through the prism of sport, but as a Black woman I also find myself viewing sport through the prism of world events. It works both ways. The Black Lives Matter movement, in its broadest sense, provides a way to explore issues of representation and visibility as some of the most urgent issues in British sport for Black athletes and Black people in wider society. I believe the struggle for racial equality that was at the heart of 2020 made that year in modern sport like no other. The power of sport was at the heart of the Black Lives Matter political protests. From the sports activism of Black British athletes articulating their experiences of racism in mainstream media, to the phrase 'Black Lives Matter' replacing Premier League players' names on the back of their shirts, to players 'taking a knee' at the beginning of games, racism was THE talking point. But as a result, I want to give you a glimpse into the hyphenated identities of Black British athletes because I know that what athletes tell me about their experiences in sport when the microphone is off and what they say when the microphone is on are two totally different things. The fact that Black athletes need – or at least have needed so far – to separate their public athletic voice from their Black voice exposes a major tension when we say Black Lives Matter – whether we mean it is just the publicly acceptable parts of our lives that matter or our Black lives in our entirety. One last thing, I am a proud Black woman of mixed Guyanese and English heritage. I do not try to speak for every Black British athlete, but I do speak from a Black perspective and for me Black also includes brown and mixed heritage people with links to Africa.

Let's talk about how sport has touched my life and shaped my thinking as a Black woman on the issues we are about to explore together. In many ways, it's a very classic story. It starts with a role model.

My own relationship with athletics began with Grace Jackson. No! Not the singer Grace Jones! Grace Jackson – the world-class 200m and 400m runner from Jamaica. In the 1980s she would glide effortlessly around the track in all her glory. I wanted to be her every time I was on the track. Kathy Cook was Great Britain's top 400m runner during this time, but I just didn't relate to her in the same way as I did Grace. I modelled myself on Grace, I saw myself in her, a Black woman from the Caribbean; a place where parts of my family roots are too. We didn't have a lot of money back then, but my mum would buy us the cheap £3 seats at Crystal Palace track and on balmy summer London evenings my twin, my mum and I would go and watch the likes of Merlene Ottey, Sonia Lannaman, Daley Thompson and Edwin Moses competing at the height of their powers. Those cheap seats felt like the best seats in the house as we sat among a sea of white faces having the time of our lives, cheering on our favourite athletes, circling their names in the programmes and sprinting down the famous steep steps of the stadium in the hope we could get that elusive autograph from one of the athletes. They were the best days ever.

Athletics was the gift of my childhood. My lifelong affair with athletics and sport started at Crystal Palace track; most athletes love that iconic track, such is its enduring legacy. Years later I would be competing in the London Youth Games and inter-counties meets on that very track where I saw my role models compete. The power of seeing someone excel who physically looks like you inspires you to think that you too can achieve the same feats, and that's what Grace Jackson did for me all those years ago. The power of the Black role model is immense.

By default, Black athletes excelling in the sporting arena take on a greater significance because of the lack of high-profile leadership roles occupied by Black women and men in wider British society. The irony is that while these athletes' success is something positive that needs to be celebrated, at the same time that very success can blind people to the racism all Black people face in society. For the Black athletes themselves it can take a heavy toll: they are expected to be the very symbol of success while living in a broader world where Black people are all too often not allowed to succeed.[1]

Global success and stardom in the sports arena increase the visibility of Black athletes but this comes at a price. Despite Olympic victory, fame, world records, titles, accolades, achievements and medals, Black athletes are first and foremost Black and will always face discrimination to some degree within a state of double consciousness. This concept was coined in 1903 by civil rights leader and intellectual W.E.B. Du Bois to describe the sense of having two social identities: 'It is a peculiar sensation, this double-consciousness, this sense of always looking at one's self through the eyes of others, of measuring one's soul by the tape of a world that looks on in amused contempt and pity.'[2] Double consciousness is a very relevant concept in today's global society. The burden of double consciousness damages the Black identity. It's why athletes often can't be their full selves.

When I organise events with Black athletes, I frequently see this double consciousness up close as they smile in public but share with me their frustrations, anger and hurt when the media chooses to portray their bodies as somehow 'naturally' abnormal because of their athletic excellence as opposed to athletes who have trained their bodies to reach world-class rankings. Acclaimed professor and sociologist Ben Carrington asserts that Black athletes are forced into seeing themselves through the racialised lens of the white gaze which brands Black athletes as superhuman, so wider society sees them as superhuman physically, but inferior intellectually.[3] Black athletes, therefore, become viewed merely for their physical prowess based on racial myths and stereotypes. This has a negative impact on the consciousness of the Black athlete's identity – viewing themselves outside of their own identity, through two social identities, one of their choosing and one enforced. And the one which can bring you the most praise can also do you the most harm. The double consciousness goes beyond just how your body and achievements are viewed. It extends into all aspects of your identity and your very place in the world.

In the hundreds of conversations I've had with Black athletes, they all talk about representing their country with pride. It is, of course, one of the highest honours to represent your country in a sport you love – I wanted to do it for most of my youth – but there is a tension around athletes' social identities because it's difficult to support a country that doesn't always support you. The racism that exists in British society is never far away from the Black British athlete, especially when something goes wrong. This was powerfully articulated by former sprinter and now leading sports broadcaster Jeanette Kwakye when she said, 'A black athlete skirts the very fine line between being the nation's sweetheart, and a pariah. Talented, patriotic and representing the best that a country has to offer, but one step out of turn and there comes a sharp reminder to be grateful for your opportunity.'[4] The Black identity becomes hyphenated between different dual identities, underpinned by this dubious and convenient validation and recognition from wider society at the athlete's most victorious moments.

GB heptathlete Katarina Johnson-Thompson illustrates another facet to this point in an interview in *Vogue* magazine (2020) when she says, 'You can be like Marcus Rashford, name trending worldwide, receiving nationwide acclaim as he successfully sought to end domestic child hunger as a result of the Covid-19 crisis, only to be called "Daniel" by the British secretary for health and social care, who made no effort to disguise his reluctance to mention him at all.'[5] The complexity and contradictions of hyper-visibility of Black athletes when they are winning versus the erasure of so much of their identity outside of the sporting arena is a heavy burden.

But it is a testimony to the strength of Black athletes that, despite the obstacles, they push against these challenges. And it is important that we view this double consciousness, not just in terms of racism, but in terms of the restrictions Black athletes face to present all of their humanity and not just the part of their lives broader society is comfortable with. It is why so many have told me totally different stories with the mic on and with the mic off. The fact is, so many Black sportswomen – Anyika Onuora, Rachel Yankey, Bianca Williams, Maggie Alphonsi, Anita Asante, Ebony Rainford-Brent, Kare Adenegan, Hope Powell, Ellie and Rebecca Downie, Ama Agbeze, Ramla Ali and more – have used their voices in the media to give a more rounded picture of what it means to be a Black woman in Britain. They talk about topics that affect them, including eating disorders, religion, sexual abuse, discrimination, mental health, menstruation, balancing career with jobs and family, body dysmorphia and racial inequalities. Their words go beyond inspiring young women to give a better sporting performance but serve up volley after volley of wisdom and life lessons.

When they share their truths, Black sporting role models not only inspire a future generation of athletes, they also create a space where the wider public benefit from seeing them as whole people with flaws and talents who help us to be more informed about their experiences. When we learn about an athlete's personal stories, our connection to them builds – especially when it is connected to a social and moral purpose higher than their sporting prowess. Such is the cultural power and sense of belonging that arises from sport: Black athletes become inspirational agents of survival and hope to Black communities.

This is why it is impossible for me to do the issue justice without centralising the voices and experiences of Black sports *women*, front and centre. Despite their objective success on the sports field, Black women are often the most marginalised group, whose stories, contributions and activism have been reduced and at times erased. This is because Black women experience discrimination differently because they stand at the crossroads of interlocking sets of oppression from racism, misogyny, gender identity, homophobia, ableism, transphobia, classism and xenophobia. These barriers are global, and affect Black women throughout the diaspora.

'The day I stop fighting for equality, and for people that look like you and me, will be the day I'm in my grave,' tennis icon Serena Williams told reporters following her 2019 Wimbledon final defeat by Simona Halep.[6] And in 2017 Williams boldly wrote: 'The cycles of poverty, discrimination, and sexism are much, much harder to break than the record for Grand Slam titles,' articulating the struggle for racial equality in tennis by locating herself first and foremost as a Black woman.[7] Similarly, in an article in the *Telegraph*'s Women's Sport Supplement GB Paralympian Kadeena Cox shared her experiences of the racist and misogynist abuse she receives online about her muscular physique;[8] while GB sprint queen Dina Asher-Smith has previously shared her experiences at cover shoots when photographers have lightened her complexion to make the images seemingly 'more attractive' to the public.[9]

The Black Lives Matter movement has given us a window where Black people in all walks of life, and athletes in particular, have taken the opportunity to push back against the very concept of double consciousness. They are not superhuman on the playing field and then Black when they are off it. They are not saying one thing when the microphones are on and another thing to me privately. They are bringing their entire identities and struggles to the playing field for the entire world to see. Of course, this is not the first time that Black athletes have tried to present themselves in their entirety. It is one of the most powerful things that sport can offer – not just for people struggling for justice but for everyone to understand what it means to be Black in a predominantly white society.

When Black athletes talk about their realities, it carries a significance beyond their athletic performance because of its social power to convey messages that can ignite a spark to awaken global public consciousness on important sociopolitical issues. US sportswriter Dave Zirin talks about this when he says it's not just the power of the words that athletes have, but also the extent of their reach.[10] Sport crosses divides and speaks to those who don't even like sport; it becomes a powerful form of protest because of how it engages with the mainstream and can puncture the views of those in privileged positions unaffected by systemic oppression. This is clear in the example of the 1959 Pan American Games when American high jumper Eroseanna 'Rose' Robinson refused to stand for the US flag. Her protest drew attention to racial inequality during the civil rights era. Then, more famously, in the 1968 Mexico Olympic Games when African American sprint track stars Tommie Smith and John Carlos stood on the medal podium and raised their black-glove-clad fists skyward to protest against the racism and poverty afflicting the United States and the world. The image of their raised fists became an iconic symbol of resistance and hope. As punishment, the International Olympic Committee banned Smith and Carlos from the Olympic Games for life. I centred Robinson's activism efforts first because Black women's activism is so often forgotten. Historical moments like this provided the legacy for the contemporary sports activism we see from American civil rights activist and football quarterback Colin Kaepernick, famous for taking a knee, to tennis superstar Naomi Osaka, at the 2020 US Open, donning face masks bearing the names of Black people killed by police brutality.

Through my work I try to champion my own unapologetic activism grounded in a desire to effect positive change in redressing racial inequalities. This activism is born from a deep-rooted sense of racial injustice; from as young as four, I remember my mum being abused in the street for having brown babies – me and my twin. When athletics came into my life, my sense of self was shaped and informed by the sports stars of the day and also the legends of the past. It's no surprise then that for thirty years I've had the iconic picture of the salute from African American sprinters Tommie Smith and John Carlos on my wall. In 2012 I heard Carlos speak at the Ritzy Cinema in Brixton where, after his stirring keynote address, I asked him what had been going through his head as he stood on the podium. He recalled one of his conversations with Dr Martin Luther King Jr, who said that 'The Olympic Games represents a huge stone thrown into the ocean, creating ripples that can change the world and in demonstrating this act of protest he stands for those who can't stand up for themselves.' That is athlete activism at its best. Afterwards Carlos signed a copy of his book, writing, on the first page, 'We live to make history'; the book is one of my prized possessions. I told him about my poster of him and Smith and how it has motivated me to use my voice in the pursuit of racial equality; he told me that Black lawyers have told him the same thing – they would carry the picture in their law books and would look at it for inspiration. I've also had the honour of interviewing Dr Tommie Smith, on the fiftieth anniversary of the salute, when his majestic spirit and words of wisdom uplifted hundreds of people in the Manchester University auditorium. The activism of Smith and Carlos has inspired and fuelled my resilience and that of thousands of people in all kinds of ways, while inspiring the athlete activists of today.

During a speech at a Black Lives Matter rally in June 2020 sixteen-year-old tennis sensation Coco Gauff quoted Martin Luther King and conveyed her anger at the killing of George Floyd. 'Black lives have always mattered. They mattered then, they matter now and they'll matter in the future.'[11] This anger is often the birthplace of activism. For many Black people, it's a traumatic and triggering experience to be confronted with images of Black people being murdered because of the colour of their skin. Witnessing these atrocities serves to remind you that the next potential victim could be you or a member of your own family. As a Black woman I can attest that the pain is visceral, the rage of the injustice intense. In the aftermath of the killing of George Floyd, athletes worldwide mobilised themselves, participating in their own forms of boycotts and social justice campaigns. This included British athletes. Anger served to fuel sports activism as part of articulating the injustice of oppression in the realities of everyday living for Black people and through the lens of what is – let's be clear – life or death both in the US and the UK. For every George Floyd, Breonna Taylor and Jacob Blake, Britain has a list of names too, which includes Sean Rigg, Cynthia Jarrett and Joy Gardner. Sports activism becomes a tool of self-determination in processing individual and collective anger as a part of the continuous healing journey for Black people. Activism is significant because it becomes a place where athletes are choosing not to be a victim in the face of physical and psychological oppression where rage can be all-consuming.

World-renowned sports sociologist Dr Harry Edwards says that we are currently in the midst of the 'fifth wave of athletic activism', the key difference being that athletes have moved beyond individual protests to team boycott efforts, which send a clear message to gatekeepers that business will only return to normal once assets are allocated to resolve the issue.[12] These waves of activism have increased as the world has become ever more divided, with many athletes stepping up and using their platforms, from the likes of Colin Kaepernick, Serena and Venus Williams, Megan Rapinoe, Simone Biles, Maya Moore, Raheem Sterling, Ibtihaj Muhammad, Naomi Osaka, Caster Semenya, LeBron James, Alysia Montaño, Lewis Hamilton, Coco Gauff and Eniola Aluko – the list goes on and on. These athletes have been galvanised by some of the biggest social and political challenges of our times, from gender, racial and LGBTQI+ equality, unequal pay, body image, working conditions, abuse and basic human rights. Some chose to be activists, and others have been forced into taking a stand in the pursuit of equality, but all risked backlash and condemnation.

This is the space in which athletes find themselves – they can take their sporting excellence and then, by presenting their full selves, use it for a social good bigger and more powerful than their sporting performance, channelling the expression of the social inequalities they face through a different medium. This is less sporting activism and just a more accurate representation of the daily reality Black athletes face in a white supremacist society. The global Black Lives Matter movement has shone a new light on the duality of the lives of Black athletes – on the idea that in part of your life you can be an athlete while in another part of your life you can be an activist. Instead, I am beginning to think that what we are trying to achieve is that, for those Black athletes who want to, they should be able to present their entire identities; for many that means no longer concealing the real issues they believe in.

Sport creates the platform, and the athlete uses their position in tandem with the media to shine a light on racial injustice and, in doing so, they are making demands of the system to reform and do better. England under-21 hockey player Darcy Bourne did just that with her placard, carried in the Black Lives Matter protests in London, declaring 'WHY IS ENDING RACISM A DEBATE?'[13] There is no debate for those of us from the Black community weathering the impact of intersectional oppression. Eighteen-year-old Bourne's image, taken by *Vogue* photographer

Misan Harriman, went viral on social media. Martin Luther King III, son of the late civil rights leader, shared the image, as did many other high-profile global figures including British *Vogue* editor Edward Enninful. In doing this, they were also sharing Bourne's story as a Black sportswoman in a predominantly white sport, highlighting the gaping racial and ethnic disparities in women's hockey – a sport where 35 per cent of the GB squads are made up of white women from private schools.[14]

During the height of the Black Lives Matter movement in the summer of 2020, the Women's Sport Supplement of the *Daily Telegraph* – a conservative British broadsheet newspaper – dedicated the whole sixteen pages to the voices of Black women in sport and the negative experiences of racism and discrimination they experience in sport and in wider British society. Articles showcased Black sportswomen and their campaigning work to challenge intersectional oppression. For example, the activism of the only Black Team GB swimmer – twenty-three-year-old Alice Dearing – has led her to co-found the Black Swimming Association, which aims to challenge the cultural stereotype that Black people can't swim. This kind of media coverage – dedicated to giving a voice to often voiceless Black sportswomen – is a rare occasion, and to be given such national coverage was a positive step and long overdue. As award-winning sportswriter and author of *No Win Race* Derek A. Bardowell so eloquently explains, 'If black lives matter, they should matter all the time, not just in moments of crisis.'[15]

In 2017 the England Football Association (FA) experienced one of those moments of crisis when former professional footballer Eniola Aluko publicly held them to account at a Department for Culture, Media and Sport Committee inquiry into racial discrimination and bullying; many people supported her in this quest, including me. Aluko, alongside fellow footballers Lianne Sanderson and Drew Spence, experienced racism in the form of racial abuse and stereotyping under the then England women's team manager, Mark Sampson. In standing up to the FA, Aluko showed us that the truth should be uncompromising; her actions served to embolden and sustain Black women to own and use their power and agency. There were real-life consequences to Aluko's activism, including vitriolic media backlash, and, lest we forget, Aluko never played for England again despite being one of the best players in the country at that time.

So far, I have centred Black women. However, I must include the efforts of Black British men who have changed the public narrative, discourse and shifted government policy through their own different forms of activism – motor racing champion and history-maker Sir Lewis Hamilton and premiership footballers Raheem Sterling and Marcus Rashford. From Rashford's influence, activating the government and stakeholders to feed some of the nation's poorest children, to Sterling's calling out the racist bigotry in the media and demanding greater sanctions for racist fan behaviour, to Hamilton's mobilisation of a new commission to tackle racial inequities in Formula 1, their contribution is seismic.[16] What gives the work these sporting stars do so much power is that they are speaking from a place of personal experience. Activism becomes less about individual choice and more about what these people are presenting as their full selves, acting on their own truths. Galvanised by Black Lives Matter, they are finally, unapologetically, saying the same things when the microphone is on as when the microphone is off.

Finally.

Job done? Is my own activism complete? Is double consciousness ended?

Sadly, no. In many ways, this is only the start. Two reasons. Access and power. Let me explain.

There was a round of polite applause around the plush banqueting hall; I was on my feet giving my own standing ovation to honour champion jockey eighteen-year-old Khadijah Mellah at the 2019 Sports Journalism Awards. From Peckham via Brixton to Glorious Goodwood, Mellah started riding in 2012 before saddling up on a thoroughbred racehorse for the first time in April 2019; five months later she rode to victory, winning the Magnolia Cup at the world-famous Goodwood racecourse. In so doing, she became the first British jockey to win a horse race while wearing a hijab. I was in awe of her achievements, knowing all too well the barriers she would've had to face to achieve this feat as a Muslim woman in a white-male-dominated sport. I gave an extra whoop to my applause, unfazed by the prim looks from others on my table. A complete novice, Khadijah had learnt to ride at Ebony Horse Club in Brixton, close to her home.

Conversely, I'm reminded of my talented godson Zion, who travels from Croydon to Millwall several miles away to attend his basketball club, London Thunder, founded and headed up by Steve Bucknall, one of England's first NBA basketball players. Zion takes two buses and a train; it is very common for young athletes to travel far and wide to train and compete. I did it all the time as a young athlete; nothing new here. Fortuitously, this was not the case for Mellah and, in winning such a prestigious horse race, making international and national headlines, she became a role model to thousands of young people and women trampling down gendered, racialised and xenophobic barriers, showing that Muslim sportswomen can become champion jockeys. It's all about opportunity and access.

Unfortunately, sport-for-development organisations like Ebony Horse Club are few and far between. According to Sport England's *Sport for All* research published in January 2020, people from Black, Asian or ethnic minority backgrounds are seven times more likely to live in an urban area than a white person.[17] These geographical factors can contribute to, and perpetuate, some of the socioeconomic, social cohesion and social mobility issues that influence a person's ability to engage in sport and physical activity, resulting in masses of sporting talent from Black, Asian and ethnic minority communities being lost to the system. The dedicated future champions may find a way, but the barriers are just too high for many who simply want to enjoy themselves.

Despite the fact that the media often stereotypes Black people as being naturally sporty, Sport England research shows Black children are less likely than their white counterparts to meet the UK Chief Medical Officers' guidelines of partaking in at least sixty minutes of physical activity a day; only 40.4 per cent of Black children compared to 45 per cent of children as a whole aged between five and sixteen years old. It is so engrained in the public consciousness that Black people are 'sporty' that people often don't believe these figures. But while Black young people are over-represented in track and field athletics, basketball and dance, they are significantly under-represented in activities such as rugby, swimming, cricket and tennis. Our sporting success might be visually conspicuous but the barriers to us leading a healthy, sporty life – due to structural racism which includes limited talent pathways, access to facilities, cost of and access to specialist equipment – are sadly hidden. No surprises here.

The picture only gets bleaker as we get older. Research reveals the stark ethnicity gap in sport, highlighting that only 56 per

cent of Black people reach the UK Chief Medical Officers'
guidelines of 150 minutes of physical activity per week; 62 per
cent of adults overall in England meet the guidelines. To break
this down even further, 51 per cent of Black women meet the
guidelines compared to 65 per cent of Black men. As with any
industry – be it sport, education or business – if the governance
and leadership fail to understand the ways in which oppression
intersects, it also fails to cater for the people it serves, which
creates a sports landscape only accessible by those in privileged
positions. These statistics paint the picture but, on the face of it,
the UK is a successful sporting nation, second on the Olympic
medal table in the 2016 Rio Olympics: a nation of winners,
you might think. Yet these winners do not reflect the British
population and, least of all, Black people. This is a surprising
revelation for some, given that there's an assumption that sport
is supposed to be a 'great leveller', where performance is the
deciding factor for success. Access and opportunity are serious
fault lines in British sport. The rewards that sport offers – and
the new microphone it offers to help shape the world we live
in – should be available to all, and this is a key next step in the
Black Sports Lives Matter movement.

The second key next step is to deal with power. Again, I want
to begin with an example.

In 2020, alongside all the athletes using their voices, Chris
Grant, one of the UK's most senior Black administrators in
sport and independent board member of Sport England, used
the press to call for a South African-style truth and reconcili-
ation commission to tackle structural racism in sport. He said
that 'the inequalities are so deeply rooted within sport's structures and assumptions that the situation amounts to a kind of
apartheid hiding in plain sight'.[18] This headline came out at the

same time as footballer Raheem Sterling told the BBC, 'The only disease right now is the racism that we are fighting.'[19] Grant also asserted that it's not the job of the athletes to fix racism, it's the job of the leaders of sport to fix a system that continues to uphold systems of bias and oppression, creating racial inequities. He's right.

Indeed, in many ways, it is easy to be fooled by the dominance of Black female athletes on the field of play into thinking that opportunities and life chances for Black women are improving. You would be wrong. Despite our visible achievements, Black women account for just 1.2 per cent of positions on the boards of thirty-eight sports organisations.[20] In June 2020, Dame Heather Rabbatts – the FA's first female board member and the first Black board member – talked about the UK Sports Governance Code's targets for gender diversity on sports boards, saying, 'What it hasn't done is benefited – at all – Black women. And you have to be specific about that case and you have to be specific about requiring sports bodies which are, for example, in receipt of public funds, that there is a requirement to have Black representation alongside some of the other diverse criteria that you should be looking to achieve.'[21] It is now widely accepted that gender targets in sport have mainly benefited white women. This lack of Black leadership shapes the structures in which the athletes find themselves – from whether they have to defend their actions or suffer penalties from their 'activism', to dealing with the access issues I outlined earlier. Sports can give the visible impression of Black female empowerment and progress, but scratch the surface and the stark reality of racism and under-representation is hiding in plain sight.

If you believe Black lives matter, this means you must value the lives of Black athletes in their entirety, not just their sporting achievements. We must break down the idea that you can separate the sportsperson from their activism or keep sports and politics separate. When Black athletes are able to represent their true selves and not say one thing off mic and another on mic it not only enriches society, but it forces society to wake up to racial injustice. We saw this vividly at the 2020 Euros football tournament when the England team took the knee before each match. We saw it when, after they lost to penalties in the final, the Black players responded publicly to the racism they received. This is because Black sportspeople in their full humanity no longer need to separate their sporting achievements and their racial identity.

We are witnessing a new era of Black collective identity in British sport. Yet whilst I take pride from their courageous actions, I am scared that this is a moment and not a movement the way we need it to be for change to happen. And because, as one of my friends reminded me, racism is patient. I want Black people to have the freedom to present all aspects of their lives, for Black people to have equal access to sport as well as to have positions of power in sport. Black athletes are writing their own history on their terms and, in so doing, being the change they want to be in wider British society. As Marcus Rashford declared after the Euros final: 'I will never apologise for who I am . . . I'm Marcus Rashford, 23-year-old black man, from . . . South Manchester. If I have nothing else, I have that.'[22]

BLACK BRITISH EDUCATION MATTERS

The continuing struggle against racism in schooling

KEHINDE ANDREWS

Exclusion rates for Black Caribbean students in English schools are up to six times higher than those of their White counterparts in some local authorities. And while representation rates of Black students at higher education institutions are relatively high, less than 1 per cent of university professors in the UK are Black.

Kehinde Andrews is a leading figure in the debate on Black education in the UK and developed the first Black Studies degree in Europe.

During the 2020 Black History Month debate in the House of Commons, Equalities Minister Kemi Badenoch responded to a campaign to transform the content of schooling by declaring that 'our curriculum does not need to be decolonised, for the simple reason that it is not colonised'.[1] It was a stark reminder of the limits of expecting diversity in the seat of power to solve the problem of racism. Badenoch is one of the handful of Black women to serve as a cabinet minister but this does not prevent her from defending the deeply Eurocentric curriculum that has again become the focus of large-scale campaigns. If we were to receive a complete history of Britain's imperial past we would all understand that Badenoch's reactionary views are following a long tradition of Black people who embraced the racist status quo in order to secure their own position. Colonialism could not have happened without the collaboration of all too many Black people. So in some senses Badenoch is a living history lesson. But the sad irony remains that the opportunity for Badenoch to reach her career heights in the mother country only exists because of the struggles for justice from Black communities.

Education has been a key site of that resistance, given the stark inequalities and how important gaining the right credentials are for improving your life chances. Through creating alternative spaces of education, to forcing the mainstream system to reform, Black communities have resisted racism in schooling. Unfortunately, for all the gains that have been made, we continue to experience vicious racial inequalities and are subject to a deeply colonial curriculum. Renewed campaigns in schools and universities build a rich tradition of Black education movements that cannot be separated from the story of Black Britain.

How the Black child was made educationally subnormal

Campaigns to transform the education system have a long history in Britain. It was not until the mid-1960s that there were significant numbers of Black young people in the British school system but it was apparent very quickly that there was a problem. Migrants to any country move for better job options and education opportunities for their children and when the Windrush generation decided to settle in Britain they had reasons to be optimistic. As colonial subjects, the school systems in the Caribbean were based on those in the mother country, so it was assumed their kids would benefit greatly from the move. But as Guy Reid-Bailey, one of the activists in the 1963 Bristol Bus

Boycott, told me in an interview for the *Guardian*, they quickly found that the country was a 'mother with no affection for Black people'.[2] Rather than the schools being a safe haven, they were a hostile environment where it was a battle to survive. Bernard Coard's seminal *How the West Indian Child Is Made Educationally Sub-normal in the British School System*, published in 1971, shone a light on the extent of the problem, with up to 70 per cent of African Caribbean boys in some London boroughs being declared special needs.[3] Black children were seen to be a problem, with an alien culture, speaking broken English, and were expected to be at the bottom of the class. Talented young people were leaving school with no qualifications and schools were almost universally seen by the university, in the words of Maureen Stone, as 'colonisers'.[4] The purpose of the school was not seen as being to educate but to transition Black children into the lower rungs of society, maintaining our colonial place at the bottom of the social hierarchy.

The experiences of that first critical mass of Black students in the British school system set the framework that we are still having to battle within. Low teacher expectations are credited as one of the biggest impacts on discriminatory outcomes.[5] Unsurprisingly, students tend to meet the level that the person with all the power in class has laid out for them. This creates a self-fulfilling prophecy where Black children are deemed to be educationally inferior and that creates the conditions where racialised test scores become the reality. For all the howling about the supposedly new problem of so-called White working-class boys, there still exists steep racialised inequality in school exam performance.[6] This is only exacerbated at university level, where White students are significantly more likely to leave with a good degree than those of an ethnic minority.[7] It is a damning indictment of universities that even those groups who outperform their White counterparts at school level (e.g. Indian and Chinese students) fall into the achievement gap in higher education.

Regardless of what happens at university level, the presence of high-achieving minority students at school level has actually increased the institutional racism faced by Black students. If other groups can do well then it cannot possibly be racism, especially with those poor forgotten White working-class boys. But this masks the problem because racism has never worked on a simple Black/White binary and this is exemplified in school discrimination. From the outset Caribbean children were seen as deficient, backwards because of their culture and language. Migrants from nations with official mother tongues were put into English-language programmes, whereas Caribbean children were chastised for their supposedly broken English. Even though the vast majority of Black schoolchildren are now born in Britain, it is not hard to draw a direct connection between those early generations' experience and what happens in the classroom today. Black young people come into the class representing the unruly, deviant street culture and language, subjects to be tamed rather than students to be trained.[8]

In the US the sociologist Elijah Anderson argues that the 'iconic ghetto' is the frame through which all Black people are seen.[9] The first assumption is not only that we come from the hood (or the ends) but that we embody the supposedly lawless, primal instincts that represent inner-city Black communities on television. From here we have to prove we can 'dance', that we are above the stereotype, in order to be given a chance to succeed. Anyone who has spent any time working in an oppressively White institution will appreciate the feeling of being seen as special, somehow different from the anonymous mass of Black 'them'. Ralph Ellison captured this perfectly in his classic *Invisible Man*, where he painstakingly explored the damage of being seen only as a stereotype, that feeling of being looked through rather than at. Walking the corridors of my university, I know exactly how he felt, with my colleagues always refusing to look up at me because I am a Black man; it is best not to make eye contact because that will only attract dangerous attention. I have lost count of the number of times I have had to wave directly in the face of a colleague to say hello and seen the instant shock and fear in the approach. It is just for an instant until they recognise me, and you get the relieved 'oh, it's YOU'; they always neglect to add 'I'm so glad it's not THEM'. It used to be upsetting but I actually appreciate the anonymity of invisibility, except when I need cheering up and then I might metaphorically go 'BOO' to an unsuspecting colleague.

If I, one of the minuscule number of Black professors in the UK, daily experience the stereotype then imagine what it is like for young people in school. I will never forget how from day one when I started secondary school we were streamed into sets based on our presumed ability. It was like our names had been put into a racist sorting hat from Hogwarts. We had only just arrived and yet we were judged; unsurprisingly, there were very few Black children in the top sets with me and successively more as the degree of difficulty got lighter. I was able to dance, to be one of the exceptions that proved the rule, and therefore the expectations of me were high so I duly performed. But I saw how so many of the children who looked like me never received the benefit of the doubt. They were perceived to be a problem from the outset and were treated as such throughout their time in the school. Black children remain less likely to achieve the higher grades at GCSE, more likely to be pushed into vocational qualifications[10] and more likely to be excluded.[11] Unless you genuinely believe that this is because we are genetically inferior or that absentee fathers, welfare-dependent mothers and the devil's music are corrupting the youth, then this is a clear, persistent problem of racist exclusion.

Coard was also heavily critical of the curriculum, which at that time was full of overtly racist concepts and imagery. We may have moved from Enid Blyton books with Golliwogs and Little Black Sambo being on the reading list but we delude ourselves if we believe that we have made much progress. In 1971, Coard cautioned that 'When the pictures, illustrations, music, heroes, great historical and contemporary figures in the classroom are all white, it is difficult for a child to identify with anyone who is not white.'[12] We may now have Black History Month, forcing the schools to showcase a few token Black people once a year, but the unfortunate truth is that Whiteness is the default in the schools. This plays out in the reading materials, with only 4 per cent of children's books in 2017 featuring an ethnic minority character at all, and only 1 per cent where they are the main character.[13] Much has been made of a History curriculum that continues to centre on the narrow island story of the uniqueness of Britain. I could probably teach the classes on the Tudors and Stuarts and the whitewashed portrayal of the Second World War that my kids will have to endure. They have become so ingrained they are second nature. There has been some optionality brought into the subject where students *can* study some aspects of the transatlantic slave trade, US civil rights and globalisation. But these are very much optional for schools; only 11 per cent of GCSE History students in 2019 studied any contributions Black people have made to Britain, and less than a tenth studied modules focusing on the British Empire.[14] The problem is not just the

History curriculum, it is the Whiteness that seeps through the core of the curriculum, in what is taught, who is adulated and who is ignored. Some schools make a much greater effort than others, and there are some wonderful teachers creating oases in which their students can be nourished. But we must face up to the fact they are bucking the trend, going against the framework that they are forced to operate in.

University academics like to point fingers at the schools and their significant problems but, as I already alluded to earlier, these issues are only compounded in higher education. Not only do we see the same, and more extreme, patterns of discrimination in attainment and dropout rates, the universities are actually the source of the problem. The reason that most schools do not opt for the paltry optional courses that represent the faintest sprinkle of diversity is because their teachers are not familiar with the subject matter. School curricula are a direct product of the Eurocentric parade of dead White men that masquerade as the foundation for knowledge in the university. In 2017 Cambridge was celebrated for announcing that its History students would be required to take at least *one* exam in a subject outside of the West. If we are lauding progress that meagre, then we can only be in the midst of a crisis. It is not just in history but across the board that the university curriculum perpetuates the myth that Black people cannot think, that we are indebted to White saviours for pulling us up out of our barbarism. In 2015 we saw the #WhyIsMyCurriculumWhite campaign emerge and spread across campuses because students were tired of the constant assault they are subjected to. #RhodesMustFall followed in 2016 in order to remove the symbolic presence of the violent racist Cecil Rhodes from Oxford University buildings, and to challenge the university to rethink its basic assumptions.[15] There has since been a variety of campaigns to 'decolonise the curriculum', which has become somewhat of a buzzword in the sector that is at least starting to acknowledge that there is a serious problem.[16]

The reason that these protests have only recently occurred – and much later than in the United States, which went through this process in the sixties – is twofold. Demographics is important because it was only in the sixties that large numbers of the children of the colonies were entering British schools. The US was built on slave labour so could not offshore its colonial violence or population and therefore there have been millions of African Americans in the nation state from the outset, struggling for access to institutions like universities. Therefore, widening participation for universities is much more recent in Britain. The first genuine attempt was only made in 1992, with the creation of a raft of new universities (like the one I currently work for, Birmingham City University). Even here we can see the implicit racism – in order to increase diversity there was no attempt to change the complexion of the student body at the elite universities; they simply created a second tier of higher education to include the poor and minority students. Although Black students are over-represented in the university sector as a whole, they remain significantly under-represented in the elite, so-called Russell Group institutions.[17] In fact, the university league tables are the perfect illustration of the racialised nature of the system, with the less diverse institutions at the top and the most colourful at the bottom. This undoubtedly is one of the reasons that Black graduates are significantly less likely to be employed at all or to find graduate-level jobs, because their degrees are more likely to be from the less respected universities.

These inequalities are only starker at the staff level. Only

0.7 per cent of academics are Black, and there are just 140 Black professors in the entire country.[18] In my department we currently employ more full-time Black academics (seven) than a lot of universities do in total. It is also no coincidence that I work at a post-1992 institution, which is where you will find a disproportionate amount of the academic staff diversity. Put it this way, I never would have had the chance at an academic job without the post-1992 sector and, even at this stage of my career, I strongly doubt that an elite university would offer me a post, unless I were willing to take a demotion. Make no mistake, academia is defined by its Whiteness in terms of the knowledge produced; those creating the updated frameworks for understanding; and the experiences of students having to endure the process.

One of the depressing ironies of the Black experience in Britain is that we have fought hard for recognition and access – particularly in the field of education – but are still subject to the same racist treatment. On the one hand, we have forced the doors open enough for me to write this piece as a university professor, something almost unheard of when I was born. But on the other hand, if I were to recount the struggles, ordeal and just dumb luck to be in this position, it would be abundantly clear that I am fortunate enough to be one of the very few exceptions that prove the rule. We are quick to warn our young people that their dreams of being a footballer are little more than fantasies, but the truth is their odds of becoming a professor are so low they don't even qualify for dream status. Having said all of this, one thing that we should never do is disempower our young people in the field of education. As problematic as our experiences in mainstream school have been, and remain, Black education has a strong foundation that continues to thrive.

Black education

It is vitally important that we always remember that schooling is not education. Universal secondary schooling is less than eighty years old in Britain, and the majority of children in the world do not have access to full-time free school. Above all else, as we have found during lockdown caused by the Covid-19 pandemic, the main purpose of universal schooling is childcare, so that adults can go out and contribute economically. Even Conservative governments have been dragged into the twenty-first century and now support free nursery places for three-year-olds so that women can have better access to the labour market. The other primary function of schools is to prepare young people for the world of work. Now that literacy, numeracy and even computing skills are requisite for the modern workforce, we are seeing increasing emphasis on all of these in the system. Universal schooling is certainly a largely progressive force, and I have definitely been a beneficiary. But we kid ourselves if we believe that the purpose of the school system is to act as a great equalising force in society. By allowing everyone access to a deeply unequal system (private schools, grammar schools, postcode lotteries) and then awarding supposedly standardised achievements, the impact is actually to justify inequality:[19] of course, those unruly Black children, who had the same opportunities as everyone else yet failed, deserve to be at the back of the queue. By filtering students into their place in society, the school system works to maintain the status quo, not to subvert it. Expecting the schools to produce racial equality is like asking 'a chicken to lay a duck egg'.[20] But all is not lost because once we see the schools (and I include universities in this) as institutions we must endure, navigate and survive, we can look for our education elsewhere.

Schools are useful for giving us the skills we need to understand the world but we must remember that 'students do not learn to read and write, they read and write to learn'.[21] There is almost nothing that I currently get paid to write and teach about that I learnt in school, college or university. Thankfully, I was exposed to Black education, the principal success of the British Black Power movement.

Alongside campaigns to hold the schools accountable, one of the strategies of resisting racism was to create Black supplementary schools. These were incredibly grassroots programmes often organised on Saturdays, or after school – first, in people's front rooms and community centres.[22] Starting in the mid-sixties, in response to the inequalities we have already discussed, they represented the community coming together to provide what the state would not. Most ethnic minority groups have supplementary schools to cater for specific language, cultural or religious instruction that will not be found in the mainstream.[23] But Black supplementary schools were different in that they primarily focused on the basics of Maths and English due to the inability of the schools to even serve this function for Black children. This remains the case in supplementary schools; we can see the increase in parents employing tutors outside of schools as a continued indictment of the system. As well as being a mechanism to get students through the mainstream system, supplementary schools also provided Black Studies education, ranging from Caribbean history to cultural activities to Pan-African politics. Here they were catering to a complete absence from the school curriculum; as Mel Chevannes, one of the early organisers, explained, 'It is not, of course, possible to "supplement" what does not exist.'[24]

Many of the pioneers and current organisers in the

supplementary school movement would chafe at the idea of being part of British Black Power. The range of political views is so vast that it is sometimes difficult to see it as a movement. My dad was involved in the supplementary school run by the African Caribbean Self-Help Organisation that started in 1967. This was put together by a group of young people who had ties to radical groups across the world and taught classes inspired by Malcolm X, the Black Panther Party and even Marxism-Leninism. Their relationship with the state was so bad that one of the founders, Bini Brown, remembers the police harassing parents who sent their kids there and the head of the Birmingham local education authority promising to 'smash' the school.[25] The idea of Black, supposedly uneducated youth teaching the children revolution shook the powers that be. But it would be wrong to character-ise the relationship of the movement based on its more rad-ical wing. Black supplementary schooling primarily aimed to help Black children succeed in schools and therefore there is little reason for conflict. After initial disquiet about the com-munity taking education into their own hands, the programme began to receive support from mainstream schools in the form of materials, teacher time and the use of school buildings. By the 1980s the Inner London Education Authority was declaring that 'supplementary schools will have a permanent structured place in London's educational system'.[26] By the early 2000s, even the radical Saturday school that the state was trying to smash in Birmingham was receiving some funding from the local educa-tion authority. There has been much made of the split between 'official', run by teachers with a more traditional curriculum, and 'self-help', organised by volunteers and often overtly polit-ical, in the movement.[27] The reality is that all of the schools wanted to help Black students succeed in the mainstream but, as much as some more conservative elements would protest, the movement was equally unified in presenting an alternative space for education.

Simply by existing, Black supplementary schools were an indictment of the mainstream system. They were the acknowledgement of the institutional racism in the schools and the inability of Black children to get an adequate education. Even those most traditionally run supplementary schools with trained teachers and no Black Studies were calling out the mainstream. They were also providing one of the key elements of Black Studies pedagogy, the Black-led environment, which is so important to changing the nature of the learning experience. By removing the 'hidden curriculum' of racist expectations and lower expectations, the children were empowered to learn.[28] The simplest way to describe the feeling of a supplementary school is to liken it to family. Even if you are learning the same curriculum in similar ways to a mainstream classroom, the environment makes it a liberating experience. The essence of British Black Power was self-help, providing the resources and opportunities that the state refused to. Supplementary schools were and remain a key part of that legacy, and it is no coincidence that groups like the Black Panthers, Black Unity and Freedom Party and Pan-African Congress Movement put the programmes at the core of their work.

In order for Black Studies to be carried out in supplementary schools, there was a much wider project to build community education. We take for granted now that you go online and order pretty much any book for next-day delivery. I'm old enough to remember having to go into Waterstones and picking out one of the ten books in the 'Black writers' section. In the sixties there was a generation of Black young people thirsting for knowledge and they created the avenues to reach it. One of these was the formation of Black bookshops. New Beacon Books in London was one of the first, founded by John La Rose in 1966. I also vividly remember being volunteered by my parents to work in the Harriet Tubman Bookshop in Handsworth, Birmingham as a child. Books had to be painstakingly brought into the country. My dad told me of the time whilst in the US he acquired some books to bring to the UK from a man who lived up a very long flight of stairs in an apartment building. As well as importing books, Black printing presses were founded. Coard's *How the West Indian Child* was published by New Beacon Books, and Bogle-L'Ouverture, founded by Eric and Jessica Huntley in 1969, was the press that first printed Walter Rodney's work. Through the bookshops and publishing, we found and created the Black Studies knowledge that was so vital to dissemination.

Another much underrated aspect of the educational influence of British Black Power was the network of speakers who moved through the UK. Due to the sprawling nature of the British Empire, the UK has been a hub for decolonial activism. It is no coincidence that the Pan-African Congress Movement started in Westminster in 1900, and had its most meaningful congress in Manchester in 1945. The belly of the beast has been an important site of struggle bringing together figures from around the globe. Because Britain exported its colonial violence, Black life in the country is by nature diasporic; almost all of us have living connections to a former colony. These connections were crucial to British Black Power because they were a source for alternative political knowledge and frameworks. For a profile in the *Guardian* Black Lives Series, I spoke to activist Leila Hassan Howe, who was drawn into Black politics while working in the library of the Institute of Race Relations in the sixties.[29] The library housed newspapers from across the world telling of the Black struggle, and therefore attracted community activists. Hassan Howe joined the Black Unity and Freedom Party after a visiting member had given her a leaflet. This was a period where revolutionary figures like Stokely Carmichael (Kwame Ture) (United States), Amílcar Cabral (Guinea) and Herbert Chitepo (Zimbabwe) would speak in the UK. Support for Black Panther struggles and the Free Angela Davis campaign were also foundational in building British Black Power. Demonstrations, events and meetings were key ways to disseminate a different set of ideas. In 1977 the first Africa Liberation Day was launched in Birmingham, drawing thousands of people on the theme of Pan-Africanism. The event still takes place every year during the May bank holiday and I have bought more books from Pepukayi Books than from Jeff Bezos. Pop-up bookshops at events, like those run by Book Love, are a vital source of maintaining community knowledge. Even with the decline of physical bookstores, the legacy of Black bookshops is alive and well.

Another important feature of the movement for community education was the creation of our own newspapers. When Claudia Jones was exiled from the United States to the mother country due to her Communism, she founded the *West Indian Gazette* in 1958. It is widely considered the first Black newspaper in Britain, but would by no means be the last. It was vital to get the perspectives of the Black community out into the public and to share the news of the diaspora that was sorely lacking in the mainstream press. From *Black Perspectives*, to the *Abeng*, to *Race Today* and eventually the *Voice*, the idea of Black publications took hold across the country. We simply did not have access to the mainstream and therefore we built an alternative. This was the overarching purpose of British Black Power – to do for self, to not rely on a system that has never had our best interests at heart. Of all the legacies of the movement that have been lost, this is the most important one. Due to the success of educational campaigns and building work outside the system, the institutions eventually opened enough to offer the illusion that we could change them from the inside.

Colonising the school system

Organically connected to the movements to provide alternatives to the school system were those campaigns to reform the mainstream system. In Haringey in 1969, the North London West Indian Association (NLWIA) launched a fierce campaign against 'banding', the process of sorting children into classes by ability that still goes on today. It is not difficult to see the racial jeopardy for Black children deemed and treated to be educationally inferior from the outset. But stoking the flames of protest was the leaked Doulton report, written by a headteacher of a private school who was commissioned to consult on the comprehensive system in Haringey in 1969. It is either depressing or refreshing – depending on your perspective – to know that the absurdity of the private sector dictating public priorities is by no means new. In the report he outlined the impending crisis due to colonial migration where 'about half the immigrants will be West Indians at 7 of the 11 schools' in the district. This was important because of the 'general recognition that their IQs work out below their English contemporaries. Thus academic standards will be lower in schools where they form a large group'.[30] Not only was he presuming Black children were inferior, he also advocated dispersing Caribbean students across the

schools to ensure that there were not too many of the educationally subnormal in any one school draining away the teachers'
attention.

The NLWIA campaign mobilised parents and the community to demand the dropping of IQ tests to determine ability; aban-
doning the principle of banding; appointing Black teachers; the
provision of nursery places; and the incorporation of community groups into the management of schools. The Black Parents
Movement was formed in 1975 in the area following this activism, and spread as far as Manchester, committed to educational
reform. These campaigns are part of countless others across the
country and the decades. We are currently seeing renewed calls
to transform the schools and, in particular, the narrow Eurocentric ideas that masquerade as a full education. Groups such
as the Black Curriculum and Decolonise the Curriculum are
following in footsteps well ploughed by activists. The minimal
gains that have been made to the curriculum and the profession
are testament to the work that has gone before.

Campaigns against racism in universities do not have the same
history because, as we have already explored, Black students and
staff only achieved any real access at all relatively recently. But
the movements have brought attention to the issue, and universities are now almost falling over each other in their steps
to 'decolonise the curriculum'.[31] Just as with the school system,
there is a question as to the extent this is a possibility. Universities have not just been complicit in racism, they are the very
place where the idea of racism was produced and legitimised.[32]
Prior to the so-called age of reason, White supremacy was jus-
tified on the basis of religion: whether or not the savages had
souls. But Western science tied racism to biology, naturalising
racial hierarchies due to the supposed genetic superiority of the

White race. It was only after the Holocaust – when the logic of racial hierarchy was brought into Europe on bodies we would consider White – that racial science was abandoned. But in its place came cultural ideas of inferiority that still dominate in the academic world. Just as with the schools, we should not get carried away with the progress that has been made. There are now competing ideas coming out of the university, a more diverse, critical range of voices, but these remain in the minority; as we have already explored, the inequalities in the system remain rife. As the campaigns to transform the university and school system continue, we must consider how much change is possible within the system.

Black power's approach was always two-pronged, providing alternatives while also holding the mainstream to account. It is precisely this stance we have taken in developing Black Studies at Birmingham City University. Rather than try to transform the Eurocentric curriculum, instead we have drawn on the tradition of community education. Black Studies is new to the university, it is not new to the country. Our frame of reference is the books, struggles, debates and ideas that have nurtured Black communities for decades. There have been other attempts in the past to do this at a module or access course level, but this is the first degree that has brought Black Studies fully into the White institution. The aim is to break the contradiction between schooling and education – schooling being the White curriculum that you have to endure for success; education being the Black Studies you can only get in your spare time. The basis of the degrees earned with us, the credential that is so important to a person's life chances, is the extent to which students have engaged and applied Black Studies. Students have to take their learning off campus and into the real world. This is a vital lesson from community education, that knowledge is not useful for its own sake; the point is, how do we improve the conditions people face? There is no doubt that our curriculum is decolonised with its strands of political activism, Black Feminism and community engagement, all rooted in perspectives, experiences and contributions of Africans and the African diaspora. But our curriculum being decolonised says very little about the sector, or even our university, as a whole.

In many ways we are not setting out to decolonise the university, because that is a goal beyond our reach. The university continues to produce racist knowledge and outcomes because of its role in society. You cannot decolonise the university without first transforming society. Expecting an institution designed to maintain the status quo to overturn it is one of the very things that keeps us in our place. But if we understand the university as a site of privilege that gives us access to resources and finance that we can turn to the service of the wider community, then we can put our positions to good use. Essentially, we are trying to colonise the university, to infiltrate it with Black Studies knowledge and practice in order to support the vital work off campus. The university cannot be the solution to the problem of racism that it is so integral to maintain, but it may be possible to leverage parts of it against itself.

The battle in the schools is no different. There is no rational argument against the idea of transforming the curriculum. The case for a new set of teachings is often made on the behalf of Black children who need to see themselves reflected in the school. A narrow curriculum is a problem for the whole of society and, more so, for the majority who will rarely have the opportunity to have the scales of Whiteness removed from their eyes. But as we have seen, Black communities have fought hard to fill that deficit. When children grow up not understanding the history of the British Empire, they simply do not understand the world. If you genuinely believe that the industrial revolution could have occurred without slavery and colonial exploitation, you are the victim of a bad education. Even so, and with the deficits so glaring, Education Secretary Gavin Williamson's response to calls for Black history and an honest account of the British Empire to be made compulsory in the curriculum was that 'we should be incredibly proud of our history because time and time and time again, this country has made a difference and changed things for the better, right around the world'.[33] There is zero chance under the Johnson Tory administration that there will be any changes to the curriculum, so campaigning to change it at this point is almost wasted energy. Governments do not last forever and there is definitely scope to influence the agenda for the next government. But it would be wrong for us to hold out hope, because we have been let down so many times before.

Rather than rely on the system changing from above, we must do what we can to decolonise the school curriculum. There is already some genuinely great practice taking place with some teachers doing everything within their power to provide a rounded education. With the resources available from organisations such as the Free Black Curriculum and efforts at places like the Bernie Grant Trust, we can support teachers in their efforts. We can also work to rebuild the alternative spaces of education that nurtured the community. Black supplementary schools still exist, but lack the same levels of support they previously enjoyed. It is imperative to support initiatives such as the National Association of Black Supplementary Schools (NABSS) that are trying to support Black voluntary education. As much as we are dedicated to working in the institutions, we must be committed to building in the community. At the Harambee Organisation of Black Unity, picking up the mantle of one of the long-standing self-help groups, we are opening the Garvey Education Centre on what was the site of one of the first Black nurseries. Building these alternative spaces is vital to keep Black education thriving, even if you are interested in trying to reform mainstream practice. What happens outside echoes on the inside, forcing the very limited changes we have seen.

Britain has a long and vibrant history of Black Studies education. It is a testament to how Black communities have never accepted the racism we have been subjected to, but have always struggled for change. By creating alternative spaces of education, we have produced and disseminated knowledge that has been vital to nurturing Black communities. Once again we see campaigns to transform education, building on the legacies of what have gone before. Black education has always been a site of struggle, an essential ingredient to any recipe of liberation.

BLACK BRITISH COMEDIANS MATTER

The importance of laughter

LENNY HENRY

I didn't want to write a chapter for this book. It felt a bit gratuitous. More showbiz media-types moaning about being neglected when the fact is many of us have nice kitchens, back gardens to frolic in and unlimited Spotify. Why does anybody need to feel sorry for a few Black British comedians? And who needs to read an essay written by a Black British comedian who is clearly doing OK – relatively speaking?

But then I think of the video of the killing of George Floyd and how I felt when I first saw (fragments of) it; I think of the role comedians play in society in general, and the role Black comedians play specifically. And I realise this is far more important than whether one Black British comedian was passed over for a job or didn't get his or her own sitcom. This goes to the very heart of the role comedy plays in society, and so, in writing this essay, I spoke to three of the most important Black British comedians at the moment – Gina Yashere, London Hughes and Mo Gilligan – as to why Black British comedians matter.

Over the last twenty years Gina has become one of the most successful Black British comedians. She has redefined both British comedy and discussions around Black British identity as a gay woman, which she has written about in her memoir Cack-Handed.

London Hughes was the first Black nominee of the prestigious

Edinburgh Comedy Award for Best Comedy Show in 2019 and bagged a Netflix comedy special.

Mo Gilligan has helped reshape what success looks like for a Black British comedian, gaining a global audience by uploading comedy sketches to social media without ever appearing on TV. Now, with his own Channel 4 show and Netflix special under his belt, he's the twenty-first-century Black British performer of whom every commissioner, green-lighter and programme-maker wants a piece.

All four of us have very different types of humour but during our conversations we unearthed some strikingly similar experiences; but most importantly, these conversations were of great help to me in my mission to articulate the question:

Why do Black British comedians matter?

To answer the question, I need to return to the harrowing footage of the killing of George Floyd.

When people ask me about George Floyd, I remember experiencing fragments of the horrific video that was made available via YouTube. I remember the triggering effect of watching moments of a man about to die and then actually dying under a policeman's knee. I found it, I still find it, incredibly disturbing (I still haven't watched the video in full – it's too much), and all the more disturbing because if I shave my head and regrow my goatee beard, I look (a bit) like George Floyd . . . in a certain light.

It has become somewhat of a cliché when people say 'representation matters' when it comes to diversity and the importance of role models. Women's rights activist and tennis legend Billie Jean King famously said, 'You have to see it to be it', meaning that to believe something is possible you have to *see* it first. But the idea also works in reverse in a troubling way that is sometimes difficult for Black people even to admit to ourselves:

When we see it, we feel it. When we see people who look like us being shot or abused or bullied on TV – there's a vicarious pain. We feel ourselves under that oppressive knee.

We do not just see ourselves in the positive role models; our children do not just identify with the positive characters on TV. We also can't help but see ourselves in the deaths of Breonna Taylor, Atatiana Jefferson, Stephon Clark, Botham Jean, Tamir Rice. When we hear the N-word being directed against a Black footballer, we feel its power also being reflected towards us. When we see an injustice inflicted on us as a group, we often feel it on a personal, individual level.

The George Floyd video shocked everybody around the world, but it shocked me in a deeply personal way. When I saw what I was able to watch of the video, I identified with George Floyd on a visceral level. I felt powerless. I felt alone. I felt voiceless. There is no clearer illustration of Black people's impotence in society than seeing the reasonable pleas of a Black man being ignored to the point of him being killed in broad daylight.

I didn't just feel sadness and pain for seeing a Black man being killed, I felt a deep sense of affinity for George Floyd, and the overarching feeling was one of powerlessness.

In contrast, I feel there is almost nowhere I am more powerful than when I am doing comedy.

The Black British comedian Ishmael Thomas, who was a regular on the BBC's sketch show *The Real McCoy* back in the 1990s, once said, 'There's nothing more dangerous to the powers that be than a stand-up comedian. You're speaking truth directly to the audience and delivering that truth while their guard is down because they're laughing. There's nothing scarier to the establishment than that.'

Black comedians have a long history of exercising this power, speaking our truth, and scaring the powers that be.

Richard Pryor was doing jokes about the police and choke-holds in the 1970s. Richard Pryor was doing Black lives matter before Black Lives Matter. Way before. Richard Pryor was talking about the difference between Black people and white people. He had an entire routine about, when a white middle-class person meets a policeman, they're like, 'Hi, Officer Thompson. Going bowling this evening?' Whereas when a Black person sees a police officer, they are saying to the officer, 'I am reaching into my pocket for my driving licence, because I don't want to be in "no accident"!'

Even though that was over thirty years ago, Richard Pryor was talking about police brutality and Black people getting shot in the street. Wrapped up in the veneer of comedy, he was able to talk about these issues on stage to a predominantly white audience, which meant that people were listening to him.

Comedians are testing people's boundaries as to what they think is funny and what isn't. Comedians can push those boundaries and make people think again about race, religion, sexism, or whatever subject matter they choose to talk about.

Comedians can walk on stage with a mic and, metaphorically, drop bombs – because a brain, and a mouth, and a microphone are incredibly powerful things.

Funny is power.

A comedian on stage with a mic is more able to broach unsayable subject matter than any politician, for instance. It's why politicians seek out people in the entertainment industry, particularly comedians, to enhance their cause; they know comedians can change the narrative and flip the script on how society views issues, and even how we, as a nation, view ourselves.

Comedians have power. Black comedians matter.

It is this ability, this power, to speak our truth that makes Black comedians so important. We are in a unique position that both speaks truth to power and through laughter comforts the afflicted. We are effectively both a weapon and a medicine. We are unique.

Talking to Gina Yashere, London Hughes and Mo Gilligan, I was struck by how they all recognised the power their comedy has to bring relief to people's daily hardship. Laughter really can be the best medicine, but in talking about their comedic influences, they, like me, mostly cited performers who were overtly political in their humour – mostly African American comedians – the only difference was that many of mine, like Richard Pryor, were from the 1970s and '80s, while they talked about comedians from the 1990s and name-checked comedy shows like *Def Comedy Jam*, *Fresh Prince of Bel Air* and *In Living Color*.

But I think it is wrong to try to categorise Black comedy as political or unpolitical. When I was working in New York, American comedian and writer Rick Siegel said to me, 'The effect when a big Black guy walks on stage is palpable. You can see the audience leaning forward, as in, "What's this guy going to say?"' Because our mere presence on any platform, saying whatever we want to say, is unique and almost by definition challenges the status quo.

This does not mean all our comedy needs to be overtly political. I'm just highlighting and recognising that our reality is powerful.

A writer and social commentator such as Afua Hirsch can write the 376-page book *Brit(ish)* dissecting the place of Black people in British society; historian David Olusoga can write volume after volume of the historical presence of Black people in the UK.

Alternatively, Mo Gilligan can walk on stage and perform a simple sketch about a school bully, which he does on his Netflix special, and we as an audience instinctively recognise that all the characters in the sketch are clearly from different ethnic backgrounds and yet it feels uniquely British.

Mo's characters couldn't be anything other than British; he brilliantly achieves in just a few minutes what many anti-racist campaigners, academics and commentators have been trying to achieve for decades. We are Black, we are British, and we are part of the very fabric of this society. And he does it all while making us laugh and, without us even realising, he changes our view of British society.

As Mo himself said when he spoke to me for this essay, 'What I am ultimately doing is paying homage to the people I grew up with' – referring to the specific characters he simply describes as the 'guys from my environment'.

Comedy both normalises Black people's reality while, at the same time, exposing it to people who may otherwise never come into contact with our experiences and our communities.

It is a point Gina Yashere makes when she describes how she used to do one set of jokes for a Black audience and another set of jokes for a white audience until the day her agent took her to one side and had a word with her: '. . . and he's like, "Why the f*** are you saving all the good stuff for the Blacks?"' Gina describes it as 'the best advice I ever got' as the realisation dawned on her, 'Oh, we're not living in different planets. We're all in England, we all are part of the same country. We're not aliens, we all live together, they will understand this. And then I started doing the same jokes to the white audience. Obviously,

I'd explain a couple of things in a different way to set up the jokes, as they may not know the specifics of my culture. But the characters that I was doing then, like the portrayal of my mom from my set, I reckon is universal, yeah? 'Cos everybody's got a mum.' For me, what Gina so beautifully illustrates is that our global humanity can be recognised through the simple act of joke-telling. Literally 'Everybody's got a mum.'

So much of my worldview has been shaped by jokes that have resonated with me and given me the ability to articulate feelings that have lain dormant within me. These jokes legitimise our experiences. And when we laugh collectively, we know that other people are experiencing the same thoughts and feelings.

We are not alone.

It builds and supports our communities. That is why I believe Rick Siegel was right: the audience leans forward when a Black comic enters because they want to know how he or she (and we) are going to change the world.

Now that is power!

It is a power we wield as Black comedians whether we want to or not. Gina Yashere describes it this way: 'I never saw myself as a political commentator. But just by virtue of who I am, I'm literally a walking political state. I just talk about my experiences. And it's my experiences that encompass my gayness, my Blackness, the fact I am a woman; simply reflecting this reality is political. And that's basically what I've done, I've never set out to be the spokesperson for Black lesbian identity. It wasn't a conscious thing. I'm just going to talk about my experiences from where I'm coming from. And I will explain why I feel a certain way, and why Black people feel a certain way to my audience and then, hopefully, they can come into my world and see it from my perspective. So that's what it was about – just talking about my experience and being able to come out that opened up that world for me, because then I was completely free, completely free to talk about anything I wanted to talk about.'

Every time I watch a Gina Yashere comedy show, she gives me a small glimpse of how she sees the world; the same is true for every Black comedian, and that is powerful. But what I have also learnt (just like Spider-Man's alias Peter Parker) is that with great power comes great responsibility.

I used to do a character called Joshua Yarlog. He was a Zimbabwean impressionist and did impersonations of people he'd seen on British television. The big joke was, because he was from Zimbabwe, all the impressions sounded the same. Also, the routine wasn't just about Joshua; he had a cameraman called Tunde and a soundman called Ziggy and they were making homemade, no-mod-cons, broke-ass television. Subconsciously, in many ways I think it was a metaphor about my own loneliness in an industry where there weren't very many Black people in positions of power in TV, let alone running their own TV channels.

However, instead of speaking my reality and view of the world, I reinforced other people's view of Black people. Because my writers and I knew it would get a knee-jerk, huge laugh from the mainstream (predominantly white) audience, in the first appearances as Josh, I stupidly wore a grass skirt and tribal makeup. I feel reticent to even write about this part of my show-business career. To admit your mistakes is always difficult, especially when those mistakes are made so publicly.

It took another Black man to help me realise what I was doing wrong: Gyearbuor Asante, who used to play Matthew (or as Desmond used to say it – Machu) on the long-running Channel 4 sitcom *Desmond's*. Gyearbuor took me to task for the faulty characterisation of a 'third world person' in the reception at London Weekend TV for a full hour. It was one of the ugliest experiences I've ever had, and I definitely didn't thank him at the time. However, a little while later, I realised how right he was.

As a result of my increasing fame – appearing on Saturday night TV and playing characters like Joshua Yarlog – I was booked to do a show at a naval base in the south of England. When I walked on stage, I saw that the entire front row was made up of white guys blacked up with shoe polish on their faces, wearing grass skirts and carrying spears. I was really, really upset, literally shaking. I had to walk off the stage because I was so offended by what I'd seen. But it not only made me realise just how powerful images are and how powerful your choices are as Black comedians, but also the importance of not being the 'only one' in the room. If Gyearbuor Asante had been my mentor or producer, I doubt I would have made the same mistakes.

Which is why I believe as a Black comedian you are either speaking your reality or someone else's. It's fine to talk about race, but it's not fine to be racist. It's fine to talk about sex, but it's not fine to be sexist. You have to make your choices, and the choices have to be informed by your political awareness. And that is why our comedy is inherently political.

London Hughes tells the story of going to the BBC and the producers wanting her to do sketches about claiming her 'giro'.

'I had no idea what a giro was. And they were like, "Whaaaat? *Come on, London!* You know, what a giro is" . . . and I honestly did not. I said, "What? D'you think just because I'm Black that I know what a giro is?"' (Dear reader, at this stage I should explain that 'giro' is slang for a welfare cheque; giro's etymology is Italian in origin, meaning a circulation of money.) And why *would*

London Hughes know what a giro is, as no one in her family had ever claimed one.

The fact is when London tells her own truth, tells the world from her perspective as a Black woman, she is award-winning – as demonstrated by her one-woman show (I'm just gonna write this – like pulling a plaster off) 'To Catch a Dick'. That's the title of London Hughes's hit show. It's not about how they caught Richard Nixon . . .

We can make a joke which basically 'slut shames' Black women for being sexually active. Or we can joke about Black women's sexuality in a way which empowers them, as London Hughes does. We can mimic the character of a Nigerian parent which confirms the worst negative stereotypes, or we can pay homage to our own mothers which introduces and informs everyone to key archetypes in our lives, in the way that Gina Yashere does.

Performing our reality destroys racist narratives and stereotypes. This is not the same as saying we need positive role models. Mo Gilligan described it to me this way: 'We like to see ourselves represented in comedy but in the right manner, in a positive light and in a funny way.' For me, a positive light is not the same as a 'positive role model'. If all our Black characters had to be 'positive role models', there would be no quicker way to destroy our humour. There is a strength in simply reflecting our reality, which is what Mo is doing and that is what I believe the best Black comedians do. But the tragic fact is that there are not enough Black British comedians. Or I should rephrase that – there are not enough of us who are given the opportunity to speak our reality.

From the time I was sixteen up until very recently, I've pretty much done a TV series every year, from the mid-seventies to the mid-noughties, but I've been the exception. In that time there have been very few sitcoms that featured Black or brown people as their focus point on British TV, and even fewer sketch shows.

(Shout out to *The Real McCoy*, *Desmond's*, *Goodness Gracious Me*, *Little Miss Jocelyn*, *The Javone Prince Show*, *The Kumars at No. 42*, and the beat goes on . . .)

If we believe Black British comedy matters, we must look at the reasons why so we can increase the number of Black British comedians.

First, we need to look at the career paths of Black comedians. To understand the obstacles facing us, I need to briefly explain how the standard career path of white, predominantly male, comedians works and how this can hurt Black people.

In the UK there are several 'comedy circuits' – venues up and down the country where stand-up comedians can perform. There's the 'alternative comedy circuit', the 'Northern comedy circuit', the 'university comedy circuit' and the 'Black comedy circuit'. These circuits are useful for comedians not just in terms of paying the bills but also in honing one's craft.

If all goes to plan, from these comedy circuits you then progress to the Edinburgh Fringe where you perform, hopefully get noticed by TV executives, and network with anyone and everyone in the world of comedy.

You might then get to write a joke for some of the long-running comedy strands on BBC Radio 4 and TV and, if fortune is really going your way, you might even be a panellist on shows like *8 out of 10 Cats* or *Have I Got News for You* or *Would I Lie to You*.

Then, eventually, once you've been through ALL THAT, you are finally recognised, get your own show and hit the big time.

Easy-peasy lemon squeezy.

That's a very basic description of the standard career path for white middle-class male comedians.

It might not happen in the exact order I have outlined – you might get to write a few jokes for radio before going to Edinburgh, for example; these things do not happen in neat succession but usually overlap. But the overall picture is one that most comedians in the UK will recognise.

Also, some comedians in privileged positions can jump a few of these stages. I heard a story about somebody who'd been to Oxbridge, and while listening to a Radio 4 comedy programme, said, 'I can do better than that. I'm going to ring my friend who's the producer of that programme and get a job.' Not *ask* for a job. *Get* a job. This guy rang his contact at Radio 4 and got the job!

However, when it comes to Black, brown or disabled comedians, not only have I never heard of a comedian being able to jump any of these stages, I have yet to meet a single one where this career path has worked in their favour. We are literally having to make it up as we go along. Do you have any idea how difficult it is for individuals to create their own career paths?

London Hughes described to me how she had a rude awakening when she realised the standard career path was not going to work for her; she says (only half ironically), 'I just *assumed* after winning the Funny Women Award in 2009, that I was gonna have this amazing career in comedy, because clearly I'm good enough, right?

'If you look at old interviews after I'd just won, the journos are saying things like, "So, what's next for you?" And I'm like, "Yeah man, I'm gonna have my own TV show, I'm gonna have movies." I'm *so* naive. Systemic racism didn't even factor into my brain at that point. The way I thought of it was just like, "If you are a nice person and are talented, you will go far." And I was *all* those things. And I had proved that I was good enough. Of *course*, I'm going to be a comedy great.'

In London's case, it took another experience to make her realise she would never make it in the UK. She tells the story of teaming up with Whoopi Goldberg – 'The biggest Black female comedian on the planet' – and shooting a taster tape for the two of them to do a travel show. Every UK broadcaster saw that sampler tape and turned it down. It was after that 'failure' that London realised if she could not make it in the UK with the support of one of the biggest stars in the world, she would never make it – and she left for the US.

Black British talent hitting a glass ceiling and moving to the States to find success is a familiar tale, and the sad reality is my conversations with all three Black British comedians were over Zoom as they ate breakfast in the US.

But while these stories are often framed in terms of the injustice done to the individual comedians, it is so much more than that. For every Black British comedian who is able to make it in America, there are countless more whose talents are neglected, overlooked or dismissed.

The end result is our stories not being told; our reality not being recognised. Our power being curtailed.

A large part of the reason why the standard career paths don't work for us is due to the gatekeepers at each level – from the TV and radio producers to the heads of writers' rooms, from the commissioning editors to the channel controllers. And these gatekeepers are notoriously 'undiverse'. As I outlined in the book I co-wrote with Marcus Ryder, *Access All Areas*, they are disproportionately from the 3.1 per cent – the proportion of the UK population which is white, able-bodied, heterosexual, male and from London.

Now I have to be careful here, because I have to work with the gatekeepers and, as we also said in *Access All Areas*, it's very difficult for people of colour to whistleblow on an institution they are hoping to work for. And the fact of the matter is it isn't about specific individuals – some of my best friends are white, able-bodied, heterosexual men from London (please read my next pitch. No, I'm serious, *please* read it . . .) – it is about a general culture which is created when you don't have diversity/ inclusion in positions of power.

It is a culture that promotes people and comedians they recognise and, all too often, overlooks comedy they do not recognise, despite the best of intentions. The running joke between Black British comedians is how gatekeepers are always telling us, 'You're pushing against an open door,' and yet we keep asking ourselves, 'Hang on a minute, if the door's open, why am I still pushing?'

I would be dishonest if I pretended that most Black comedians didn't have their own personal horror stories when it came to gatekeepers. More than ten years on, Gina Yashere's anger still burns when she talks about her experience during one meeting with a gatekeeper at a time when she was performing sell-out shows all over the UK.

'I remember going into a meeting at Channel 4 and trying to pitch a show with me at the helm. And this woman said to me, and this was in my f***ing face, Lenny, "We've already got Richard Blackwood." She said that to my f***ing face! So, this is what I was up against and trying to overcome. You know, to them, I was only *Black famous* or the *hood famous*, as they call it in America. So, I was already selling out theatres to the Black audience, but I was trying to encompass everyone, in order to get to that next level.'

Her obstacle was a gatekeeper who couldn't see past the Richard Blackwood scenario . . . the 'One in/One out' problem.

If we believe Black comedians matter, we need to change the diversity of our gatekeepers.

But what I am also learning from the next generation of Black comedians, who are coming up like wildfire, is that we need to forge career paths that change our relationship to gatekeepers, and that means examining what we mean when we use the term 'gatekeeper'. When we use that term, we are in fact describing a power relationship. A gatekeeper has the higher status and power; we are lower status and at a disadvantage when we show them our wares.

Today's younger Black comedians are subverting that narrative. Mo Gilligan became famous through posting his videos online and grew his audience directly. As he described it to me, 'I gained enough audience to say, you know what, I'm gonna do it this way. So, I never was in a place of having a gatekeeper because I'm bringing my own audience. And as far as we're concerned, we don't even need to go through the gate. We're already in the building. They need my audience, you know, they want that eighteen to twenty-five demographic, I have it right here on Instagram. So, let's find a way that we can make something together that can work.'

This is not a confrontational relationship, where Mo is angry with the gatekeepers, and saying 'f*** you!'; nor is this a relationship where he's having to beg for acceptance. Mo has effectively shifted the power balance when he enters the boardroom to negotiate with a gatekeeper – they are two equals discussing business rather than a boss deciding whether or not to throw a minion a bone.

And whether it is in comedy or in other parts of our lives – that is *all* under-represented groups are asking for: equality.

So, let's end how we began. What is there to joke about in events such as Black Lives Matter, police brutality and the tragic last few moments of George Floyd's life?

Mo Gilligan told me he likes to explicitly separate politics from his comedy. 'When it comes to speaking on, like, real issues, I think I always try to separate that from my comedy. Because when I am serious, I want to be taken seriously; when I am making jokes, I want people to laugh.'

While I respect that position, for me, and some other comedians, I think it is harder to draw a neat line. But there is a line.

A death at the hands of police brutality will never be funny.

I think the way the government and the police have dealt with it, the laissez-faire attitude of our governing bodies towards their constituencies, the forces of law and order that work for them – it's OK to make jokes about all those things; it's how Chris Rock, Wanda Sykes and many more pay the rent.

Gina Yashere, now based in the US, also feels that the death of George Floyd, and the discussions and activism that followed, illustrated the importance of Black British comedians to not only cement our place in British society, but also to help build bridges with Black people internationally and across the diaspora.

'In my comedy I'm telling African Americans, Black people in America, we feel you, we have the same experiences. Racism is systemic. It is embedded in the psyche, in the very fabric of our societies. Black people still die at the hands of police officers in England even without guns. If they don't beat us to death, they hang us in cells, they strangle us. It still happens. So Black

British comedians do matter. We have to speak out. Our voices must be heard. And we need these platforms. We're not getting the same platforms.'

Without a safe space in the centre space, there is no platform from which to speak.

Black British comedians matter because our comedy enables us to be seen.

I was going to finish this piece with a clever turn of phrase by saying Black British comedians matter because we provide not only a punchline for Black lives but also – and more importantly – a lifeline.

But then London Hughes put it best: 'Black comedians matter because Black laughter matters.'

BLACK BRITISH LIVES MATTER

Your responsibility doesn't start where my survival ends

MARCUS RYDER

*While this book attempts to give voice to the discussions sur-
rounding why Black British lives matter, all too often for Black
people police brutality and our experiences of racism are painful
issues to articulate and explore. In this very personal concluding
essay to the book, Marcus Ryder wanted to reflect on this
experience.*

*Marcus Ryder has over twenty-five years' experience of working
in television and journalism and is a leader on the issue of diversity
in the media.*

1989

I am an eighteen-year-old Black man. It is about seven o'clock
at night. My parents are going through a messy separation
which would eventually lead to an even more acrimonious
divorce. I have just gone to the family home where my father
is still living to pick up a few belongings and now I am making
my way to my mother's new rented flat about twenty minutes'
walk away.

I am feeling sorry for myself, in the way only a self-absorbed
adolescent can when their parents are going through the next
stage of their relationship which would see them never talk to

each other again – except through their respective lawyers – after more than twenty years of marriage.

I am not thinking about my parents – or at least I am not thinking about the turmoil they must be going through. I am eighteen. I am thinking about myself. I am thinking how unfair my life is that I am now living between two homes.

I am thinking about the fact I am failing Chemistry A-level and just can't grasp the concept of valency.

And, I am wondering if Nichole Mayfield-Stewart really was too busy to come to the phone when I called her the day before or whether she has broken up with me and I just don't realise it yet.

Like I said, I was a typical self-obsessed teenager.

I remember all these things thirty years later because the evening is indelibly tattooed in my memory due to what happened next.

It is early spring and dark. As I walk along the main road, there is a stretch of wasteland just to my right.

A car screeches to a halt beside me and four white men, wearing jeans and light jackets, jump out and start running towards me, shouting. I don't know how they got out the car so fast but two are in front of me, running up to my face. I look towards the car and two are behind me. I look to my right and see the wasteland.

I brace myself and take a step to get ready to run into the wasteland. I hear one of the men shout something about police.

The wasteland is pitch black.

Where I am at that moment is bathed in streetlight. There are no other pedestrians but cars are going past quite regularly.

If I do not outrun them in the wasteland, it will just be me and four white men under the cover of darkness. They are shouting something about police and they might be police – I don't know. But I make the split-second calculation that it is probably better to stay in the light.

I don't run.

I just stand still.

The four white men have now surrounded me and one of them tells me they are police officers. He shows me a badge. I can't really see it; even if I could, I don't really know what I would be looking for.

I accept him at his word.

He jokes that he thought I was going to run, and it wouldn't have been good for me if I'd run. He's laughing. I don't really see the funny side of it. I just look down.

He tells me there has been a spate of burglaries in the neighbourhood and I match the description of the person committing the burglaries.

I listen.

They need to look in my bag, and search me 'just to make sure you are not carrying a weapon'. I'm not really sure what a weapon has to do with burglaries but I hand over my bag. Two of the men take it away and look in it. The other two get me to turn out my pockets and open my jacket and they do a cursory body search. I am not carrying a weapon but if I had been they would not have discovered it the way they searched me.

They ask me a few questions about where I am going and where I live. Due to my parents' marital situation, they are surprisingly difficult questions to answer and I find myself divulging far more personal information than I want to, trying to explain, and even justify, why I am walking along a busy high road at seven in the evening.

The two officers with my bag return it to me.

All four of them politely thank me for my time and get back in their car and drive off.

I walk to my mother's flat. I don't tell her what happened. I am not entirely sure why, but I do not want to relive the whole experience again and I know my mother will just have a lot of questions that would require too much emotional effort to answer. Worse yet, I am worried she might make us go down to the police station and complain about what has happened to 'her little boy'. I don't need that. I don't need to see more police. And, on top of that, what will it achieve?

So, when I reach her flat, I just eat dinner, fail at my Chemistry homework, and go to bed.

1992

Three years later, I attend an anti-racism demonstration in Woolwich. It is actually a counter-demonstration march. The British National Party (BNP) has been given permission to march on the first anniversary of Rolan Adams's death. Rolan Adams was a fifteen-year-old Black teenager who was killed by racist thugs two years before Stephen Lawrence's murder, and in the same area of London.

The anti-racist march is to protest against the BNP's march. The BNP don't mention Rolan Adams by name but, by the date and area they have chosen to march, the message is clear enough.

I attend the anti-racism march with four friends. We witness a few scuffles between the police and some of the other marchers. The confrontations are far off in the distance, we can't even get close as other police are blocking us. To be honest, I am not even sure I want to get close.

The whole march seems to be a non-event. We never even see the BNP. After a few hours, we go back to our car to drive home.

Anyone who knows Woolwich in South-East London will know it is a series of dual carriageways with multiple round-abouts.

As we start to pull off, we see a van full of police officers on the other side of the dual carriageway. We all stare at the police in the van. The police stare back.

We start driving home.

The police van reaches the first roundabout and turns around to follow us. It flashes us. We pull over.

A few of the police get out of their van and approach us, telling the five of us to get out of the car. They split us up and then question us individually. I am questioned by two officers by the police van, its doors still open. They ask me my name, my age, where I am from, where I live, why I am there. I duly answer all their questions.

All of a sudden something happens – I see several of the police officers manhandling one of my friends towards the police van. The friend keeps asking what's going on, what has he done?

They bundle him towards the police van. The two officers questioning me are taken by surprise, as am I, and we are directly in the path of getting my friend into the van.

The result is they bump into us and a number of us fall down.

It's confusing but, the next thing I know, I am handcuffed and being walked into the police van where my friend is already sitting quietly – also handcuffed.

We are taken to a police station.

A few hours later my mother picks us up.

My friend thanks me that I was in the police van with him. If I hadn't been in the van, he fears what the police would have done to him. I have no idea if he's being overdramatic, and I hadn't intentionally got into the van. But I accept his thanks all the same.

My Jamaican mother tells me off for even attending an anti-racist march.

We do not talk in the car on the way back home.

2021

I am collecting the final completed essays for the anthology I am editing with Lenny Henry on Black British Lives Matter.

I am worried.

We do not have an essay that directly addresses police brutality of Black people. Possibly the core issue of the Black Lives Matter movement. Numerous essays touch on the issue, not least 'Black British Police Matter' and 'Black British Lawyers Matter'. Also numerous essays discuss the murder of George Floyd and the parallels in Britain. But there isn't one that directly talks from the victim's perspective – from a Black person's perspective.

I am eating breakfast and I tell my Black British wife that I think we need an extra essay.

We argue.

Hannah tells me that all we ever talk about is police brutality against Black people. There are more than enough essays and articles written about the issue. It dominates and suffocates all other discussion around Black Lives Matter.

She tells me society's responsibility for the racism it inflicts upon Black British people does not start where our survival ends.

I cite the facts:

Black people are more than twice as likely to die in police custody as our white counterparts.

According to an independent review into deaths in police custody in 2017, 16 per cent of people who died after the use of force were Black – more than twice the percentage originally arrested, and five times more than the number of Black people in the population.

And, if you forget about deaths but just look at Black people's interactions with the police, the numbers are even worse.

In 2018/19 Black people were more than nine times as likely as white people to be stopped and searched by police.

And the police were more likely to use force against us – more than five times more likely compared to white people, to be precise.

My wife sighs – she knows my love of statistics – and she has heard all of these, or similar, before.

'When Stephen Lawrence was knifed to death, Doreen Lawrence did not set up an anti-knife charity. She didn't even set up an anti-racism charity,' my wife tells me. 'Doreen set up a charity for aspiring young architects because that was Stephen's ambition and that was the life that was cut short – that was the Black British life that mattered. These essays focus on the architects of the future, they do not dwell on the knife.'

'But this book is about capturing the unique experience of Black British people,' I reply. 'Police brutality is part of our reality.'

'There is more to our reality – and it feels that is all I hear about.'

We finish our breakfast in silence.

Now

We should not be silent. Twelve names that should not be forgotten.

An incomplete list of Black people who have died in police custody in Britain:[1]

CHERRY GROCE (1985)

CYNTHIA JARRETT (1985)

JOY GARDNER (1993)

ROGER SYLVESTER (1999)

SEAN RIGG (2008)

JIMMY MUBENGA (2010)

DAVID 'SMILEY CULTURE' EMMANUEL (2011)

MARK DUGGAN (2011)

SARAH REED (2016)

MZEE MOHAMMED-DALEY (2016)

DALIAN ATKINSON (2016)

TREVOR SMITH (2019)

NOTES

BLACK BRITISH WRITERS MATTER

1 Toni Morrison, 'A Humanist View', speech given during Black Studies Center public dialogue, Part 2, Portland State University (30 May 1975).

BLACK BRITISH HEALTH MATTERS

1 Viet-Hai Phung et al., *Ethnicity and Prehospital Emergency Care Provided by Ambulance Services*, Race Equality Foundation (May 2015).

2 'ICNARC Report on COVID-19 in Critical Care' (10 April 2020).

3 Public Health England, *Beyond the Data: Understanding the Impact of COVID-19 on BAME Groups* (2020).

4 The Food Foundation, *The Broken Plate* (2018), https://foodfoundation. org.uk/wp-content/uploads/2019/02/The-Broken-Plate.pdf.

5 Aviva, *Health Check UK Report* (Autumn 2016).

6 S. K. Malone et al., 'Ethnic Differences in Sleep Duration and Morning-Evening Type in a Population Sample', *Chronobiology International*, 33(1), 10–21, https://doi.org/10.3109/07420528.2015.1107729.

7 T. Bignall, et al., *Racial Disparities in Mental Health: Literature and Evidence Review*, Race Equality Foundation (2019).

8 'Black Women in the UK Four Times More Likely to Die in Pregnancy or Childbirth', *Guardian* (15 Jan. 2021), https://www.theguardian.com/ global-development/2021/jan/15/black-women-in-the-uk-four-times-more-likely-to-die-in-pregnancy-or-childbirth.

9 H.M Harb et al., 'Ethnicity and Miscarriage: A Large Prospective Observational Study and Meta-analysis' (2014), https://doi.org/10.1016/j.fertnstert. 2014.07.276.

10 Nadine White, 'Black Women Were Tortured to Develop Gynaecology Methods. Midwives Want them Remembered', HuffPost (29 July 2020).

11 Rohan Deb Roy, ' Decolonise Science: Time to End Another Imperial Era', *The Conversation* (5 April 2018).

12 A. Singhal, Y.-Y. Tien, R. Y. Hsia, 'Racial-Ethnic Disparities in Opioid Prescriptions at Emergency Department Visits for Conditions Commonly Associated with Prescription Drug Abuse', *PLoS ONE*, 11(8) (2016), 1–14, https://doi.org/10.1371/journal.pone.0159224.

13 Emily Gersema, 'Racism Has a Toxic Effect', Science Daily (31 May 2019), https://www.sciencedaily.com/releases/2019/05/190531100558.htm.

14 Boris Johnson, 'Rather than Tear Some People Down We Should Build Others Up', *Telegraph* (14 June 2020).

BLACK BRITISH ARCHITECTURE MATTERS

1 Stuart Hall, 'Cultural Identity and Diaspora', in Jonathan Rutherford (ed.), *Identity: Community, Culture, Difference* (London: Lawrence & Wishart, 1990), p. 225.

2 'Fred Moten on Figuring It Out'. The Poetry Project – event funded in part by Poets & Writers, Inc., through Public Funds from the New York City Department of Cultural Affairs, in Partnership with the City Council, 2015.

3 Stuart Hall, 'Racism and Reaction', *Five Views of Multi-racial Britain* (London: Commission for Racial Equality, 1978), p. 31. See also Stuart Hall, 'The Narrative Construction of Reality: An Interview', *Southern Review*, 17, no. 1 (1984), pp. 3–17.

4 Paul Gilroy, *There Ain't No Black in the Union Jack: The Cultural Politics of Race and Nation* (London: Routledge, 1992), p. 204.

5 Stuart Hall quoted in Alison Donnell (ed.), 'Introduction' in *Companion to Contemporary Black British Culture* (Abingdon: Routledge, 2002), p. xii.

6 Kobena Mercer, *Welcome to the Jungle: New Positions in Black Cultural Studies* (New York: Routledge, 2006). See also James Procter, *Writing Black Britain, 1948–98: An Interdisciplinary Anthology* (Manchester: Manchester University Press, 2006), pp. 1–11.

BLACK BRITISH LAWYERS MATTER

1 Ministry of Justice, *Statistics on Race and the Criminal Justice System* (2018), https://assets.publishing.service.gov.uk/government/uploads/system/uploads/attachment_data/file/849201/race-cjs-2018-infographic.pdf.

2 There were six stop and searches for every thousand white people, compared with fifty-four for every thousand Black people. Stop and search rate per thousand people, by ethnicity: Home Office, 'Stop and Search' (22 Feb. 2021), https://www.ethnicity-facts-figures.service.gov.uk/crime-

justice-and-the-law/policing/stop-and-search/latest#by-ethnicity.

3 There were thirty-two arrests for every thousand Black people, and ten arrests for every thousand white people. Arrest rate per thousand people by ethnicity: Home Office, 'Arrests: 3. By ethnicity' (17 Sept. 2020), https://www.ethnicity-facts-figures.service.gov.uk/crime-justice-and-the-law/policing/number-of-arrests/latest#by-ethnicity.

4 Sir William Macpherson of Cluny, *The Stephen Lawrence Inquiry: Report* (Feb. 1999), paragraph 6.11, https://assets.publishing.service.gov.uk/government/uploads/system/uploads/attachment_data/file/277111/4262.pdf.

5 Macpherson report, paragraph 22.

6 Macpherson report, paragraph 24.

7 Macpherson report, paragraph 25.

8 Macpherson report, paragraph 26.

9 'What is the Gangs Matrix?' *Amnesty Magazine* (18 May 2020), https://www.amnesty.org.uk/london-trident-gangs-matrix-metropolitan-police.

10 Vikram Dodd, 'A Thousand Young, Black Men Removed from Met Gang Violence Prediction Database', *Guardian* (3 Feb. 2021), https://www.theguardian.com/uk-news/2021/feb/03/a-thousand-young-black-men-removed-from-met-gang-violence-prediction-database.

11 Dodd, 'A Thousand Young, Black Men'.

12 Ministry of Justice, *Black, Asian and Minority Ethnic Disproportionality in the Criminal Justice System in England and Wales* (2016), table A2.1, p. 37, https://assets.publishing.service.gov.uk/government/uploads/system/uploads/attachment_data/file/639261/bame-disproportionality-in-the-cjs.pdf.

13 Centre for Justice Innovation, *Building Trust: How Our Courts Can Improve the Criminal Court Experience for Black, Asian, and Minority Ethnic Defendants* (2017), p. 11, https://justiceinnovation.org/sites/default/files/media/documents/2019-03/building-trust.pdf.

14 C. Thomas, 'Ethnicity and Fairness of Jury Trials in England and Wales 2006–2014', *Criminal Law Review*, 11 (2017).

15 Ministry of Justice, *Statistics on Race and the Criminal Justice System* (2018).

16 Ministry of Justice, *Statistics on Race and the Criminal Justice System* (2018).

17 Baber Yasin and Georgina Sturge, *Ethnicity and the Criminal Justice System: What Does Recent Data Say on Over-representation?* House of Commons Library (2 Oct. 2020), https://commonslibrary.parliament.uk/ethnicity-and-the-criminal-justice-system-what-does-recent-data-say/.

18 Sentencing Council, *Investigating the association between an offender's sex and ethnicity and the sentence imposed at the Crown Court for drug offences* (15 Jan. 2020), https://www.sentencingcouncil.org.uk/publications/item/investigating-the-association-between-an-offenders-sex-and-ethnicity-and-the-sentence-imposed-at-the-crown-court-for-drug-offences/.

19 James Ball, Owen Boycott and Simon Rogers, 'Race Variation in Jail Sentences, Study Suggests', *Guardian* (26 Nov. 2011), https://www.theguardian.com/law/2011/nov/25/ethnic-variations-jail-sentences-study.

20 Centre for Justice Innovation, *Building Trust* (March 2017), p. 7, https://justiceinnovation.org/sites/default/files/media/documents/2019-03/building-trust.pdf.

BLACK BRITISH MENTAL HEALTH MATTERS

1 Adult Psychiatric Morbidity Survey, https://digital.nhs.uk/data-and-information/publications/statistical/adult-psychiatric-morbidity-survey/adult-psychiatric-morbidity-survey-survey-of-mental-health-and-wellbeing-england-2014.

2 Michael Buchanan, '"Discriminatory" Mental Health System Overhauled', *BBC News* (13 Jan. 2021), https://www.bbc.co.uk/news/health-55639104.

3 Charlotte Carter, 'Mental Health Act Overhaul Will Not Tackle Racial Disparities Without Societal Change, Experts Warn', Community Care (20 Jan. 2021), https://www.communitycare.co.uk/2021/01/20/mental-health-act-overhaul-will-tackle-racial-disparities-without-societal-change-experts-warn/.

4 Carter, 'Mental Health Act Overhaul'.

5 Carter, 'Mental Health Act Overhaul'.

6 Speaking on *Women's Hour*, BBC Radio 4 (2 April 2014).

7 Woody Morris, 'Black Lives Matter in Rural England', *BBC Newsbeat* (6 July 2020), https://www.bbc.co.uk/news/av/newsbeat-53283565.

8 BJCT, 'BJTC Alumni on Black Lives Matter: Marverine Duffy' (June 2020), https://bjtc.org.uk/2212/it-needs-to-be-made-clear-that-when-a-bame-journalist-is-hired-its-not-just-a-diversity-hire-this-is-a-mindset-that-needs-to-be-quashed-bjtc-a; Charlotte Tobitt, '"Culture of Fear and Cliquiness" in UK Newsrooms Must End to Move Diversity Conversation Forward', Press Gazette (9 July 2020), https://www.pressgazette.co.uk/culture-of-fear-and-cliquiness-in-uk-newsrooms-must-end-to-move-diversity-conversation-forward/.

9 Dixon-Fyle, S., et al., *Diversity Wins: How Inclusion Matters*, McKinsey

(2020), https://www.mckinsey.com/featured-insights/diversity-and-inclusion/diversity-wins-how-inclusion-matters#

10 Cabinet Office, *Race Disparity Audit: Summary Findings from the Ethnicity Facts and Figures website* (Oct. 2017), https://assets.publishing.service.gov.uk/government/uploads/system/uploads/attachment_data/file/686071/Revised_RDA_report_March_2018.pdf.

11 S. McManus, P. Bebbington, R. Jenkins, T. Brugha (eds), *Mental Health and Wellbeing in England: Adult Psychiatric Morbidity Survey 2014* (Leeds: NHS Digital, 2016), https://files.digital.nhs.uk/pdf/q/3/mental_health_and_wellbeing_in_england_full_report.pdf.

BLACK BRITISH CHARITIES MATTER

1 Lizzie Dearden, 'Black Lives Matter: 210,000 People Have Joined UK Protests and Counter-demonstrations since George Floyd's Death', *Independent* (15 June 2020), https://www.independent.co.uk/news/uk/home-news/black-lives-matter-protests-uk-george-floyd-police-statue-arrests-a9567496.html.

2 Nadine White, 'Black Lives Matter Sparks "Largest Racial Justice Movement in UK History"', HuffPost (13 Nov. 2020), https://www.huffingtonpost.co.uk/entry/black-lives-matter-petitions-protests-racial-justice_uk_5fa12dc2c5b6c588dc9561f2.

3 Toni Morrison, 'Racism and Fascism', *The Journal of Negro Education*, 64, 3 (Summer 1995: Myths and Realities: African Americans and the Measurement of Human Abilities). Accessed 26 Jan. 2021.

4 Sanjiv Lingayah et al., *Common Ground, Contested Space*, Runnymede Trust and Voice4Change England (Dec. 2020)

5 Sanjiv Lingayah, 'Understanding How Britain really Thinks about Race Is Vital to Tackling Racism', *Independent* (30 Nov. 2020), https://www.independent.co.uk/voices/britain-race-racism-black-lives-matter-b1762975.html.

6 Afua Hirsch, 'On Race in 2020, We Took a Step Forward – From Minus 10 to Zero. We Can't Afford to Go Back', *Guardian* (1 Jan. 2021), https://www.theguardian.com/commentisfree/2021/jan/01/race-2020-step-forward-structural-racism-government.

7 'Kimberly Latrice Jones BLM Video Speech Transcript', Rev.com (8 June 2020), https://www.rev.com/blog/transcripts/kimberly-latrice-jones-blm-video-speech-transcript. Accessed 26 Jan. 2021.

8 George Padmore Institute, 'Ephemeral Material Collected by John La

Rose, 1952–1966', https://catalogue.georgepadmoreinstitute.org/records/ JLR. Accessed 26 Jan. 2021.

9 Rebecca Cooney, 'Charity Boards Less Diverse than UK's Biggest Companies, Says Report', *Third Sector* (19 April 2018), https://www.thirdsector.co.uk/charity-boards-less-diverse-uks-biggest-companies-says-report/ governance/article/1462582.

BLACK BRITISH BUSINESS MATTERS

1 Toni Morrison, 'A Humanist View', speech given during Black Studies Center public dialogue, Part 2, Portland State University (30 May 1975).

BLACK BRITISH ATHLETES MATTER

1 Baroness McGregor-Smith, *Race in the Workplace: The McGregor-Smith Review* (Department for Business, Energy and Industrial Strategy 2017), https://assets.publishing.service.gov.uk/government/uploads/system/ uploads/attachment_data/file/594336/race-in-workplace-mcgregor-smith-review.pdf.

2 Stuart Hall, 'Tearing Down the Veil', *Guardian* (22 Feb. 2003), https://www.theguardian.com/books/2003/feb/22/featuresreviews.guardianreview30; Delgreco K. Wilson, 'The Re-Emergence of Black Consciousness Within the Sports Community', The Black Cager (16 Nov. 2015), https://delgrecowilson.com/2015/11/16/the-re-emergence-of-black-consciousness-within-the-sports-community/.

3 Ben Carrington, *Race, Sport and Politics: The Sporting Black Disapora* (Los Angeles and London: Sage, 2010).

4 Jeanette Kwakye, 'As a Black Woman, You Have to Leave Part of Yourself Back in the Changing Room – but Attitudes Are Changing', *Telegraph* (25 June 2020), https://www.telegraph.co.uk/athletics/2020/06/25/black-woman-have-leave-part-back-changing-room-attitudes-changing/.

5 Katarina Johnson-Thompson, '"I've Been a Black Woman Longer than I've Been an Athlete": Katarina Johnson-Thompson on Her Personal Battle Against Racism', *Vogue UK* (30 Aug. 2020), https://www.vogue.co.uk/ arts-and-lifestyle/article/katarina-johnson-thompson-racism.

6 Leah Asmelash and Nadeem Muaddi, 'Serena Williams Says the Day She Stops Fighting for Equality "Will Be the Day I'm in my Grave"', CNN (13 July 2019), https://edition.cnn.com/2019/07/13/us/serena-williams-wimbledon-equality-trnd/index.html.

7 Sean Gregory, 'Serena Williams Finishes the Fight for Historic Win at Australian Open', Fortune (28 Jan. 2017), https://fortune.com/2017/01/28/serena-williams-australian-open/.

8 Ben Bloom, 'Kadeena Cox Interview: "A Cyclist Said Racism Does Not Exist in Britain. Are You Serious?"', Telegraph Women's Sport Supplement (25 June 2020), https://www.telegraph.co.uk/womens-sport/2020/06/25/kadeena-cox-interview-cyclist-said-racism-does-not-exist-britain/.

9 Dina Asher-Smith, 'Think Racism Hasn't Affected Me? It's There Almost Every Day', Telegraph (25 June 2020), https://www.telegraph.co.uk/athletics/2020/06/25/think-racism-hasnt-affected-almost-every-day/

10 Dave Zirin, 'The Sports Strikes Against Racism Have Not Been Coopted', The Nation (31 Aug. 2020), https://www.thenation.com/article/society/nba-blm-strike/; Dave Zirin, Game Over: How Politics Has Turned the Sports World Upside Down (New York: The New Press, 2013).

11 'Coco Gauff Demands Change in Powerful Black Lives Matter Speech', BBC Sport (4 June 2020), https://www.bbc.co.uk/sport/tennis/52919468.

12 Ruairi Carberry, '"Owners Need to Get on the Same Page as Athletes": Dr Harry Edwards on US Boycotts', OTB SPORTS (1 Sept. 2020), https://www.otbsports.com/other-sports/sports-boycott-usa-1069593.

13 'Black Lives Matter: State of Sport in the UK – and What Needs to Happen Next', Telegraph Sport (23 June 2020), https://www.telegraph.co.uk/sport/2020/06/23/black-lives-matter-state-sport-uk-needs-happen-next/.

14 Michael Short, 'Sport Inequality: Some Sports "Dominated" by the Privately Educated – Social Mobility Report', BBC Sport (24 June 2019), https://www.bbc.co.uk/sport/48745093; The Sutton Trust and the Social Mobility Commission, Elitist Britain 2019: The Educational Backgrounds of Britain's Leading people (2019), https://assets.publishing.service.gov.uk/government/uploads/system/uploads/attachment_data/file/811045/Elitist_Britain_2019.pdf.

15 Derek A. Bardowell, 'Racism Is a Permanent Stain on Sport. Maybe this Time It Will Be Different', GQ (2 July 2020), https://www.gq-magazine.co.uk/sport/article/racism-sport.

16 'Raheem Sterling Speaks Out on Racism following the Death of George Floyd', BBC Sport (8 June 2020), https://www.bbc.co.uk/sport/football/52959292.

17 Sport England, '"Sport for All" Highlights Ethnicity Gap in Sport' (27 Jan. 2020), https://www.sportengland.org/news/sport-for-all.

18 Sean Ingle, 'Britain's Sporting "Apartheid" Must End', says Sport England's Chris Grant', *Guardian* (7 June 2020), https://www.theguardian.com/sport/2020/jun/07/britains-sporting-apartheid-must-end-says-sport-englands-chris-grant.

19 *Newsnight*, BBC (7 June 2020).

20 Ben Rumsby, 'Special Investigation: Just Five Black Women Among 415 Leading Sports Board Members', *Telegraph Sport* (25 June 2020), https://www.telegraph.co.uk/womens-sport/2020/06/25/special-investigation-just-five-black-women-among-415-leading/.

21 Rumsby, 'Special Investigation'.

22 Skysports.com, 'Marcus Rashford: England Forward Sorry for Penalty Miss but "Not for Who I Am" after Racist Abuse' (13 July 2021), https://www.skysports.com/football/news/12016/12354589/marcus-rashford-england-forward-sorry-for-penalty-miss-but-not-for-who-i-am-after-racist-abuse.

BLACK BRITISH EDUCATION MATTERS

1 Hansard, HC vol. 682 (20 Oct. 2020), https://hansard.parliament.uk/commons/2020-10-20/debates/5B0E393E-8778-4973-B318-C17797DFBB22/BlackHistoryMonth.

2 Kehinde Andrews, 'Guy Reid-Bailey: The Man Who Sparked the Bristol Bus Boycott and then Fought to Desegregate Housing', *Guardian* (17 Dec. 2020), https://www.theguardian.com/world/2020/dec/17/guy-reid-bailey-the-man-who-sparked-the-bristol-bus-boycott-and-then-fought-to-desegregate-housing.

3 Bernard Coard, *How the West Indian Child Is Made Educationally Subnormal in the British School System* (London: New Beacon Books, 1971).

4 Maureen Stone, *The Education of the Black Child in Britain* (London: Fontana, 1981).

5 Dr Remi Joseph-Salisbury, *Race and Racism in English Secondary Schools* (London: Runnymede Trust, 2020), https://www.runnymedetrust.org/uploads/publications/pdfs/Runnymede%20Secondary%20Schools%20report%20FINAL.pdf.

6 Department for Education, 'GCSE English and Maths Results: 2018 to 2019 school year' (6 April 2021), https://www.ethnicity-facts-figures.service.gov.uk/education-skills-and-training/11-to-16-years-old/a-to-c-in-english-and-maths-gcse-attainment-for-children-aged-14-to-16-key-stage-4/latest#by-ethnicity.

7 Universities UK and NUS, *Black, Asian and Minority Ethic Student Attainment at UK Universities: #Closing the Gap* (London: Universities UK and National Union of Students, 2019), https://www.universitiesuk.ac.uk/policy-and-analysis/reports/Documents/2019/bame-student-attainment-uk-universities-closing-the-gap.pdf.

8 Dimela Yekwai, *British Racism, Miseducation and the Afrikan Child* (London: Karnak House, 1998).

9 Elijah Anderson, 'The Iconic Ghetto', *The ANNALS of the American Academy of Political and Social Science*, 642, 1 (July 2012), pp. 8–24.

10 Matt Ford, 'Quantifying the Ethnic Penalty' (London: Centre for Crime and Justice Studies, 2015), https://www.crimeandjustice.org.uk/sites/crimeandjustice.org.uk/files/09627251.2015.1080942_0.pdf.

11 Department for Education, 'Pupil Exclusion' (2020), https://www.ethnicity-facts-figures.service.gov.uk/education-skills-and-training/absence-and-exclusions/pupil-exclusions/latest#temporary-exclusions-by-ethnicity.

12 Coard, *How the West Indian Child*, p. 30.

13 Centre for Literacy in Primary Education, *Reflecting Realities: Survey of Ethnic Representation within UK Children's Literature 2017* (London: CLPE, 2018), https://clpe.org.uk/library-and-resources/research/reflecting-realities-survey-ethnic-representation-within-uk-children.

14 Anna Leach, Antonio Voce and Ashley Kirk, 'Black British History: The Row Over the School Curriculum in England', *Guardian* (13 July 2020), https://www.theguardian.com/education/2020/jul/13/black-british-history-school-curriculum-england.

15 Rhodes Must Fall, *Rhodes Must Fall* (London: Zed, 2019).

16 Gurminder K. Bhambra, Dalia Gebrial and Kerem Nişancıoğlu (eds), *Decolonising the University* (London: Pluto, 2018).

17 Runnymede Trust, *Aiming Higher: Race, Inequality and Diversity in the Academy* (London: The Runnymede Trust, 2015), https://www.runnymedetrust.org/uploads/Aiming%20Higher.pdf.

18 Richard Adams, 'Fewer than 1% of UK University Professors Are Black, Figures Show', *Guardian* (27 Feb. 2020), https://www.theguardian.com/education/2020/feb/27/fewer-than-1-of-uk-university-professors-are-black-figures-show.

19 Ivan Illich, *Deschooling Society* (Harmondsworth: Penguin Education, 1973).

20 Malcolm X, Speech at the Militant Labor Forum, New York (29 May 1964).

21 Beverley M. Gordon, 'African-American Cultural Knowledge and Liberatory Education: Dilemmas, Problems, and Potentials in Postmodern American Society', in Mwalimu J. Shujaa (ed.), *Too Much Schooling, Too Little Education: A Paradox of Black Life in White Societies* (Trenton: Africa World Press, 1998), p. 66.

22 Kehinde Andrews, *Resisting Racism: Race, Inequality and the Black Supplementary School Movement* (London: Institute of Education Press, 2013).

23 Amanda Simon, *Supplementary Schools and Ethnic Minority Communities: A Social Positioning Perspective* (London: Palgrave, 2018).

24 Mel Chevannes and Frank Reeves, 'The Black Voluntary School Movement: Definition, Context, and Prospects' in Barry Troyna (ed.), *Racial Inequality in Education* (London: Routledge, 1989), p. 147.

25 Andrews, *Resisting Racism*, p. 44.

26 Andrews, *Resisting Racism*, p. 5.

27 Stone, *The Education of the Black Child in Britain*.

28 Peter Figueroa, *Education and the Social Construction of Race* (London: Routledge, 1991).

29 Kehinde Andrews, 'Leila Hassan Howe: "My life was made hell. You'd just hear a tirade against immigrants"', *Guardian* (8 Oct. 2020), https://www.theguardian.com/society/2020/oct/08/leila-hassan-howe-black-power-london-revolution-black-lives-matter.

30 A.J.F. Doulton, Haringey comprehensive schools. BEM 1/2/5(16) (London: GPI Archive, 1969), p. 3.

31 J. Arday and H. Mirza (eds), *Dismantling Race in Higher Education: Racism, Whiteness and Decolonising the Academy* (London: Palgrave, 2018).

32 Ibram X. Kendi, *Stamped from the Beginning: The Definitive History of Racist Ideas in America* (London: Bodley Head, 2017).

33 Nick Duffy, 'Gavin Williamson Rejects Calls to "Decolonise" History Curriculum, Saying Britons Should Be "Proud of our History"', inews (19 June 2020), https://inews.co.uk/news/education/gavin-williamson-british-history-decolonise-blm-reject-empire-451290.

BLACK BRITISH LIVES MATTER

1 Paula Akpan, 'Say Their Names: Twelve Victims of Police and State Brutality in the UK', *Vice* (25 June 2020), https://www.vice.com/en/article/qj4j8x/remembering-police-brutality-victims-uk